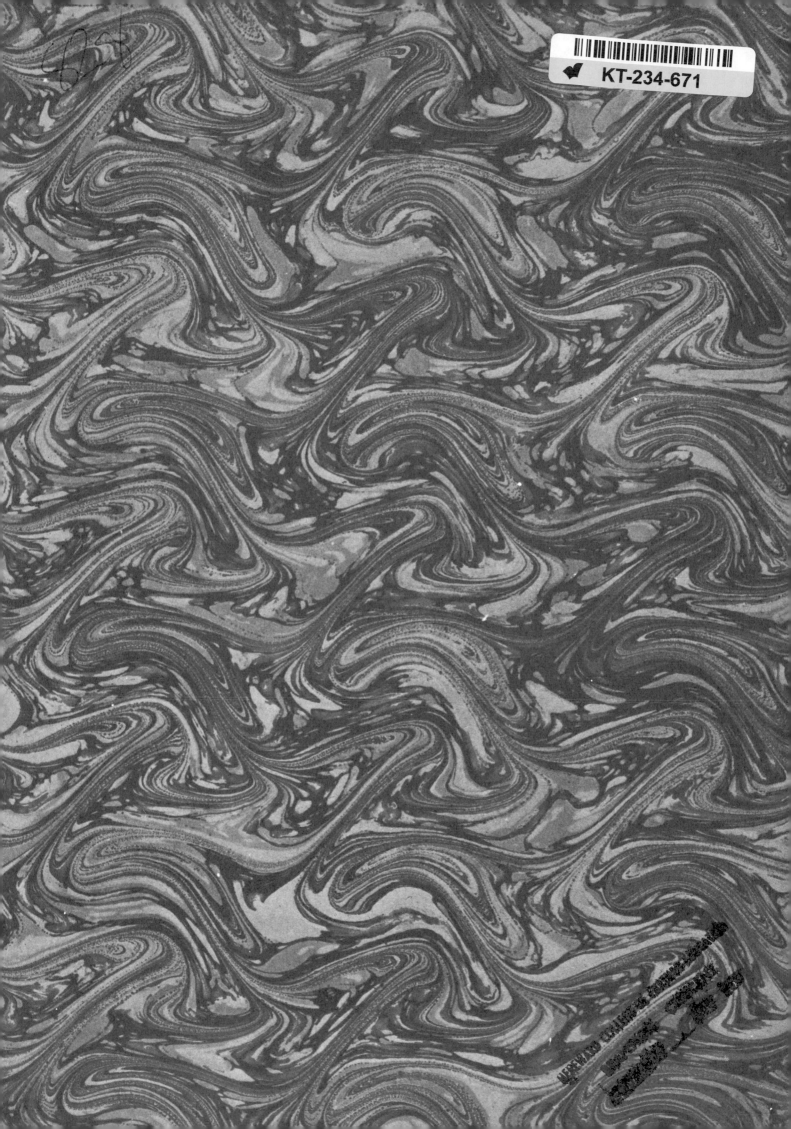

Rudyard Kipling

Title page
Rudyard Kipling at fifty-eight, in the year of his installation as Rector of St Andrews.

Front cover
Rudyard in 1899, the portrait by which he is best known, by Philip Burne-Jones. National Portrait Gallery.

27. APR. 1989

Rudyard Kipling

MARTIN FIDO

HAMLYN
London / New York / Sydney / Toronto

To my Mother

Published by
The Hamlyn Publishing Group Limited
1974
London   New York   Sydney   Toronto
Astronaut House
Feltham, Middlesex
England

ISBN 0 600 35329 X

Printed in Spain by
Printer Industria Gráfica sa, Tuset 19
Barcelona, San Vicente dels Horts, 1974
Depósito Legal B–21082–1974
Mohn Gordon Ltd, London

Contents

Colour Plates
Kipling in 1899, the portrait by which he is best known, by
Philip Burne-Jones. National Portrait Gallery Front cover/
Bombay, 1878. The railway station 33/Captain J. A. Wood
winning the VC at Reshire Fort 33/Jamrud Fort, 1879 36/
The Victoria Memorial, Calcutta 36/The Khyber Pass 37/
William Morris 40/W. E. Henley 41/Edmund Gosse 41/
Rudyard Kipling, 1891 44/Caroline Kipling, 1899 45/
Soldiers Three 48/Boer War cartoon, 1901 97/The
Absent-minded Beggar 97/The Advance to Relieve
Kimberley 100/Bateman's 100/An early Lanchester 101/
Kipling's study, Bateman's 104/Kipling in 1920 108/
Indian elephant and British lion 109/Workless 128

Above, *Rudyard Kipling at the age of three.*

Left, *John Lockwood Kipling, his father.*

Right, *his mother, Alice Kipling, née Macdonald.*

Babies in Bombay and Bewdley

DECEMBER 30, 1865. A HOUSE ON THE ESPLANADE at Bombay. A narrow neck of land, with the open sea on one side and a busy harbour on the other. Palm-groves by the sea. Arab dhows in the harbour. Parsee Towers of Silence standing near the house: places of death, where the Parsee dead were exposed on flat surfaces, high above the living world, to be picked clean by kites. A kid in the throes of death in the garden of the house on the Esplanade, sacrificially slaughtered by a servant as an offering for the safe delivery of the woman of the house. The woman inside near to death, suffering a grievous first labour, almost given up by her doctor. In this exotic setting was Joseph Rudyard Kipling born.

The sacrifice of the kid was, he liked to think, propitious; his life had been 'bought' by the killing of an animal, like that of his creation, Mowgli. Alice Kipling, his mother, survived too, though she was never to find childbirth a happy experience. Her second child, born in England in 1868, was delivered with a black eye and a broken arm, and barely survived. And in 1870 her final pregnancy terminated in the swift death of a second son.

Kipling's parents were both children of Methodist ministers. It was the Methodist connection that had led to their meeting in England, although by the time of their marriage both had quietly dropped the evangelical faith in which they had been reared. Alice was the eldest daughter of a large family. Like all Methodist ministers' offspring, they spent a roving childhood, moving from place to place as the 'Circuit System' translated their father from one chapel to another every three years. By the time she was twenty-seven, Alice Macdonald had lived at Sheffield, Birmingham, Leeds, Wakefield, Huddersfield, London, Manchester, and Wolverhampton.

But the constant removals did not lead to instability in the Macdonald family, any more than the narrow income of a Methodist minister led to insecurity. The Rev. George Macdonald was contented with his library of two thousand books, and such very occasional luxuries as a trip to Chatsworth, or three-shillings-worth of cigars once in his life. His wife, Hannah, brought up her children to love one another, and discipline themselves to enjoy what might otherwise have seemed an overcrowded and underprivileged family life. They would have to live with one another, she told them, and so positive quarrelling was forbidden. 'If you want to be rude to anyone,' she would say, 'let it be to a stranger. Perhaps you will never meet again.' Nor did she encourage or tolerate tale-bearing. As a result, the five daughters and two sons who survived into adult life remained good friends, in spite of all family strains, and the four girls who married made quite notable matches, and gave their children secure confidence in family ties.

Alice was a slim, good-looking girl, with dark brown hair, grey eyes, and a fair skin. Her eyes, with their dark lashes and shapely brows, were her best feature, and attracted many young men as she grew up. She was engaged three times before she settled down to marry John Lockwood Kipling; her youngest sister commented sharply about her youth that 'Alice never seemed to go on a visit without becoming engaged to some wild cad of the desert.' Her father warned her against the danger of becoming a flirt: a serious charge in strict evangelical Victorian circles, for it was obviously unkind to excite members of the other sex in a society where the mildest sexual satisfactions were tabooed outside the confines of matrimony. Alice was impenitent: 'P-H-L-U-R-T' she spelled out; 'What is that?' And she received a really severe paternal reprimand when she arrived home unwarrantably late from a party in London, having walked about the city with a young man who was seeing her home.

Her younger sisters saw her as a daring and dashing figure. She herself revolted against the strictness of her evangelical upbringing as strongly as was compatible with retaining a contented foot-hold in a happy family. Two things suggest that Methodism was, in the end, profoundly distasteful to her. When the children discovered a lock of John Wesley's hair, lovingly preserved in an inscribed envelope, it was Alice who called it 'a hair of the dog that bit us', and, to the horror of the others, threw it on the fire. And when her son wrote his bitter autobiographical story *Baa Baa, Black Sheep,* he had the idealised portrait of Alice write to her husband, 'Don't you remember our own upbringing, dear, when the Fear of the Lord was so often the beginning of falsehood?'

Not that anyone would ever have characterised Alice Macdonald as a rebellious liar. Many of her spirited pranks were in perfect harmony with a respectable, but by no means narrow or intolerant Victorian household. Thus, when the girls and a

visiting young man wondered whether mouse was edible, Alice caught one, and baked it in a pie, of which her sister Georgiana bravely ate a part. And, perhaps surprisingly, for one so lively, light-hearted, quick-witted, and unserious, she was the daughter whom her father called 'the Peacemaker', for her skill in soothing family disputes.

In the spring of 1863, after her father's final professional move to Wolverhampton, Alice accompanied her brother Fred to a picnic on the shores of Lake Rudyard, in Staffordshire. Fred was a Methodist minister at Burslem, and the picnic was arranged by the Misses Pinder, daughters to the Burslem potter whose firm was Pinder, Bourne & Co. After the young people had eaten, they all went for a walk in a field where an old, broken-down horse was grazing. One of the firm's young designers, who was at the picnic, quoted Browning's *Childe Roland*: 'Thrust out past service from the devil's stud'. Alice recognised and capped the line: 'He must be wicked to deserve such pain'. From this introduction dated the engagement between Alice Macdonald and the short, golden-bearded, blue-eyed, prematurely bald, pottery designer, John Lockwood Kipling.

John Lockwood Kipling was a gifted young man in his middle twenties, who had yet to make his mark on the world. He was a Yorkshireman, and his father's ministry had kept him in circuits in Yorkshire and Lincolnshire. John Lockwood went to Woodhouse Grove Methodist school, near Leeds, and was not very happy there. When he was fourteen, he visited the Great Exhibition of 1851, and the display

of contemporary artefacts filled him with enthusiasm for plastic craftsmanship. Within a few years he was studying art and sculpture in South Kensington under Sir Philip Cunliffe-Owen, supporting himself by giving French lessons, and working as a stonemason on the new Victoria and Albert Museum. When he was about twenty-two, he left London and went to work for Pinder, Bourne & Co., bringing with him a wide range of craft skills, and the high esteem of Sir Philip.

Cunliffe-Owen, indeed, thought so highly of Lockwood Kipling that, two years after the picnic at Lake Rudyard, when the distant Sir Jamsetjee Jeejeebhoy was in search of a 'Professor of Architectural Sculpture' for his newly-founded Bombay School of Art, Sir Philip recommended the young designer as 'one of his best boys'. Lockwood was only too happy to accept. The post was not only more high-sounding, but indubitably more secure and better paid than any job he could hope to hold in England. What may have pleased him as much as anything was the fact that he could afford to marry, now, on the strength of his prospects.

He had entered into Alice's fourth engagement soon after the picnic, and had been taken home to meet the rest of the family. He found them at family prayers when he first visited the Macdonald parents in their home, and took it as a good omen that almost the first words he heard in the house were the scriptural text, 'There came a man sent from God, whose name was John.' Such inoffensive humour over matters of piety was entirely acceptable in the

Above *A view of Bombay taken from the Clock Tower at the turn of the century. Looking towards the anchorage.*

Macdonald family, and Alice's sisters Agnes and Louisa were delighted with her new young man. He enjoyed their company as much, and said that Aggie, the acknowledged family beauty was 'tyrannously pretty', with conversation like 'champagne'. George and Hannah Macdonald felt they had never met a young man they liked so much on a short acquaintance. So there were no family problems to hinder an early wedding.

Alice, for her part, may have been less delighted with the Kipling family. She rapidly resolved that old Mrs Kipling was dull, and persuaded her husband to maintain ties with his family that were more dutiful than affectionate. But Alice always liked to be the emotional centre of any scene, and usually persuaded her audience that this was her rightful place. It was in keeping that she should persuade her husband – not to mention her son's audience in posterity – that the Macdonald family were really interesting: the Kiplings were no more than dreary Yorkshire Methodists.

Actually, the only real glamour inhering in the Macdonald family in 1865 was vicarious and potential. The girls were far from dull. They all wrote poetry, and had short effusions published in respectable magazines like *Temple Bar*. They could almost be said to compose music. But compared with those truly remarkable parson's daughters, the Brontës, they were the most ordinary of creatures. What they did achieve, in the end, was a succession of interesting marriages. Alice was not the first. Georgiana had already been married for five years by the time Alice was united with her Mr Kipling. Georgie's husband was a young painter; a schoolfriend of her eldest brother Henry with the undistinguished name of Ned Jones.

When Ned went up to Oxford, he became friendly with another young man named William Morris. Both had artistic ambitions; both were enthusiastic admirers of the revolutionary Pre-Raphaelite brotherhood, headed by Dante Gabriel Rossetti, Holman Hunt, Ford Madox Brown, and young John Millais. Jones left Oxford without taking his degree, and began painting in London, living in lodgings very close to the Macdonalds' current home. Soon Morris came down and joined him, and the two lived and worked in a dream of artistically idealised medievalism, with furniture designed by Morris after old patterns. Together they went with Rossetti to paint Arthurian murals on the walls of the Oxford Union. Together they visited the lively and artistically interested Macdonald sisters, although brother Henry, their original source of introduction to the family, had gone to America in a fruitless attempt to carve out for himself a business career that should enable him to marry.

Below *Edward Burne-Jones at the age of thirty-seven. Rudyard's amiable Pre-Raphaelite uncle, painted by fellow Pre-Raphaelite G. F. Watts.*

By 1857 Jones was engaged to Georgiana, the quietest and most serious of the Macdonalds. It was not until 1860 that his earnings were secure enough for him to marry. But by that time he was a rising painter – Tennyson and Ruskin had dubbed him 'Gigantic' – and he was preparing to dignify his name to Burne-Jones. As the first married sister, Georgie now took precedence in her family, and the Burne-Jones home at The Grange, Fulham (a house formerly owned by the novelist Richardson) became the central meeting-point for the Macdonald tribe.

The younger sisters, Agnes and Louisa, married after the Kiplings had gone to India. Agnes, like her sisters, married into the art world. Her husband, Edward Poynter, was a friend of Ned Burne-Jones, though unlike Ned he favoured traditional and classical forms of art, and was to become President of the Royal Academy. The gulf between academic painting and Pre-Raphaelitism did not lead to any estrangement between the brothers-in-law, and it is interesting to note that three Macdonald sisters had made marriages covering the broad spectrum of mid-nineteenth century art: the *avant-garde*, the traditional, and the craftsmanlike. Kipling's father, significantly, was the craftsman.

Louisa broke with family tradition by marrying into the business and public life community. Alfred Baldwin was the politically ambitious son of an ironmaster at Bewdley, in Worcestershire, where the Macdonald parents moved in their retirement. Louie made the only predictably prosperous marriage in the family; but the promise of Burne-Jones and Poynter was amply fulfilled, and their

Borah Bazaar, Bombay, with its shops opening directly on to the busy pavements. A photograph taken during the 1880s.

wives lived to see them win knighthoods. In compensation, Louie and Alice bore sons of greater distinction than the family had previously seen: Stanley Baldwin and Rudyard Kipling. Aunts Georgie, Louie and Aggie were important figures in the life of Rudyard Kipling, and he was always on close and affectionate terms with his cousins Stan Baldwin, 'Ambo' Poynter, and Phil Burne-Jones. Indeed, so vital were the ties across the Macdonald marriages that Rudyard was even able to maintain friendly relations with the liberal scholar J. W. Mackail, who ultimately married his cousin Margaret Burne-Jones, although liberal scholarship and the adult Kipling were normally anathema to one another.

Bombay at the time of Rudyard Kipling's birth was entering on its period of great prosperity. It had long been the least important of the three Presidencies into which British India was divided. Calcutta and Madras looked back to Clive's victories and the conquest of the Mahrattas. But Bombay was Portugal's casual gift on the marriage of Charles II to Catherine of Braganza, and remained a backwater until nineteenth-century industrialism brought it wealth. Cotton-milling gave the city an importance that increased as the American Civil War cut off Lancashire's normal supplies of raw material. And the development of a railways system converging on Bombay as the major west coast port made it the gateway to Suez when the canal was opened in 1869.

Here Lockwood Kipling undertook duties appropriate to an acquaintance of William Morris. He was to foster and revive Indian arts and crafts, and relate them to the new industrial age. There was no question of reacting against industrial progress. In British India, of all places, it was a matter for pride; public evidence of the superior culture and civilisation of the white Sahibs. But the values of traditional cultures had their place and Lockwood Kipling, sculpting monuments, sketching remains, studying the ancient trades of India, and organising exhibitions of the older way of life, was trying to help that way of life to adapt itself to new methods without being totally superseded. It was far from ignoble work, and laid a foundation of cultural attitudes which would find strong expression in his son's writings: a mixture of headstrong enthusiasm for the technological future with nostalgic admiration for the folk-loric past. Both strands can prove so strong in Rudyard's writing that he sometimes seems bafflingly inconsistent: *Below the Mill Dam*, for instance, a story which appears to demand instant building in brick over the English countryside, to prove that quiet streams can produce electric power, hardly strikes one as being the work of the author of *Puck of Pook's Hill* or *Friendly Brook*, where superstition and a kind of animism are treated with respect as outcrops of England's historically green and pleasant land. But the amalgam makes sense when related to the context of a mid-Victorian Bombay School of Art.

Significantly, Rudyard's earliest memories combined the romantic with the practical. 'My first impression', he wrote when he was seventy, 'is of daybreak, light and colour and golden and purple fruits at the level of my shoulder. This would be the memory of early morning walks to the Bombay fruit market with my *ayah* and later with my sister in her perambulator, and of our returns with our purchases piled high on the bows of it.'

The Goanese *ayah* was a Roman Catholic, and Lockwood and Alice might not have been pleased to know that she encouraged the little boy to pray publicly and popishly with her in front of a wayside cross. Alice would certainly have been furious to know that the *ayah*, on the day when a vulture dropped a dead child's hand in the garden from one of the Parsee Towers of Silence, told little Ruddy about it. For Alice had told her son not to ask questions about what was going on in the garden that day. (But he wanted to see the hand).

After the manner of insensitive nurses, the *ayah* told Ruddy that the stuffed leopard's head in his nursery was watching him to see that he went to sleep. Kipling never underestimated childhood terrors, and he was always grateful to Meeta, the Hindu bearer, who freed him from dread of the dark

Kipling's Aunt Georgie. Lady Burne-Jones.

Aunt Louie. Mrs Alfred Baldwin.

Aunt Aggie. Lady Poynter

by saying that it was only 'the head of an animal'.

Real animals played some part in his infant life. The household boasted three dogs: Bogy and Toby, the terriers, and Chang the pekingese, which was Ruddy's favourite. His father had given him a little whip with which he clumsily drove the others off if they came too close while Chang was eating. But he was less bold when a hen attacked him on the way to the School of Art: it was 'a winged monster, as big as myself', and he fled weeping. His father called him a baby, and cheered him up with a comic drawing of the tragedy.

In 1868 Alice took the two-year-old Ruddy back to England. She was not risking a second confinement in India, and went to stay with Georgie at The Grange for the birth of her daughter, Alice – or 'Trix', as she was known in the family. Ruddy was sent to Bewdley to stay with Louie and Alfred Baldwin.

Rudyard's first impression of the land of his descent was understandably unfavourable: 'a dark land, and a darker room full of cold, in one wall of which a white woman made naked fire, and I cried aloud with dread, for I had never before seen a grate.'

A sense of the climatic inhospitability of the country stayed with him well into maturity, and found amusing expression in the mouth of 'Shafiz Ullah Khan', narrator of *One View of the Question* in *Many Inventions*:

> 'Further, and for visible sign that the place is forgotten of God, there falls upon certain days, without warning, a cold darkness, whereby the sun's light is altogether cut off from all the city, and the people, male and female, and the drivers of the vehicles, grope and howl in this Pit at high noon, none seeing the other. The air being filled with the smoke of Hell – sulphur and pitch as it is written – they die speedily with gaspings, and are buried in the dark.'

To the Baldwins, the little visitor from Bombay was less than welcome. Edith, the youngest and unmarried Macdonald sister, was living at Bewdley, where the Macdonald parents were becoming increasingly old and infirm. Bedrooms were not plentiful, and Ruddy had to share a bed with his Aunt Edith. He kicked. And, used to having

adoring Indian servants at his beck and call, he demanded water at intervals throughout the night. In a land where servants were (as he had noticed) white, and little children were expected to be seen and not heard, he was a spoiled nuisance. He complained, after surveying his grandparents' bedroom, 'They've gone and tooken the best rooms for themselves.'

His Aunt Louie's familial affection was strained almost beyond endurance. After he had been at Bewdley for a month or so she confided to Aggie, 'Now for the first time I can truly say I am very fond of the child' – a remarkable admission of reserve among the close Macdonald kin. And after the Kiplings' departure Louie confessed that Ruddy, Alice and the noisy baby Trix had been intolerable: 'Her children turned the house into such a bear-

The Grange at Fulham, the home of Georgiana and Edward Burne-Jones, and the centre of the Macdonalds' family life. The house was previously owned by Samuel Richardson.

garden, & Ruddy's screaming tempers made Papa so ill, we were thankful to see them on their way. The wretched disturbances one ill-ordered child can make is a lesson for all time to me.' Alice's lackadaisical refusal to exercise effective maternal authority even caused some friction between herself and the placid Hannah, and it was no real kindness to Ruddy and Trix, who would, in a few years, desperately need aunts and a grandmother concerned for their happiness rather than their appearance of good order.

In spite of his screaming fits, Ruddy probably enjoyed himself, like most habitually spoiled infants. He asserted himself vigorously on the street in Bewdley, stamping along and shouting, 'Out of the way, out of the way, there's an angry Ruddy coming!' His great idol was Reuben, the Baldwin's coachman, in imitation of whom he adopted a gruff Worcestershire accent. And his essential good nature emerged in his gentleness with his one-year-old cousin Stan. It was only the adult world which he expected to tyrannise. The stickily sentimental stories *Wee Willie Winkie*, *Tods' Amendment*, and *His Majesty the King* – almost the only cheap Victorian *bijoux* in his prose output – show that he retained an immature ideal of pampered infancy as charming, at least until he had children of his own.

Back in Bombay the servants remained his adult intimates. Meeta now became his hero, and Hindustani again became his first language. Lockwood and Alice enjoyed the comfortable life of upper-class English parents, with their children out of the way until the afternoon, when they were cleaned up and brought in by the servants, with the injunction, 'Speak English now to Papa and Mamma.' Then Alice would sing to them, accompanying herself at the piano, and say goodbye before going out to 'Big Dinners'.

For the rest of the time, Ruddy and Trix ranged free and unchecked around the house and the School of Art. Mr Terry, Lockwood's assistant, let them play with clay. Meeta and the *ayah* told them Indian folk-tales, and sang them Indian nursery songs which stuck in Kipling's memory:

This is a handful of cardamoms,
This is a lump of ghi:
This is millet and chillies and rice,
A supper for thee and me!

And in the evenings the children would walk in the palm grove by the sea with the *ayah* until the wind blew the great nuts down and all three scampered to open ground together. 'I have always felt the menacing darkness of tropical eventides,' recalled Kipling, 'as I have loved the voices of night-winds through palm or banana leaves, and the song of the tree-frogs.'

It was an idyllic early childhood, and Ruddy and Trix felt no forebodings in 1871, when the whole family came back to England for Lockwood's six-months' home leave.

A Sinner in Southsea

Ruddy was six and trix three on that memorable furlough of 1871. The relatives were all visited again, and this time Alice must have been less demanding on behalf of, or inert about her children, for Hannah wrote at the end of their visit to Bewdley, 'We have never had one misunderstanding nor one sharp word. We met in peace and we parted in peace, for which I say, thanks be to God.'

But an amicable renewal of family contacts was not the only purpose of the trip home, nor was Lockwood taking a well-earned rest without thought for the future. All Anglo-Indian families had to consider the problem of their children's education in the home country. There were no satisfactory schools in India, and had any been established, it is unlikely that snobbish Victorian society would ever have granted them the prestige they might deserve.

From the point of view of most mid-nineteenth century Englishmen, India was a country for the second-best of Britain. The Indian army was believed to be inferior to the home army, in spite of the fact that most generals of any real ability (like the Duke of Wellington) spent some early part of their careers in India, where they learned military skills in skirmishes with hostile local chiefs, rather than the strategically useless skills of gambling, duelling and whoring imparted in fashionable British regiments. The Indian Civil Service – an organ of government since the Mutiny of 1857 – had demonstrated the necessity for transferring the remaining responsibilities of the old East India Company to the state if British dominion in India were to continue – did not offer so desirable a career as the home civil service, where Dickens' 'Tite Barnacles' clung incompetently to the government jobs nepotism had won them. Thackeray's fat and foolish nabob, Jos Sedley, exemplified adequately the stereotyped English view of an Anglo-Indian: a man too inept to succeed in Europe but astute enough to amass a fortune by misgoverning ignorant 'natives'. And Thackeray had himself been born in India, so he could be taken as reasonably authoritative.

In these circumstances, any education offered in India would surely have been undervalued. The teachers would have been described as second-rate, and the pupils dismissed as unfit for secure middle-class occupations. Parents concerned for their children's futures were therefore bound to make arrangements to send them home for schooling in England at some point. Thackeray had been sent home to Charterhouse, and although he was miserably unhappy in an English boarding school after the warmth and freedom of an Indian early childhood, he felt no later resentment about so inevitable a process. Rather he came to adopt the metropolitan English view that almost all things Indian were ludicrous. Certainly he took it for granted that British rule in India made it unavoidable that Anglo-Indian children should be separated from their parents round about the age of eight, and sent to live in the cold and unfriendly country mysteriously called 'home' by those who lived and worked in Bombay. To children like Ruddy and Trix, living close to the servants, it seems likely that going to England represented going *belait* (west) rather than going home.

Nevertheless, the little Kiplings had no suspicion that they were to be left in England at the end of the summer of 1871. Their parents gave them no warning that a parting was to take place; that Papa and Mamma were going back to the beautiful house in Bombay, while Ruddy and Trix stayed in a smaller, colder, less comfortable house in an unfriendly town by the sea, under the care of two remote adult strangers. What Lockwood and Alice thought they were doing in disappearing without adequate warning or farewells, one cannot imagine. It has been charitably assumed that they hoped to save the children the needless pain of anticipation. What they achieved, in fact was a shattering dislocation that left Rudyard and Trix feeling deserted, with chilly strangers confirming that the desertion had really happened. In his fictionalised account of the experience (*Baa Baa, Black Sheep*), Kipling stated to the full the feelings he was left with, though his unwillingness to ascribe any blame to his parents leaves a touch of one-sided strain in the writing:

'When a matured man discovers that he has been deserted by Providence, deprived of his God, and cast without help, comfort, or sympathy, upon a world which is new and strange to him, his despair, which may find expression in evil living, the writing of his experiences, or the more satisfactory diversion of suicide, is generally supposed to be impressive. A child, under exactly similar circumstances as far as its knowledge goes, cannot

The boy who went to live in the House of Desolation. Rudyard Kipling at the age of six.

Jos Sedley and Becky Sharp in Vauxhall Gardens, one of Thackeray's drawings for his Vanity Fair. *Sedley typified the inept and unsuccessful Englishman who could somehow manage to make money in India, misgoverning another race.*

very well curse God and die. It howls till its nose is red, its eyes are sore, and its head aches. Punch and Judy, through no fault of their own, had lost all their world.'

But there is nothing strained about Kipling's objectified description of 'Punch' miserably trying to console 'Judy' on the cold seashore after they have wandered, lost for an hour, under the impression that the sea must lead them to Bombay.

Obviously one asks *why* were Ruddy and Trix with strangers? What had become of the intimacy of the Macdonald tribe, who should surely have taken the children in? And why had they been sent home so early? Ruddy might well have hoped for another year, or even two, in the Indian sun; Trix was being flung out into the cold at a truly extraordinarily early age. The questions are important, as Lockwood and Alice have frequently been presented – not least by their son – as utterly ideal parents. In *Baa Baa, Black Sheep* the children's parents are innocent, well-meaning figures, and the mother steps in finally as a warm and loving saviour. Yet even in this work of filial piety there is a tiny hint of parental irresponsibility and self-indulgence:

'Don't forget us,' pleaded Mamma. 'Oh, my little son, don't forget us, and see that Judy remembers too.'

'I've told Judy to bemember,' said

Punch, wriggling, for his father's beard tickled his neck. 'I've told Judy – ten – forty – 'leven thousand times. But Ju's so young – quite a baby – isn't she?'

This implantation of an obsessive memory of Mamma as a *duty* (and one in which, of course, Punch fails) surely cannot be reconciled with the defence of the quick, unemotional parting. All in all, Lockwood and Alice leave a nasty impression of having put their own ease of mind before their children's needs.

Alice did explain to a friend that 'she had never thought of leaving her children with her own family, it led to complications'. Does this mean that she could not face another round of quarrels with her sisters over the undisciplined brats she would be dumping in their houses? That Hannah's principle of quarrelling only with strangers took precedence in her mind? That she believed a hired foster-parent would be more amenable to her own theories (if any) of upbringing? Or (as one suspects) that despite her demand that the children continue to extend to her the gratification of their love, she was not willing to stand up to any one on their behalf, and not willing to hear her sisters' adverse opinion of the children's behaviour in their homes? Certainly none of the other Macdonalds can be blamed for what happened: they showed themselves willing and kindly hosts to the children over the next six years, and made responsible, uninterfering investigation into the situation Lockwood and Alice left behind them.

What Lockwood and Alice did was to leave the children in the care of foster parents whom they discovered through a newspaper advertisement. Captain and Mrs P. A. Holloway of Lorne Lodge, 4 Campbell Road, Southsea, supplemented the income of retirement by taking in child boarders for colonial parents, and sending them to a local school. Their house was not large, and two children at any one time were enough for them. Their own son, Harry, was twelve when Ruddy and Trix were added to the household; he was to be at work in a bank before Rudyard reached the same age, and finally left Southsea.

To all external appearances the arrangement was entirely satisfactory. Mrs Holloway was a good household manageress. The children were properly fed and presentably turned out, and it seemed as though, under less than doting care, their behaviour was improving signally. Captain Holloway was just such a romantic old salt as an imaginative boy might delight in: he had been a midshipman at the Battle of Navarino, and bore on his ankle the scar inflicted by a harpoon-line when a whale had dragged him near to death under water. Yet his manners and attitudes were those of the respectable lower middle-class suburbs, and he was utterly reliable with children. He took Ruddy for long walks around the naval areas of Portsmouth and Southsea, taught him sea-shanties, and, delightfully, said things like, 'Shiver me timbers!'

Hannah Macdonald, and Aunts Georgie, Louie and Aggie, all came down to see that the Kipling children were well cared for. All were entirely satisfied. The children were 'much improved in manners, and seem very happy', wrote their grandmother, and added, 'They seem to be attached to Mrs H., and she seems very fond of them.' Louie, too, noted in her diary that 'the little Kiplings were very well & happy, improved in every way, & Mrs Holloway a very nice woman indeed'. When, after about a year, Captain Holloway died, Alice wrote sympathetically from Bombay that she would try to find Mrs Holloway some more child-boarders from among her own acquaintance.

So that Kipling's own direct and unambiguous denunciation of his six years at Lorne Lodge comes as something of a shock:

> 'Then the old Captain died, and I was sorry, for he was the only person in that house as far as I can remember who ever threw me a kind word.
>
> 'It was an establishment run with the full vigour of the Evangelical as revealed to the Woman. I had never heard of Hell, so I was introduced to it in all its terrors.'

And this is not the remembered protest of a spoiled Bombay brat, reacting against a brief period of childhood in which he was not idolised. This is the voice of a man who recollects being bullied and harried by adult ignorance, stupidity and cruelty into a nervous breakdown at the age of eleven.

What went wrong? To begin with, Mrs Holloway dominated the house. The old sea-captain was described in *Baa Baa, Black Sheep* as 'big, bony, grey, and lame as to one leg'. His wife was the stronger personality, and as she already had a son of her own it was Trix, the sweet little girl, who won her instant sentimental affection. Ruddy's self-willed conduct was not something Mrs Holloway was prepared to tolerate – and who can blame her? But who can forgive her for failing to distinguish between the naughtiness that was acceptable to the Kiplings, and the unhappiness that his parents' sudden desertion occasioned the little boy? Why should her standard of 'naughtiness' have been drawn so much more rigidly than that of the Baldwins or Hannah Macdonald? Who can sympathise today, with her self-righteous evangelical confidence that her own repressive Christianity as imposed on the children was a greater blessing than the love and security offered by their aunts and uncles? She went so far as to tell Alice directly that her own church-going made her a better influence for the children than kind Aunt Georgie. What excuse can be made for her humiliating the six-year-old Ruddy when she found that his parents had neglected to teach him to read? And then, having corrected this failing, bitterly opposing his sitting reading to himself?

Lorne Lodge, Southsea.

Did she envy the little boy with the superior social standing, whose prospects were so much better than her son Harry's? We may deduce from his fiction that Rudyard could not disguise the rather unpleasant prejudices of his class, and thereby gave Mrs Holloway some natural offence: 'Aunty Rosa' is understandably sour when the 'black sheep' says,

> 'If I was with my father . . . I shouldn't *speak* to those boys. He wouldn't let me. They live in shops. I saw them go into shops – where their fathers live and sell things.'

And it would seem difficult to know for sure where justice lay in the tension between the couple when Captain Holloway punished Harry for bullying 'strangers' children', and Mrs Holloway accused him of cruelty to his own. It would *seem* difficult – if we had not the concrete evidence of Rudyard's nervous collapse after a few years of the sole care of Mrs Holloway and her son.

Mrs Holloway's utterly unforgivable offences can be quickly listed. First and worst, she isolated Rudyard emotionally, even trying to turn Trix against her brother. By showering sentimental affection on the little girl she quickly won her superficial love, and from then on Trix was unhappy about Ruddy's 'naughtiness' and, confused herself as to what her brother was doing that made him so wicked, she unwittingly contributed to the miasma of unfocussed guilt and self-hate which made his life wretched. It was a mark of Trix's tractability that

Robinson Crusoe and Friday. Defoe's immortal hero gave Kipling, miserable in the care of Mrs Holloway, the same pleasure in escape from reality that boys have enjoyed since the famous romance was first published in 1719.

she temporarily adopted an immature piety in imitation of Mrs Holloway, just as it was a mark of Rudyard's remarkable psychological sturdiness that he resolutely rejected it as an unnecessary evil emanating from an unnecessarily evil woman.

By the standards of the 1870s, Mrs Holloway's deplorable habit of caning her child boarders may not have seemed extraordinary. Kipling himself suggests that her husband had caned his son, and that although this occurrence alarmed little Rudyard at the time it did not detract from his respect for the sea-captain. Still, humane and kindly people did exist in some mid-Victorian homes. Kipling's uncles would never have dreamed of hitting their difficult nephew with a stick, and Dickens, in his delineation of Mr Murdstone, Mr Squeers and Mr Creakle, had shown a wide public that beating children was evil, especially if accompanied by cold 'christian' moralising. Kipling was to add some memorable sentences to the necessary English 'hate' literature opposing corporal punishment, an achievement seldom credited to him when readers are either rejoicing over or excoriating the heroic whackings of *Stalky & Co.*

'Aunty Rosa pounced upon him unawares and told him he was "acting a lie".

'"If you're old enough to do that," she said – her temper was always worst after dinner – "you're old enough to be beaten."

'"But – I'm – I'm not an animal!" said Punch aghast.'

and

'Aunty Rosa told him that God had heard every word he had said and was very angry. If this were true why didn't God come and say so, thought Punch, and dismissed the matter from his mind. Afterwards he learned to know the Lord as the only thing in the world more awful than Aunty Rosa – as a Creature that stood in the background and counted the strokes of the cane.'

Under the pressure of Mrs Holloway's suspicious and nagging régime, Rudyard became, predictably, a nervous and habitual liar. It was utterly indefensible, then, for Mrs Holloway to stitch a large placard reading LIAR to the back of his jacket, and send him to school in it. Nor was her habit of giving him Collects to learn for each offence one calculated to increase his devotion to the Church of England, though the writer was, of course, pleased that he knew them in later life.

Harry Holloway, a dark, oily boy when the little Kiplings came into his home, was as pious as his mother, and temperamentally a bully. He shared Rudyard's bedroom, and asked him terrifying questions about his daily doings. If he could trap him into making self-contradictory statements, he would report to his mother that Rudyard had been lying again, and bring down another round of punishments and penalties. Fortunately, work at the bank exhausted him sufficiently to remove this source of strain before Rudyard left the house but it was bad enough for him to call Harry (secretly) the 'Devil-boy', just as he called his mother a *kuch-nay*, or person of so little worth as to have no caste at all. The house was named 'The House of Desolation' by Rudyard and Trix. They never changed their name for it when they reached adult life, nor could they ever bring themselves to go and look at it again when they found themselves in Portsmouth. The whole experience was traumatic and injurious.

But, for all his suffering, Kipling was not mentally crippled by Southsea. There were moments of relief, and times of actual happiness in his life between the ages of six and twelve. Once he could read, he read voraciously. His parents sent him books from India, and among the jumble of Victorian children's fantasies and magazines he discovered the odd poem by Tennyson and Wordsworth, and the delightful ballad 'Farewell, Rewards and Fairies'. *Robinson Crusoe* gave him ideas for a game of isolation from the unhappy world, and he would fence himself off in 'a mildewy basement room' with a piece of old

*Rudyard Kipling's cousin, Stanley Baldwin,
at the age of nine.*

19

packing case, before settling down to trade with savages, his trading post being an old tin trunk, and his merchandise a coconut shell with red cord threaded through it.

But the times of greatest happiness and escape came at Christmas and other holidays when Ruddy went to stay with the Burne-Joneses in Fulham. Aunt Georgie loved her tamed nephew, and made him very happy. Cousins Phil and Margaret Burne-Jones were dear friends, and Ruddy, already experimenting with language, addressed them nobly as 'Son and Daughter of my Uncle'. The uncle himself amused the children with his drawings, and joined in their evening play.

Burne-Jones had an impish and often childlike sense of humour; his sweetness and charm were a delight after the sterile, loveless order of Lorne Lodge. Usually he worked through the day, but Rudyard never forgot the day when he came down from his studio with a tube of 'Mummy Brown' paint in his hand, announcing that it was made of dead Pharaohs, and taking the children with him to bury it peacefully in the garden.

Associated with Uncle Ned was his fellow artist, 'Uncle Topsy', as the children knew William Morris. He too was a willing playmate, always consumed with some passionate interest of the moment. His powerful enthusiasm was so infectious that Rudyard found it hard to concentrate on pumping the organ-bellows in the studio for his aunt if Uncle Topsy came in. But how different was The Grange from Lorne Lodge: The Grange, where furniture could legitimately be tipped up and used for sliding and tobogganning! The Grange, where the children pumped the organ while Aunt Georgie played, and, 'If the organ ran out in squeals the beloved Aunt would be sorry. Never, *never* angry!'

Uncle Topsy's most mysterious enthusiasm was one which led him to bound up to the nursery on a day when there were no grown-ups to be found, and seat himself on the rocking-horse to tell Ruddy and Trix a wonderful story he just *had* to share with someone. Some of its 'fascinating horrors' stayed with Rudyard for life, and he later realised that he had heard from Morris a retelling of an Icelandic saga.

But escape to The Grange always came to an end. There was always Mrs Holloway and her canings and her inquisitions to return to. If Rudyard cried (as he did) on waking up and finding himself at Southsea, questionings and punishments would begin. If he talked about the books that delighted the artistic household at Fulham, he was accused of showing off. It was a wretchedly unfair position for a boy who had met many of the greatest names of art and literature of his day, and made little more of them than that 'a person called Browning' was unwilling to play with children, and a place called Oxford was inhabited by 'an ancient of days' called, for some unknown reason, the 'Provostoforiel'.

The end was heralded by the weakening of Rudyard's eyesight. Mrs Holloway took advantage of this not unusual occurrence in a ten-year-old to forbid him to read. This exclusion from his private world of escape led him to read desperately in secret by worse and worse lights. His school work suffered, and his reports became so bad that he threw one away and claimed he had never received it. (It was for this commonplace panic behaviour that he was placarded through the streets of Southsea as a LIAR). And then came the evidence that his mind could take no more strain. He began to see shadowy shapes of things that were not there, and flinched from them. Even

The Battle of Navarino, 20 October 1827. The boy Kipling was delighted to find that Captain Holloway, of the house in Southsea where he was boarded, was an old seadog who had fought in the famous engagement.

Mrs Holloway was able to distinguish between hallucinatory delusion and 'showing off' or 'lying': for one thing, Rudyard's shapes frightened him more than she did. Aunt Georgie noticed that something was wrong when the boy stayed at Fulham, and wrote to Alice about his inexplicable unhappiness. A doctor reported that he was 'half-blind', and at last, in 1877, after Mrs Holloway had made one last effort to separate Ruddy and Trix, Alice Kipling came home.

She found the children nervous and remote from her, clinging rather anxiously to Mrs Holloway (the devil they knew) who tearfully protested her affection for them. Rudyard was frightened by his mother's return, for he had come to believe all the evil Mrs Holloway spoke of him, and expected his parents to represent that even more exacting authority which would produce yet more frightful punishment than Lorne Lodge afforded. He had, after all, never dared to tell Aunt Georgie about his misery, being sure that this would only lead to the exposure of his own wickedness and mendacity, and his banishment from The Grange. So when Alice Kipling came upstairs to kiss him goodnight he was sure she could only be leaning over to hit him in the dark – an unfairness even Mrs Holloway had never attempted. And he threw up an arm to fend her off.

Alice took the children away for long months of holiday that were to lead Ruddy to recovery and happiness. They stayed on a farm in Epping Forest where Ruddy immediately made friends with a gipsy, and delighted in his tales of dishonest horse-trading. The naturally boisterous spirits which had been crushed by Lorne Lodge returned, and the farmer found him a handful, objecting particularly to his experiments with milking cows as they stood in the fields. When cousin Stan Baldwin came to stay the two little boys ran wild. Alice had suffered distress enough at Ruddy's tendency to come indoors with his boots covered in manure or pig's blood. Stan and Ruddy together got splendidly muddy and splendidly stung when they attacked a wasp's nest by a pond with switches of broom. Nobody was pleased when the two stole a foot-long roly-poly pudding from the kitchen. And Alice, incapable as ever of imposing any discipline at all, sent for her unmarried sister Edith to help. Edie was immediately treated to a taste of children's conduct under Alice's care when fish was carried in for dinner on the night of her arrival. Ruddy, Stan and Trix rose as one, holding their noses, and declared that it stank. Edie restored order without terrifying her sister's offspring, and the rest of the glorious holiday at Epping was less startlingly eventful, if no less memorably enjoyable.

After Stan had returned to Bewdley, the Kiplings went to a lodging-house in Brompton Road. Here Ruddy suffered the first of the attacks of insomnia to which he was to be a prey for the rest of his life. Finding himself sleepless, he reflected charitably that

As a boy, Kipling knew many of the writers and artists of the 1880s, and was struck by the extensive corrections he saw on a manuscript page of Dickens' David Copperfield.

his pet toad Pluto, captured in Epping Forest, might also be restless and thirsty. So he crept into his mother's room and broke the water jug in an attempt to settle Pluto.

Alice gave her children season tickets to the Victoria and Albert Museum to keep them occupied, and as became their father's offspring, they revelled in it. Among the treasures and mechanical marvels Ruddy noticed the manuscript of one of Dickens' novels. And this holiday year showed him his *métier*.

'By the end of that long holiday I understood that my Mother had written verses, that my Father "wrote things" also; that books and pictures were among the most important affairs in the world; that I could read as much as I chose and ask the meaning of things from anyone I met. I had found out, too, that one could take pen and set down what one thought, and that nobody accused one of "showing off" by so doing.'

Before returning to India, Alice settled Rudyard in with three ladies – the Misses Craik and their widowed sister Mrs Winnard – who were to replace Mrs Holloway as his holiday protectors while he went to boarding school. They were charming, cultivated people, who revered Carlyle, and were on terms of intimacy with Christina Rossetti, Jean Ingelow, and other admired writers of the 1880s. Rudyard was hardly the perfect boarder for them but he was happy there, and enjoyed meeting William and Alice De Morgan, who let him play with the paints they used for glazing their fashionable artistic tiles.

Trix, astonishingly, was sent back to Lorne Lodge, where Rudyard sometimes visited her during the holidays. It still seems never to have been suggested that relatives might take the children, though Trix in adult life felt that they ought to have been sent to Lockwood's mother in Skipton. But Lockwood's relatives never entered into Macdonald calculations. And the move to boarding school put the House of Desolation out of Rudyard's mind for the next few years.

*Kipling at School, a drawing by C.G.Beresford
from his* Schooldays with Kipling.

A Schoolboy with a Moustache

AFTER THE DISASTER OF SOUTHSEA, LOCKWOOD and Alice were more careful in selecting a school for their sensitive son. A family friend, Cormell Price, was a schoolmaster by profession, already known to little Ruddy as 'Uncle Crom'; and the boy was despatched to him for what were to prove his only years of formal education.

Cormell Price had been at school in Birmingham with Ned Burne-Jones. Afterwards he had gone to Oxford, where he became friendly with William Morris and was accepted by the younger Pre-Raphaelites as one of themselves. But he did not become a painter or a poet. After a half-hearted attempt to train for medicine, he went to Russia as private tutor to the children of a wealthy family. For the rest of his life he was to be Russophile, liberal, and anti-jingoistic.

On his return to England he continued teaching. He became a housemaster at Haileybury, the most Anglo-Indian of the public schools, and successfully established its 'modern' side. When, in 1874, a group of army officers decided that they wanted a cheap school to prepare their sons for the dreaded Army Examinations that were replacing the old nepotic system of purchased commissions, it was to Cormell Price they turned as a possible headmaster. So Price took his distinguished-looking beard and monocle to Westward Ho!, in Devon, where with a nucleus of old pupils from Haileybury he founded the United Services College.

English 'public schools' are actually private boarding schools, catering to boys aged between thirteen and eighteen. Many of them were founded several hundred years ago. By the early nineteenth century they were disgracefully and dangerously ill-disciplined and disorganised. Dr Thomas Arnold, headmaster of Rugby School, devised a system of allowing certain older boys limited privileges, provided they carried out disciplinary and organisational duties, and supported the tone of 'muscular Christianity' he favoured. Rugby's reputation soared, as a consequence. Arnold's methods were almost universally copied by the existing Public Schools, and a host of new institutions following his example were founded in the late nineteenth century.

Price's great achievement as a headmaster was to give the parents what they wanted without damaging the boys' sense of dignity or reality. This was no simple task. The parents wanted a cheap crammer, while the more able of the assistant masters wanted to imitate the educational reforms Arnold of Rugby had brought to the public schools. Price, who fully appreciated the benefits of the Arnoldian system was none the less firm in refusing to admit the rigid Anglicanism and loudly-proclaimed spirit of public service that underlay Arnold's superficies of monitors and reading parties. Nor did he let the boys deceive themselves into thinking that their little academy was in any prestigious sense a Public School. It was a limited liability company, owned by some of the parents, and its most important feature was the Army Class in which senior boys were coached for the examination on which their careers depended.

On the other hand, he did allow a form of school spirit to flourish. Although the enthusiastic assistant masters were discouraged from making sports matches, house loyalty, and character building the centre of life at Westward Ho!, Price's easy-going tolerance of boyhood and its limitations gave his pupils a sense of social and intellectual superiority over the inmates of more obvious crammers, where work was forced into unwilling and incapable heads, and a tremendous emphasis on a well-drilled cadet force was expected to impress the army examiners with the officer material put before them.

Early in 1878 the small, rather tubby, bespectacled Rudyard arrived at the bleak row of five-storey boarding houses that had been knocked together into a rudimentary school by the seaside, and was assigned to Mr M. H. Pugh's house for small boys. Pugh was a decent, well-intentioned, conscientious, unimaginative man, of limited scholarly abilities. He took his ideals of housemastership from his more go-ahead colleagues, and followed them to the best of his ability. During Kipling's time at the school, his special house for small boys was transformed into a normal house of mixed ages, and he was to remain Kipling's housemaster for the rest of his school career. Pictures of him show a thin-faced, anxious man, nervously trying to live up to the standards imposed by more confident pedagogues. Readers of *Stalky & Co.* will recognise Mr Prout's unhappiness about a house that will not evince sterling house spirit. The boys, of course, paid most attention to his large frame, resting on outsize feet, for which physique they nicknamed him 'the Hefter'. The adult Kipling remembered him as a man whose 'errors sprang from pure and excessive goodness'.

Within two days of his arrival in Pugh's house, Kipling had made a friend. George Beresford was an Irish boy; quiet, serious, and superior, with a passion for books. He was quick to notice that the new boy with the spectacles and the astonishingly early growth of thin black moustache also showed signs of a literary bent and the two became close companions for the rest of their schooldays.

The first term was not easy. The school had not been running long; it was cheap; and the boys were a mixed lot. Under Cormell Price's light disciplinary hand, a fair degree of bullying passed unnoticed by his authority. For although his nickname actually was 'Proosian Bates', this had more to do with a confused understanding of his tutorship in Russia than with any 'Prussian' discipline the liberal Pre-Raphaelite might have imposed on his boys.

Beresford and Kipling missed the extremer boyish cruelties of the school's opening years, but were still in danger of being picked on by bigger boys who disliked an uppity manner in their juniors, or just wanted to impose their personality on any one weaker than themselves. There was no system of compulsory fagging, although a tradition of calling the younger boys 'fags' existed. Senior boys who wanted odd jobs done by junior 'varlets' had to bargain for the work with promises of food. Kipling gained nothing by this: he was too clumsy and untidy to be trusted with any cooking or washing up.

Any boarding school of the late nineteenth century maintained its discipline on a firm basis of beating. But Cormell Price was too liberal-minded and cosmopolitan for this to become orgiastic or cruelly ritualised at the United Services College. Prefects were allowed to administer three strokes of the ground-ash for any infringement of their particular privileges (pipe-smoking being their most jealously defended perquisite), and similarly punished any failure to attend compulsory games. Housemasters were free to cane boys themselves, and for certain serious offences, like drinking or sodomy, were expected to pass offenders on to the headmaster, who might inflict a public caning, or expulsion, or both.

Kipling, naturally, loathed the humiliation of being beaten, and quickly adopted a permanent strategy of caution and diplomacy to ensure that he rarely, if ever, endured it. He was lucky that Cormell Price was already a friend, and an avuncular friend of a kind that would have found it repellent to thrash Lockwood's Ruddy. He was lucky, too, that there was only one master – the chaplain, 'Belly' Campbell – who laid about him indiscriminately with a stick.

Campbell, by all accounts a rather horrible man, was also the only member of the staff who employed the kind of heavy moral blackmail Rudyard had endured in the House of Desolation. He suffered from an obsessive concern that there might be homosexual activity among the boys, and tried to persuade the other masters to join him in uttering dire and pious warnings. Fortunately, his colleagues overwhelmingly rejected his approach, and pretended that the copious fresh air and exercise available to the boys left them too tired for any sexual desire. In adult life Kipling supported this pretence, though a chance remark in *Stalky & Co.* shows that it was only a pretence.

Still, Campbell's presence made life uncomfortable with reminiscences of Mrs Holloway's cosmic picture, and it was a relief when he left the school after two years. Characteristically, he improved the occasion with a gushingly sentimental sermon regretting his departure, and hoping that no boy had any hard feelings against him. He even managed to weep a little at the thought that his well-intentioned concern for the boys' souls might have seemed unacceptable when translated into excited beatings. The school was touched by the performance, and might have forgiven the man from the bottom of its adolescent heart, had not Kipling cut through the humbug with the caustic observation, 'Two years' bullying is not paid for with half an hour's blubbering in the pulpit.'

Rudyard was growing more robust and confident. Simple fighting and bullying; beatings given without accompanying moralising; blows accepted as immediate pain, without the threat of future humiliation or damnation: these were sufferings which the 'Black Sheep' could absorb and accept. He was the only bespectacled boy in the school, and for this he was nicknamed 'Giglamps'. His eyesight excused him from some games and made him poor at others. He was inky and bookish and round-shouldered. And for all these things he suffered some teasing. But no one seriously suggested that he was a worthless human being, and he was secure in the knowledge that the ultimate source of power in his little world, the Head, thought him a delightful and valuable person.

This experience was vitally and positively important in Kipling's development. He was to become a writer whose deep love of rough and apparently insensitive masculine society suggested to critics that he was himself insensitive. His casual attitude to punitive thrashings, given and accepted with a gentlemanly handshake; his undoubted delight in the idea of violent practical jokes; his willing acceptance of soldiers casually destroying anonymous 'enemies'; these things have been taken as evidence that his sensitivity had soured, and he become temperamentally cruel. But these attitudes must be seen against the background of Westward Ho! *Stalky & Co.* should not be dismissed as a novel which merely exults in savagery and immaturity. Schooldays, for Kipling, were a time in which he discovered that rough camaraderie permitted a respect for the individual which was a wonderful release from religious repression. Casual violence had nothing to do with bitter and embittering hatred but narrow piety had. Kipling's ebullient

The United Services College, Westward Ho!

appearance of insensitivity is actually a form of generous sensitivity. And there is no hypocrisy, sycophancy or masochism in his famous verse-tribute to his cane-wielding schoolmasters:

> There we met with famous men
>   Set in office o'er us;
> And they beat on us with rods –
> Faithfully with many rods –
> Daily beat us on with rods,
>   For the love they bore us.
>
> Wherefore praise we famous men
> From whose bays we borrow –
> They that put aside To-day –
> All the joys of their To-day –
> And with the toil of their To-day
> Bought for us To-morrow!

On one point, if only one, the adult Kipling would have been in complete agreement with Max Beerbohm: he would have dismissed as outrageous and offensive impertinence G. B. Shaw's assertion that 'Those who can, do: those who can't, teach.' Kipling was aware that the West country schoolmaster might make no stir in the great world *'Men of little showing'*, he called his teachers. But he never doubted that he owed them much, and he was supremely lucky in learning English and Latin literature from a really first-class teacher, Mr William Crofts.

Beresford, inclined to be smart and supercilious, failed to recognise the quality of Croft's teaching. But he left an account of a lesson on *Lycidas* that is more impressive than he intended, particularly when it is recalled that Crofts prepared and carried out this work for and with a group of incipient army officers, none of whom might be expected to take easily to his own scholarly love of literature.

> 'The subject was Milton's *Lycidas*. The class worked on it exhaustively, reading it forwards and backwards, ticking off every word, then studying the poem's complete history and derivation, speculating on

what the first draft of it was like, trying to discover by internal evidence the successive steps of correction and polishing, searching laboriously through all previous literature to discover the plagiarisms and the sources of them, then searching further to find if these sources were plagiarisms and to discover their sources, and so on back and back. They paraphrased the poem, and wrote it in the prose styles of all the greatest masters. They turned the prose back into verse and compared it with the original. Milton would have learned a lot if he could have attended that class.'

Beresford, a self-satisfied, half-baked intellectual, who early delighted his friend 'Gigger' Kipling by calling the masters 'ushers', and meaning it, learned little from Crofts. Kipling learned all he could. He learned to cope with the taxing work Crofts put before him, and when necessary to cheat his way round Crofts' private tests, on which nothing but personal honour rested. He learned to listen to Crofts' throwaway remarks, and take in the apparently irrelevant observations through which Crofts showed that literature was for him an essential part of life and not a mere discipline through which boys must drudge. He accepted Crofts' habitual sarcasm as evidence that he had shown himself worthy of some personal attention, and enjoyed the varied mastery of language Crofts displayed in putting down all boys in general, and Kipling in particular. They had a notable disagreement in class over Walt Whitman. Crofts' tastes were old-fashioned and decided: to him, Whitman seemed a mere charlatan whose reputation had been inflated artificially by the back-scratching London intellectuals with whom Kipling and Price associated during the holidays. But he played fair when he critically disembowelled Kipling's idolised *Leaves of Grass* in class: he evinced no personal envy of Kipling's private association with the fashionably great. And it is safe to assume that Kipling learned two important lessons from the superficially humiliating set-to: that it was important to base one's literary preferences on one's real feelings, and not metropolitan trends; and that it was necessary to read poetry before dismissing it. Crofts may have detested Whitman but he owned a copy of his works, and knew his way around it well enough to prove his hostile points by selective quotation. For years after he had left school the young Kipling posted his anonymous journalism from India to Crofts, valuing his opinion and correction above anyone else's.

This may seem surprising to readers who have recognised in Crofts a shadowy original of the Mr King of *Stalky & Co*. But the apparently different estimates of the man can be reconciled. When Kipling wrote *Stalky & Co*. he permitted himself a clear and direct recall of schoolboy society, as he had experienced it subjectively, in common with his peer group. Of course Beetle (Kipling), M'Turk (Beresford), and Stalky (L. C. Dunsterville) regard themselves as being above the common herd and hold themselves a bit aloof from their schoolfellows. But in so doing they are only obeying the normal and recognisable cliqueishness of adolescence: other boys in the school – footballers, prefects, or amateur naturalists, say – might equally well have seen themselves as a separate and superior in-group. And, no doubt, did. But what Kipling is careful to exclude is any way in which Beetle feels himself to be separate from Stalky and M'Turk. The individuality of Kipling is only expressed in such ways as the schoolboys Dunsterville and Beresford might have appreciated. And they would not have appreciated any high degree of admiration for Mr Crofts.

The attitude Kipling shared with his friends was a rejection of Crofts' public school professionalism. Crofts was a Brasenose College man, and accepted the high nineteenth-century Oxford ideal of education of the whole man for public service. Thus he wanted to follow Arnold's methods and aims. Kipling and his friends objected to the outer forms in which this inner spirit came clothed. With boyish realism they grasped that 'house spirit', team games,

'The Head with a beard'. Cormell Price, the enlightened and successful founder of the United Services College.

'Belly – irritated'. The chaplain at the College for two years, 'Belly' Campbell was the only member of the staff whom Beresford and Kipling actively disliked.

and a public appearance of College superiority were mere trappings. Instinctively, they preferred Cormell Price's liberal realism about the place to Croft's ambitious hope that the United Services College might grow into a serious rival to Blundell's and other such older and wealthier foundations. Some snobbery inheres in the public school ideal of social leadership, but the schoolboy Kipling had already noted the fraudulent element in the British class system. The lower orders, he told his friends, did not really exist, for everyone talked about them, however far down the social scale one went; yet no one admitted to being one of them.

Crofts was the very latest model of a modern public school housemaster. He ran his house, like his private rooms, on meticulously orderly lines. He kept himself spruce and fit, and, with becoming modesty, concealed from the school the fact that he was an athlete of distinction – twice winner of the

Diamond Sculls. But Kipling and his friends preferred to oppose Crofts' outward sense of 'good form' using it as an obvious enemy against which they could exercise and improve their gifts of guile and self-preservation. When the time came, Kipling might acknowledge Crofts' importance to him personally. But thinking as a schoolboy rather than an incipient writer he knew that his primary response to Crofts' was one of total rejection of the sterile trappings of public school spirit as exhibited in the man's housemastership.

A more easily congenial master was the chaplain who succeeded Campbell. Mr Willies, the Reverend John Gillett of *Stalky & Co.*, was easy-going and uninterfering. He liked Kipling, and quietly encouraged his literary interests. The Padre's books were at young Gigger's disposal, and, as the boy grew older, he was often welcome into the Padre's study for a thoughtful, untheological chat over a dubiously legal briar pipe.

Willies' orotundity, and perhaps his cloth, preserved him from the more earnestly athletic side of the school's life. But he did enjoy swimming off the Pebble Ridge, a high bar of smooth-washed boulders lying to the eastern end of Westward Ho! Kipling's giglamps might disqualify him from participation

'King – on top of his form'. The Mr King familiar to readers of Stalky & Co *was based on William Crofts, who taught English and Latin at the United Services College. But the character portrayed subjectively – from a schoolboy's standpoint – in* Stalky, *had little resemblance to William Crofts, a gifted teacher who strongly influenced the direction of Kipling's life.*

'Stalky quietly competent'. Lionel Dunsterville.

in football or cricket. Stalky's insistence that paper-chasing cross-country runs were a heaven-sent opportunity to find a quiet hedge and smoke a peaceful pipe might save his friend from long-distance loneliness; but swimming was the one sport in which Kipling could excel. He loved to accompany the chaplain on his bathing-parties, and then, while the other boys enjoyed glimpses of Lundy Island in the lift of the waves, he concentrated on reciting Swinburne, and trying to link the poet's complex metres to the combined rhythm of his own strokes, and the crashing rise and fall of the breakers.

For Kipling was undisguisedly and unashamedly the school's intellectual and poet. A passion for reading had brought him together with Beresford, and the two ostentatiously isolated themselves from the mob by their shared knowledge of strange gods like Ruskin and Rossetti. Although Kipling modestly concealed his relationship to Poynter and Burne-Jones with as much diffidence as he used to conceal his first Christian name (being 'John Rudyard' to a school that knew not Joseph), he could not avoid showing Beresford that Gigs knew best about artistic matters. Gigs knew that it was unsafe to talk freely to any artist before you had found out whether he was an Academy man or a 'Grosvenor Gallery' man. Gigs was treated with some sort of respect by the Head which made Beresford's assumption of superiority pale into insignificance. Kipling's respect for Beresford was, on the whole, social. He was of the landed gentry, and could teach his friends about the different bores of guns and the preservation of game and the innately acquired spontaneous superiority of the upper-class Englishman.

But when the two made their major move up together inside the school it was as partners in aestheticism and maturity that they chose to dazzle the world. The move up was from being 'tramps' to being 'studymen'. 'Tramps' were ordinary boys, who passed their leisure hours in form-rooms or, in fine weather, in privately knocked-up hides, somewhere within the school's reasonably generous bounds. 'Study-men' were the school's senior fifty boys. They shared, in fours and fives, little rooms, conveniently furnished with coconut matting, plain tables, kitchen chairs, and double gas brackets. Here their chief delight was to brew up gargantuan feasts of cocoa and biscuit, supplementing the school's cheap, plain, and perhaps excessively meagre diet.

Kipling and Beresford were invited to join two slightly senior footballers, whose study-mates had departed for Sandhurst and the adult army world. Delighted, the two aesthetes swept in and took over. They cleared away the boyish jumble of athletic gear; took the cherished first-team caps off the wall, and replaced them with Japanese fans and ornate pottery brackets! A compromise between sportsmanship, artistry and gentlemanliness was achieved by making the dominant feature a set of vividly coloured papier-mâché dead game-birds. This satisfied the footballers' wish that something manly dominate the room, and Kipling and Beresford's wish that it should be something more grown-up than the trophies of mere schoolboy games.

The study boasted a great bow-window overlooking the sea, and a good deal of space. Study dramatics, therefore, became a form of horse-play the oddly matched room-mates could enjoy together, by curtaining off the window bay as a stage, and inviting outsiders to watch. They decided to make their major production a popular farce, and with simple Victorian determination set to counting puns in a number of acting texts from Samuel French's. *Aladdin, or The Wonderful Scamp* proved three puns richer than its nearest rival, and so was chosen. The footballers became Aladdin and Abanazar; Kipling took the Widow Twanky, and Beresford was left as the Executioner. With more parts than study-men to enact them, outsiders were called in. And the greatest of these was Lionel Dunsterville.

Dunsterville, a quite straightforward schoolboy, with a certain skill at practising sly pranks, has become so permanently identified with Kipling's Stalky that one northern university library catalogue nurses the delusion that his Christian names were 'Knightly Stalker'. They were not, but he and Kipling would both have loved the error. Stalky would probably have adapted easily to any company. He accepted and enjoyed Kipling's insistence that their little play, in which he enacted the Sultan, must be pronounced 'Allah-Deen'. He joined Gigger and the footballers in sending to Nathan's for expensive costumes (which the riotous actors ruined), much to the disgust of Beresford, who had made two attempts to decorate his cricket flannels into the appearance of an oriental executioner's trousers. And Stalky made a more fitting companion for the aesthetes than the footballers had done—just as he would have made a more fitting companion for the footballers than the aesthetes had done – when the study was closed.

No outrageous breach of rules led to its closure. Quite simply, a master named Osborne wanted it for his room. So the footballers went and joined up with some more suitable study-mates, and Kipling and Beresford, the most recent initiates to the glory of a study, reverted briefly to the humiliation of tramp-hood. But not for long.

Kipling realised that the tiny room which Osborne had previously tenanted (and which had been the Padre's bedroom before that) could be turned into a study for three. He and Beresford invited Dunsterville to join them, and went off to ask Mr Pugh for permission to occupy it. Thus was born 'Study No. 5' and the association of Stalky & Co.

The first thing to be done for the new study was to give it a character. 'Biscuits' Osborne (he has no place in *Stalky & Co.*) inspired the boys' immediate action. He had set about redecorating the old bow-

*A school group at the United Services College.
Kipling in the centre.*

windowed room rather after the manner of a high aesthetic scene-painter. Dadoes were being loudly proclaimed by Wilde and Whistler as the essence of interior decoration. Whether or not they meant that half the height of walls should be oil-painted with an aesthetic landscape of storks, bullrushes, chrysanthemums and water-lilies, may be another matter. But Osborne was carrying out just such a work. Obviously Kipling and Beresford were not going to admit superior taste in a mere usher. They immediately bought fashionable chocolate and grey paints, and coloured their room in what they took to be Whistler's taste. They picked out their dado and chimney-piece in stencilled Greek honeysuckle and key patterns. Then they sat back to enjoy the fruits of their cultural labours.

Alas, the first discovery they made was that their papier-mâché game-birds now looked horrid and out of place. Expensive curios from the junk shops of Bideford, together with pieces of stonework rescued from the newly-restored parish church, were needed to ornament their study appropriately. No boy would willingly reduce the essential cocoa and biscuits fund; Stalky was almost permanently penniless; and the papier-mâché birds which had cost so much when new were too utterly junk to be bought or traded by the Bideford dealers.

Beresford and Kipling might have had to abandon some of their artistic pretensions, had not Stalky showed those powers of common sense and understanding of ordinary mortals which made him *de facto* leader of his two more intelligent companions. He knew that outsiders had always envied the dead birds, and now proposed to auction them. It was essential to conceal the few antique curios the study already possessed, and pretend that dire poverty and a desperate thirst for cocoa dictated the sale. It was necessary to affect deep regret as each glossy, embossed, three-dimensional still-life found a purchaser. And then, when the money was safely in hand, it was possible to go stealthily out to town, pretending that a visit to the dentist made the extension of bounds necessary, and return laden with treasure to arouse the ire and envy of those who had financed the venture in return for tawdry cardboard cast-offs. Such was actual 'stalkiness'; the imaginative cunning and guile which Kipling exaggerated and idolised in his school stories.

Academic labours were divided between members of the study. Dunsterville, destined for a straightforward military career, mastered enough mathematics to coach his friends through their work. Beresford was the study's Latinist, and (wrongly) refused to believe that Kipling had really come to master Horace in later life. Kipling taught his friends all the French they ever knew, though Beresford snobbishly despised the Parisian accent his friend acquired.

29

Kipling's private life became increasingly literary. He scribbled endless verse. Bawdy and abusive limericks on the masters came easily. More serious attempts at poetry also seemed easy, and led his verse into dangerous facility. 'Gigadibs the literary man', Crofts called him, one day, and hurled Browning's *Men and Women* at him, that he might trace the quotation. Kipling devoured the book, and imitated the poet's unaesthetic directness.

Prose, his true *métier*, demanded more concentrated attention. Cormell Price revived a defunct school magazine specifically for Kipling to be its editor. And the boy learned about meeting deadlines, writing material to fill space left by unreliable contributors, and visiting printers to see his work set up.

Price also gave his friend's son the run of his study, and encouraged him to read whatever interested him. A wide, independent and unusual frame of literary reference was opened up to Kipling. Hakluyt and Alexander Smith; Pushkin and Lermontov; Fletcher and Marlowe; Donne, Crashaw, Dryden, Omar Khayam and Ossian; Borrow and Peacock: all began to fill his mind. Price would wander in while he read, and encourage him to think seriously of writers, dead and living.

The holidays were further occasions for artistic and literary education. He stayed with his aunts, and discovered there James Thomson's *City of Dreadful Night*, Swinburne, Tennyson and Rossetti. Early in his schooldays, an important holiday experience had been a trip to Paris with his father. Lockwood Kipling came over from India in 1878 to supervise the Indian exhibit at the Paris Exposition. He gave young Rudyard a free pass to the exhibition, and two francs a day for food. The boy discovered the excellence of cheap French food in Duval's restaurants, and soon made friends with another visiting English lad, a scholar of Christ's Hospital. The two scandalised Parisians by playing paper-chase in the Bois de Boulogne. The Bluecoat boy's uniform was even more puzzling than his untidy idea of sport: 'What,' the gendarmes demanded, 'is the genesis of this bizarre uniform? Military? Civil? Ecclesiastical?'

At the same time, Rudyard discovered the beauties of Notre Dame, the glories of the Left Bank, the book-boxes of the Quai Voltaire, and the depth of feeling left on Parisians by their defeat in the Franco-Prussian war of 1870. It was the beginning of an ardent francophilia. Lockwood Kipling saw to it that this healthy cultural growth should not be stunted by linguistic incapability. He gave his son a translation of Jules Verne's *Twenty Thousand Leagues Under the Sea,* and when he was halfway through it, took it away and replaced it with the original in French, and a dictionary. After this he put him to reading Dumas' romances in French. From then on, Kipling was to boost his status at school with his knowledge of French literature, usually regarded as slightly immoral in the 1880s.

Masculine prestige in a nineteenth-century boys'

school was difficult to achieve. Bumptiousness and obstreperousness were loathed by boys and masters alike: 'putting on Side' was one of the great offences of the time, and it seems likely that the unwilling suppression of his natural tendency to show off at school led Kipling into much of the tiresome cockiness of his young manhood, when he had been released. For how was a boy to prove his masculinity without a modicum of swagger? Athletic achievement was ruled out by Gigger's eyesight. This also kept him from expectations of a military future, from which the quieter Dunsterville could draw his confident masculinity. A gloating delight in the horrible provided a minor opening: Kipling made one contribution only to the study of Natural History at Westward Ho!, when he found a still-living frog, half eaten by maggots, and spent an afternoon extracting the parasites with a tweezer, before killing both them and the frog together. But delicately brutal cruelty was turned away to linguistic outlets once he passed early adolescence.

Kipling ultimately scored through the combination of his genes and his wits. His precocious moustache had long astonished the school and it was a proud day when he was ordered to shave his scrubby chin long before either Dunsterville or Beresford had thought of owning razors. And this sense of 'being a man' was reinforced by a constant stream of knowing self-advertisement to the effect that young Gigger knew all about women.

French literature was not his only source for such simulated knowledge. He was reading Donne in an age when few adults, and no other recorded schoolboys, had heard of him. And so, without revealing his prosaically printed sources, he hinted to his friends that he knew surprising things about that mysterious gender, segregated from the lives of boys and masters alike at the United Services College.

In the long run, this 'masculinity' was to be of grave disservice to the writer. He remained, for a long time, retarded as a kind of 'knowing' schoolboy, whose ideas of exotic womanhood were infantile. In *The Light that Failed* he veered horribly between the sickly sentiment of an overgrown calf-love, and its concomitant romanticising of the erotic in fantastic Egyptian brothels, and 'a sort of Negroid-Jewess-Cuban; with morals to match', whatever that may be supposed to mean.

Part of the problem was that Kipling actually did fall in love while he was at school, and then seven years' absence in India prevented him from outgrowing the attachment in a normal healthy way. Flo Garrard was another child boarder at the House of Desolation. Rudyard met her there while visiting Trix during the holidays, before Trix had been finally removed from Mrs Holloway's care. Flo is portrayed, as well as the young Kipling could manage, as Maisie in *The Light that Failed.* She kept a pet goat. She despised Mrs Holloway. She was pretty enough to despise almost every one if she chose. She was a year or so older than Rudyard, and despised him as mere boy, until one day, suddenly, he seemed so much more. And then Rudyard, who was sixteen at the time, felt that he was irrevocably committed; that he had found the love of his life; that he was really experiencing grown-up passion.

His family had simpler ideas about his growing up. They had privately published an edition of his *Schoolboy Lyrics* in India, and had no doubt that he would earn his living with his pen. As they could not afford to send the gifted boy to university, Lockwood and Alice decided to have him out with them. 'Uncle Crom' summoned his pupil to his study, one day in 1882, and told him that he would be going to India at the end of the summer, to work on a newspaper for one hundred rupees a month.

Rudyard rejoiced when he thought of the public side of this life: real work for real pay. But his private emotions were in turmoil. To rejoin his beloved parents would be a delight: had not Alice Kipling, alone among Collegians' parents, managed to invite herself to a study cocoa-brew when on home leave, and not disgraced herself at the time? But Flo Garrard, on the other hand: how could he leave her? He proposed to his friends that he should send a cable saying, 'I have taken a wife and therefore I cannot come.' They thought it a joke; Beresford suspected that the lure of literary London as opposed to illiterate Lahore might be giving Gigadibs pause. But when Rudyard Kipling sailed from Tilbury on his own on the P. & O. steamer *Brindisi*, one drizzling September day, he faced the prospect of a long, lonely sea-voyage with the private conviction that he was engaged to Flo.

The Pavilion of the Prince of Wales' Indian Collection at the Paris Exposition 1878. Lockwood Kipling was responsible for the Indian exhibit, and took Rudyard to Paris to see it.

The Creation of Kipling

THE NEXT SEVEN YEARS WERE THE MOST important of Kipling's life. Living and working among Anglo-Indians taught him his craft, and furnished him with attitudes and much of the subject-matter which would come to be his hallmark as a writer. And he moved in a direction that would have been utterly unpredictable when he left Westward Ho!

The United Services College intellectual had identified himself with the self-conscious aestheticism of the 1880s. The one 'imperialist' poem in his *Schoolboy Lyrics*, the ode *Ave Imperatrix*, imitated a poem of the same title by, of all people, Oscar Wilde. His adored uncles and aunts were all advanced liberals after the manner of fashionable artists. Even the Baldwins had not yet been disgusted by Gladstone into changing their politics to the Conservatism they were to typify through Stan's ultimate success. Cormell Price had influenced Kipling more than any other teacher, and he was a gentle internationalist liberal. Even Crofts, the rigid public school man, was an anti-jingoist liberal, who once appeared on a platform with Price to oppose Disraelian foreign policies. Had Kipling proceeded to Oxford, he would almost certainly have clung to the arty left-of-centre, and although his talents would still probably have left his name memorable it would have held none of the conservative, imperialist resonance it now carries.

Kipling, as we think of him, was shaped by Anglo-Indian official and military society. And this society was predominantly philistine and provincial: deeply racist, anti-democratic, and politically anti-liberal. Kipling, of course, had developed during his boyhood strong reserves of aestheticism, metropolitanism, humanity, friendliness across class-barriers, and generosity, which prevented these vices from corrupting his art. But he was infected by them, and defended them, for they were attitudes held by a society which he knew to be superciliously undervalued in the centres of artistic power.

The virtues of Anglo-Indian society which appealed to Kipling were industriousness, conscientious attention to duty, resolution in the face of adversity, and intense group loyalty. This last may have carried the largest appeal for him personally. He was to need the support of a group throughout his life, and many critics, noting his attachment to Freemasons, shop-talking engineers, small land-owners, and other exclusive groups, have taken this to be the central fact in his personality. If this is accepted, it is probably to be accounted for by his seven years apprenticeship in India rather than by his sense of deprivation and exclusion from his family at Southsea. Certainly he was no 'outsider' at the United Services College, for all his spectacles and intellectual superiority.

The Anglo-Indian community after the Mutiny of 1857 was a very tight in-group. The British saw themselves as an embattled ruling minority in a potentially hostile land. Reformers in the early nineteenth century had picked out certain aspects of Hindu culture which seemed morally offensive, and to the ultimate benefit of India had successfully suppressed those which were obviously harmful. Thus slavery was proscribed. *Suttee*, the ceremonial immolation of widows on their husbands' funeral pyres, was suppressed. And the *thuggee*, highly organised bands of murderous robbers, who killed travellers almost with impunity all over northern India, acting, they claimed, in the name of the goddess Kali, were put down by outraged British officials. Christian missionaries then managed to win the foothold that the eighteenth-century trading company had forbidden them in India. They spread the message that Indian religions were vicious superstations. And senior administrators let themselves be persuaded that Indian officials were corrupt and untrustworthy. So the higher reaches of the Civil Service and the Army in India were closed to natives. British memsahibs wanted little more than the closest possible imitation of British life in their ghettoes, and increasingly cut off their menfolk from the casual intercourse with Indian life which obtained in the early days of the East India Company.

By 1857, the British were effectively another exclusive caste in a land that was used to such divisions. But they were very much a ruling caste and they owed their power to a large extent to the anarchic misrule on the part of native princes which had increased since the Company began to trade. British India was not entirely the creation of conscious imperialist expansion: much territory had been conquered merely to safeguard trading areas from pointless and uncontrolled depredations. By the mid-nineteenth century, the greatness of the empires and principalities Britain had originally

Above Captain J. A. Wood winning the VC at
Reshire Fort. *The Indian Mutiny was a
profound shock to the English and served to
strengthen their assumptions of superiority over
a 'lesser breed'. The community young Kipling
returned to in 1882 saw itself as an embattled minority in a
potentially hostile country. From a painting by
Lionel Edwards, National Army Museum, Sandhurst.*

Top *Bombay in 1878. The railway station,
reminiscent of the Victoria & Albert Museum,
from a painting by Axel Herman Haig.
India Office Library.*

Kipling in India, aged nineteen, where he was 'Kupeleen Sahib' to his servants.

function in their own country should be the supply of cheap labour. Paternalist civil servants, on the other hand, regarded them as wayward children. Both agreed that they were not to be trusted. Yet neither could do without them in subordinate positions. In consequence, individual servants or employees might be given disproportionate sentimental esteem, while their race or caste as a whole was damned out of hand. British India's attitude to what it called its 'subject races' was hopelessly confused and irrational. The British did not even agree among themselves as to what they were doing governing India at all; most thought they didn't much like being exiled to Asia.

At least, it might be assumed, the whole mishmash of planters making money, administrators satisfying a wish for a good but useful career, soldiers gaining reasonably active experience, wives marrying good salaries and obtaining cheap servants, journalists and teachers making a living out of this distant extension of England's economy, and adventurers enjoying a society less efficiently policed than Europe – at least all these people could gain a sense of common identity by looking back to England. But no, England had a trying habit of electing Liberal governments, and Liberal governments sent out Liberal Viceroys who tried to govern the subcontinent with some regard to liberal principles and little regard for illiberal prejudices.

The British in England had never heard of any prominent Anglo-Indians. They knew nothing and cared less about the day-to-day problems of Indian government. They disapproved strongly of the Mutiny, and were glad to see it put down. But equally they disapproved strongly of planters who beat their servants to death, and would have been glad to see them put down. They could not understand why an Indian Civil Service composed of highly educated men, who had all gained their places after sitting a difficult competitive examination, was unable to permit normal British freedom to the British in India without at the same time imposing abnormal despotism on the 'subject races'. Members of Parliament – especially Liberals – would visit India, and discover that educated Indians were often more intelligent, able and pleasant than uneducated Anglo-Indian settlers. And the Anglo-Indians would curse them as 'globe-trotters', and insist pathetically, like all entrenched colonials, that only they, the men on the spot, knew what things were really like, and what policies were really necessary.

Morally and emotionally cut off from the home country, then, the Anglo-Indians became a self-conscious inward-looking group, with their own slang, their own customs, and a rather rigid insistence on conformity to the group's standards. It was in this demanding society that Kipling spent the vital seven years until he was twenty-three; and inevitably it marked him for life and narrowed his

found in India had been forgotten, and the Anglo-Indians had come to believe that they were innately superior to the native races around them.

But their superiority was not utterly secure. The Mutiny had happened. British-trained Indian soldiers had risen against their superior officers when the insensitive imposition of European standards looked as though it were really threatening traditional Indian religion, culture and self-respect.

The experience had proved traumatic for the British in India. Trusted servants had killed their masters, and were widely believed to have raped their mistresses. European children had not been spared. Soldiers had broken their oaths of loyalty. Native princes had secretly intrigued for the overthrow of the British, even while protesting their loyalty to the Governor-General.

These events brought all the undercurrents of British racism, with all their innate self-contradictions, into the open. The mutineers had committed horrid atrocities – as might be expected from barbaric savages. Therefore the forces of British civilisation must assert themselves – by tying mutineers to the muzzles of heavy guns and showering parade grounds with their blood and guts, as an object lesson to those troops who had remained loyal. Reforms which offended against Indian religious customs must be stopped. All Indian religious practices were beneath contempt, anyway. After 1857, a powerful group of the British, particularly prominent among the Bengal indigo planters, regarded the Indians as 'damn niggers', whose only mental horizons. He himself knew what would be best for him, when he wrote from India to his Aunt Edith, 'I'd give something to be in the Sixth at Harrow . . . with a University Education to follow.'

After landing at Bombay, and finding himself uttering sentences in long-forgotten Hindustani without knowing what they meant, Kipling journeyed on to Lahore in the Punjab, where his parents had been living for the past seven years. Lockwood had been transferred in 1875, and became curator of the Lahore Museum as well as becoming responsible for setting up an art school on the lines of Bombay's.

The Kiplings enjoyed rather more social success than Lockwood's quite humble standing in the strictly-tiered hierarchy of Anglo-Indian occupations justified. Both Lockwood and Alice contributed occasional pieces to the Allahabad *Pioneer*, the widest-circulating newspaper in the Punjab. In 1876 the Viceroy, Lord Lytton, summoned Lockwood to Simla. The Head of the Lahore Art School was the only man in India believed to know enough about heraldry to be entrusted with the design of

emblazoned banners for the independent Indian princes at the great Delhi Durbar to proclaim Victoria Empress of India. So the name of Kipling was humbly involved with Disraelian imperialism from the moment of its formal inception.

Alice enjoyed a minor triumph with Disraeli's flamboyant literary Viceroy – (Lytton wrote verse under the pseudonym of Owen Meredith). He complimented her on the embroidery of one of the banners, which she was known to have undertaken herself, and expressed enthusiastic interest on learning that she was Mrs Burne-Jones's sister. Although Lockwood was displeased by the shoddy workmanship of some of the pavilions at the Durbar, the gilded occasion satisfied Lytton's and India's sense of theatre, and Lockwood was awarded five hundred rupees and a silver medal for his contribution.

By the time Rudyard arrived in Lahore the Liberals were in power at home and their business-like Viceroy, Lord Ripon, did not share his elegant predecessor's interest in the arts and their practitioners. But the family were delighted at their reunion, and when fifteen-year-old Trix came out the following year, Alice was overjoyed to have what she called 'the Family Square' completed.

The cosy foursome provided a secure emotional base from which Rudyard could work. He was sure of encouragement and praise from his parents. Trix joined him in writing occasionally herself. Lockwood seemed to know more than any other man about

A Victorian engraving of the Hindu practice of suttee: *the widow joins her husband's corpse on his funeral pyre, honouring her bond in death as well as life. Originally self-immolation – following the example of the Hindu scriptures – was voluntary. But rigid custom could often force a hapless woman to endure a horrible death.*

Above *The Khyber Pass in a modern photograph, looking as romantic as in any period engraving. In Kipling's time it was regarded as the obvious route for an invading army, and Russian expansion in Asia was watched with uneasiness by the British in India.*

Opposite, top *Jamrud Fort, at the entrance to the Khyber Pass. From a watercolour by Charles J. Cramer-Roberts, 1879. India Office Library.*

Opposite, bottom *The Victoria Memorial, Calcutta. An odd survival from an age of glory, it stands in the south-east of the* maidan, *the great park of the city. Though it was not opened until 1921 it suggests very strongly the imposition of British rule in an alien land.*

native arts and crafts, and brought a tremendous enthusiastic curiosity to every aspect of life he encountered. And Alice read, praised, and occasionally censored her son's work.

Although Rudyard was happy to be living under his parents' care, and thoroughly enjoyed the feeling that, at seventeen, he was a working man with an office box and a servant, like his father, there was something a little emotionally stifling about the 'Family Square'. Lockwood had worried about the possibility of his son's staying in London, and hoped that Lahore would prove a place of less temptation. But once Rudyard was in Lahore, he began worrying all over again that India itself might hold too many temptations for a young bachelor.

Alice, one may deduce from Rudyard's writings, wanted her son never to grow up. Mothers in his stories poke their noses ceaselessly into their sons' love affairs, and are constantly gratified when these are seen to be coming to nothing. India, as Rudyard saw it, was a land where young men were forever falling dangerously in love with older married women. Alice Kipling, however, kept a watchful eye on him, and would not even let him write with the confident freedom his nature demanded. 'There's no

---

The Lahore Art School, where John Lockwood Kipling was Principal. The Persian bronze gun in the foreground is 'Zam-Zammer', mentioned in the opening chapter of Kim.

Mother in Poetry,' she said in justification of her interference. But it might have been better had Kipling been able to devote himself more decisively to Poetry and less to pleasing Mother. Mother was too determined not to allow the Donne of the 1880s to emerge from her cosy nest, and Kipling formed the characteristic habit of writing about love in the tone of a coldly amused, dispassionate gossip columnist, and of defusing sex by discussing it in the tone of a rather hearty, if remarkably broad-minded, nanny:

'Lalun is a member of the most ancient profession in the world. Lilith was her very-great-grandmamma, and that was before the days of Eve, as every one knows. In the West, people say rude things about Lalun's profession, and write lectures about it, and distribute the lectures to young persons in order that Morality may be preserved. In the East, where the profession is hereditary, descending from mother to daughter, nobody writes lectures or takes any notice; and that is a distinct proof of the inability of the East to manage its own affairs.'

A more obvious source of frustration and elderly control was Kipling's chief. Stephen Wheeler, editor of the Lahore *Civil and Military Gazette*, may have resented having Kipling wished on him as his assistant. He would probably have preferred a more experienced journalist: it was the paper's owners who had favoured Lockwood by appointing his son.

As a result, Wheeler was a grudging and demanding taskmaster. He gave the young Kipling no encouragement to indulge in any flights of fancy; he wanted to turn the boy into a competent newspaperman. Anything beyond this goal was, as far as he was concerned, as undesirable as anything falling short of it.

Kipling fretted at first, but under pressure he learned his trade thoroughly, and subsequently felt that he should be grateful to Wheeler for having kept his nose to the grindstone. But it took some effort to avoid desolating bitterness. If Wheeler were not to be cast as another Mrs Holloway he must not be permanently hated. Kipling knew the corrosive effect of misery, and acutely noted that the effect of the House of Desolation was to make him unwilling, for the rest of his life, to indulge in bitter personal hatred on his own account. 'Who having known the Diamond,' he asked, 'will concern himself with glass?'

The price Kipling paid for trying to feel grateful to Wheeler was the sacrifice of some of his love of youth. If it was worth being licked into shape, he must have been a formless young cub before the licking. And if he was the better for being older, wiser and more restrained, so would all other young men be. For the rest of his life he was liable to demand a rather preternatural and wooden virtue from the young. (*The Brushwood Boy* in the cheap romantic story of that name becomes so preposterously perfect that even Kipling notices, and has wise old senior officers wonder about the 'danger of his developing into a regular "Auntie Fuss" of an adjutant', until a spell of active service makes all well.) And he wrote story after story about the correction and instruction of over-confident young men. He was capable of pitying those whose callowness led them to ruin or suicide. But he tried hard not to think of himself as a young man: the cocksure, but shrewdly inactive, narrative voice of his early stories wants to sound thirty or more years old. In fact, of course, Kipling was less than twenty when he began to develop his authorial personality.

He learned very fast that he was too young and inexperienced to stand up to social disapproval. Shortly after his arrival in Lahore, the Indian government attempted to pass the Ilbert Bill, a measure giving native magistrates the power to try any persons charged before them. This Liberal proposal aroused a storm of hysterical protest from Anglo-India. The basic racist objection was of course that no white person should ever appear to be in a position of inferiority to any brown person. But racism is always more fun if a sexual note can be introduced. It was noted that the place of women in Hindu culture was not exactly that of Christian memsahibs. It was stated that Hindu magistrates were not proper people to try white women. It was whispered that Indian judges might abuse their official power to try and compel sexual favours from

Two thugs and a dacoit, from a drawing of 1857. Thugs killed by strangling: the drawing shows one (standing) with his roumal, *the rolled handkerchief used for murder. A companion squats next to him. The dacoit stands behind: his weapon was a stupefying drug and his victim would often be decoyed from a band of travellers by a female accomplice. Once drugged the victim could be robbed. Dacoits, like thugs, worked in groups.*

European women. Altogether a noisy and filthy campaign was mounted by the Anglo-Indians to intimidate the government: it had the short-term effect of winning their object, and forcing the mutilation of the Ilbert Bill; and the long-term effect was to antagonise the most westernised and pro-British Indians, the English-educated middle classes, and to demonstrate to them the precise mixture of riot, agitation and argument which might be used to defeat a despotic government.

All this should have had little effect on the seventeen-year-old Kipling. He was neither a politician nor a lawyer. But Anglo-India was not generous-minded. He who was not enthusiastically screaming in its midst was a form of traitor. And Kipling worked for a newspaper.

Although he was not responsible for the *Civil and Military Gazette's* political leaders Kipling, unlike Wheeler, frequented the Punjab Club where most of the local British bachelors dined nightly. When the *Gazette* moved from opposing the bill to cautiously supporting some of its proposals, the young assistant-editor was hissed by his fellow club-members. The best natured among them checked the outburst by

*William Morris, known as Uncle Topsy to the
Kipling children. The famous writer and artist
was a frequent visitor to the Grange at Fulham,
where Rudyard and his sister Trix enjoyed
holidays from the unhappiness of Southsea.
From a painting by G. F. Watts. National
Portrait Gallery.*

Above *W. E. Henley, as seen by Spy in* Vanity
Fair, *1892. The lame poet and journalist was a
rugged individualist who steered clear of the
self-conscious London literary world of the 1890s.
He was Kipling's closest friend during his
early years as a writer in London.*

Right *Edmund Gosse, as seen by Spy in* Vanity
Fair. *Some years older than Kipling, he was both
friend and admirer, and warned him, in a
review of 1890, that his work was showing
signs of haste. Gosse advised him to put his
pen down for a while.*

One of John Lockwood Kipling's drawings of Indian life, 'A wood-carver'. Simla, 1870.

saying, 'Stop that! The boy's only doing what he's paid to do.' But the damage was done.

Kipling dared not resent the uncouth mob action of the clubmen. He chose instead to resent the fact that he was employed by other men whose decisions might make him unpopular. He began to mistrust exceedingly newspaper proprietors, especially those whom he suspected of desiring honours for themselves. He later insinuated that the knighthood granted to one of the *Gazette's* proprietors was connected with the paper's *volte-face* over the Ilbert Bill. The suggestion was cheap and false: it was ungrateful to a man who had given Kipling a better start in life than his age and education apparently warranted, and it was simply untrue; the knighthood was awarded several years later by a different administration.

Kipling's urgent desire for acceptance in Anglo-Indian society was to lead him into a more serious piece of disloyal ingratitude. He wrote, in 1883, a sarcastic little review of William Morris's poem *The Day is Coming*, in which he held up Morris's high bourgeois socialism to ridicule. He sneered at Morris's dream of an end to trade and competition as absurd in 'a pushing and energetic manufacturer of carpets and stained glass', and claimed that Morris's poetry was obscure and confused – in Morris's own words, 'a weltering tangle'. Now, no one could reasonably ask that Kipling should pretend to sympathise with socialism merely because he liked William Morris. But equally, no one can admire the smug superciliousness with which kind 'Uncle Topsy' was being handled by his courtesy 'nephew'

Morris deserved fair treatment – candid disagreement and some respect for his age and achievements – from Rudyard Kipling. Cheap gibes might come from strangers; Kipling cannot and should not be lightly excused for allowing the lure of popular approval to outweigh the claims of decent civility and gratitude.

In fact, this is the first clear indication of the Achilles' heel which was to cripple Kipling's intellectual reputation for a couple of generations. Kipling learned early that a writer's integrity was of enormous importance, and must not be sold. No offer of money or position could ever persuade him to write anything he did not believe, and he was always scrupulously careful to avoid any mark of official attachment to any political party or government. But what he would not sell in maturity, he gave away while he was too young to know any better. The respect of his elders in India was something he courted like the most shameless literary whore. He simply failed to perceive that hard-working, middle-class Anglo-Indians constituted a herd, and he was sacrificing his integrity by making himself run with them. He made their loves and hates his loves and hates, and in so doing he also adopted their stupidity, their uncontrolled fanaticism, and their downright bad manners.

He never subsequently sold out. Having made himself into an ultra-imperialist colonialist he stuck to the position he had taken up in the 1880s for another fifty years. It became politically absurd; it lost him almost all the serious intellectual readership he deserved at the end of his life, but he defended it with a dogged courage worthy of a better cause. It forced yelps of stridency into his writing, for he was iterating a habit of thought that had originally been assumed, and had not sprung directly from his own observation of life. (He was, by temperament, far more individualistic and democratic than run-of-the-mill mob-imperialists). Morris was only the first victim of the savage animus with which Kipling was to support the prejudices of his earliest audience. The 'cub' had been licked into a cub's shape, and would preserve the note of adolescent waspishness for the rest of his life whenever he wrote of the liberal left.

In 1884 Kipling had his first brushes with genuine bribery, as offered by independent Indian princes. Lord Ripon was making a viceregal tour of their territories, and Kipling went along to report the viceregal progress. (He thoroughly enjoyed it – a reporter was assigned an elephant for transport.)

A matter of some weight to the independent rulers was the number of guns each might expect in his personal salute from the British. To achieve the maximum dignity it was held that a good press was essential, and so the young reporter found himself offered a basket of fruit, a Cashmere shawl, and five hundred rupees. To affront the donor, he returned the bribe by the hands of a sweeper, whose low caste rendered anything he touched unclean. Kipling's servant then warned him that he was in danger of being poisoned if he ate anything thereafter in that particular state. As Rudyard's servant was the son of Lockwood's servant, and answerable to both fathers for the safe return of his young master, he undertook to cook everything Kipling ate for the remainder of the tour. But then, he was the

Alice Kipling, seen on the extreme right, taking part in amateur dramatics in India. Alice had the double pleasure of being both a social success and the mother of a reunited family in Lahore in 1883.

than any one else about Flo Garrard, and was a little worried by what seemed to her the extravagance of her nephew's passion. Rudyard still considered himself engaged, and received presents from Flo. In 1884 he received a rather formal letter from her stating that any understanding between them was at an end. In consequence of this he felt free to pursue his own investigations among the flirtatious ladies of Simla, as far as his own timidity and his mother's watchful eye would allow. But at the same time, he evidently felt that his attachment to Flo had been serious and left a palpable bruise. In 1885 he was writing to his cousin Margaret Burne-Jones ('Dear Wop', they each addressed each other) asking her to make covert inquiries at the Slade School of Art, and

model servant who shaved Kipling before he had woken up each morning.

A more exciting bribe was offered in Lahore itself. An Afghan asked Kipling into his room, and blandly invited him to help himself to bank notes that were piled up there. Kipling refused indignantly, whereat the Afghan calmy replied that the English were fools who didn't know the value of money, and fetched out a beautiful Kashmiri girl. Kipling felt degraded by this offer, and lost his temper. Yet he was, he claimed, tempted when offered his pick of the Afghan's string of horses. Still he refused, and only accepted a cup of coffee, which he was relieved to find was not poisoned.

This rather lurid story was, oddly, told in a letter to Edie the maiden aunt. She had become Rudyard's chosen confidant in some matters. She knew more

send him such reports as she could garner about Flo.

The appointment of Lord Dufferin as Viceroy in 1884 opened a period of quiet success and happiness for the Kipling family, for like his Conservative predecessor, Lord Lytton, Dufferin took to them. His daughter went to Lockwood's drawing classes when the Kiplings were on leave at Simla. His son paid such marked attentions to Trix that the Viceroy felt impelled to ask Alice whether it might not be better for her to remove her daughter to another hill-station. This was a dangerous opportunity to give Alice Kipling; she brightly asked His Excellency why he didn't remove his son? And it was the Viceroy who gave way.

Lockwood remained a fascinating and widely informed man. His wife was a witty and charming conversationalist. Trix was growing into a beauty, though one so distant with young men that she was nicknamed 'the Ice Maiden'. Rudyard was, at this stage, the least notable corner of 'the Family Square'. But the family were pleasant enough acquaintances for the relaxed and worldly Viceroy to invite them to small, private parties at Peterhoff, the rather inconvenient house that served as the viceregal residence during those months of the year during which the government of India was carried out from the cool comfort of the hills. More senior Anglo-Indians, who had to make do with official invitations to large official parties, may have been chagrined at the humble Kiplings' social success but there was nothing they could do about it. Rudyard was getting glimpses of the highest in his society at close quarters, however, and casting a sharp, cynical, observant eye over Simla society.

Simla was a curious town. It was perched on the slopes of the Himalayan foothills in a series of descending terraces, steeply overhung, so that the houses looked ready to pitch off the edges and start sliding down the mountainside. One Viceroy's wife complained that there was only just enough room for a tennis court at Peterhoff, and after a conservatory had been added to extend the ballroom, it was virtually possible to step directly out of the house and over the terrace to the road below, in one precipitous leap. The residence of the army's Commander-in-Chief, the other great powerhouse of government, was described as looking like a series of trams piled on top of one another. And the whole town was roofed inelegantly in corrugated iron.

The town had an odd reputation. The Viceroy and his council and aides-de-camp used it as a working place. Other residents were usually on leave, enjoying a respite from the heat of the plains. Wives and daughters were likely to be sent to the hills on their own while husbands continued to work through the murderous hot weather. As the Viceroy's court was staffed by some of the most eligible bachelors on the sub-continent, the town was believed to be a hotbed of flirtation, intrigue and adultery. It provided a setting with a flavour all its own, and this the young Kipling was quick to capture. His first memorable character to reappear in a number of stories was a representative Simla figure:

> 'Mrs Hauksbee appeared on the horizon; and where she existed was fair chance of trouble. At Simla her by-name was the 'Stormy Petrel'. She had won that title five times to my own certain knowledge. She was a little, brown, thin, almost skinny woman, with big, rolling, violet-blue eyes, and the sweetest manners in the world. You had only to mention her name at afternoon teas for every woman in the room to rise up and call her not blessed.'

Alice Kipling was slightly less than delighted when her son wrote favourable stories about this daring woman, and was very much relieved when

Rudyard, as he appeared in 1891, the year before his marriage to Caroline Balestier. From the portrait by John Collier at Bateman's.

the original of Mrs Hauksbee, a Mrs F.C. Burton, was called home on leave. Lockwood Kipling made no offer to draw or sculpt in relief his idea of Mrs Hauksbee.

But Mrs Hauksbee and her friend Mrs Mallowe were useful for making the sort of points about Anglo-India that could only be made by intelligent women. Thus they noted that there were only two types of men in India: 'The Civilian who'd be delightful if he had the military man's knowledge of the world and style, and the military man who'd be adorable if he had the Civilian's culture.' The society of Anglo-India was, alas, parochial and philistine: 'One by one, these men are worth something. Collectively, they're just a mob of Anglo-Indians. Who cares for what Anglo-Indians say? . . . They have forgotten what of Literature and Art they ever knew.' Whatever Alice Kipling might say or think, Mrs Hauksbee's attitudes sometimes sound as though Rudyard may have taken much of his knowingness about women's private conversations from views his mother might be expected to hold fairly publicly.

1885 took Kipling on visits to the north that were to give him material for the hill-folk and tribesmen

Carrie in 1899. From the full-length portrait by Philip Burne-Jones at Bateman's.

a well-grown pine, as neatly split length-wise as a match by a penknife, in the act of hirpling down the steep hillside by itself. The thunder drowned everything, so that it seemed to be posturing in dumb show, and when it began to hop – horrible vertical hops – the effect was of pure D.T.'

Another vision afforded by the immense height of the mountains was an eagle, circling a thousand feet below. And a family of wild bears remained a sight Kipling remembered, though he cautiously gave them a wide berth.

Back in Lahore the round of work continued. It was a hard, demanding grind, and twice during his time in India, the strain brought on minor break-downs for Kipling. These, however, did not alarm him unduly: the punishing overwork undertaken by most Europeans meant that he was one sufferer among many, and he did not feel brought to the verge of suicide, as were so many around him. And he was grateful that he did not come close to the early death suffered by so many young Anglo-Indians, victims of cholera or typhoid.

Much of his social life was fairly formal. He joined the Freemasons – he was under age but the local lodge wanted a secretary. And under their auspices he began to meet Indian citizens of other races and creeds: 'Muslims, Hindus, Sikhs, members of the Araya and Brahmo Samaj [reformed Hindu sects], and a Jew tyler who was priest and butcher to his little community in the city'.

He dined quite often at the officers' mess, at the Mian Mir cantonment. The East Lancashires and the Northumberland Fusiliers were the regiments which succeeded each other as his hosts during his first few years in India. Another soldier with whom a couple of happy days were to be spent was Lieutenant Dunsterville, passing through Lahore to join his regiment, the Royal Sussex, at Rawalpindi. Both young men were twenty, but Kipling was now an old India hand, whereas Stalky was a 'Griff', or newcomer. Kipling enjoyed patronising him a little, and told him about his adventure in the Khyber pass. Stalky had travelled slowly through Egypt, and had much to tell Kipling about the seedy side of Cairo. Soon after his arrival at Rawalpindi he was to decide to leave the expensive British army and join the Indian army, accepting a commission in the 25th Punjabis, and so giving Kipling an opportunity to produce the slogan, 'Stalky *is* a Sikh!'

'The Regiment' and the Punjab defined two sorts of loyalty Kipling was coming to value highly. The Punjab was noted for its decentralised administration, with heavy responsibilities cast on the man on the spot. Kipling came to admire the practicality and detailed knowledge of local conditions which he detected in District Officers in the Punjab. He shared the Punjab administrators' suspicion of legislation, and vociferated their enthusiasm for quick *ad hoc* executive action.

who appear in his Indian writings. Dufferin was holding a Durbar at Rawalpindi to establish strong diplomatic relations with the Amir of Afghanistan, and Kipling went as a reporter. He gives some account of the occasion in *Soldiers of the Queen* in *The Jungle Book*. The most memorable incident from his point of view was his own, solitary venture a little way into the Khyber Pass on foot. He stopped when a tribesman fired a shot at him from the steep hillside, and after throwing a stone at his attacker, retreated with dignity.

In May he took another trip north, to the Kulu Hills and the Doon country; territory that *Kim* was to cross in the last stages of his 'Great Game'. Here Kipling's adventures may have suggested the mis-fortunes contrived for Kim's French and Russian spies, for his servant quarrelled with the coolies, and Kipling had first to pay the little hill-men extra in compensation for injuries one of their number was said to have suffered, and then had difficulty in persuading them to continue the journey with him. He also witnessed a splendidly dramatic hill thunder-storm that broke out in space *below* him, and gradually rose to the ridge he was on:

'We were all flung on our faces, and when I was able to see again I observed the half of

At times a very distinctive Punjab loyalty colours Kipling's view of India. Being in Lahore, in the Moslem-dominated section of the Punjab, he evinced a fairly consistent bias in favour of Moslem Indians. But his preferred non-Moslem Indians were clearly the good fighting Sikhs of the eastern Punjab. The story *William the Conqueror*, written after he had left India, sets out to celebrate the noble labours of British administrators, who work themselves almost to death in the humane, heartbreaking task of famine relief. But woven into the story is an extraordinary thread of Punjab self-admiration. The team of relief workers are seconded from the Punjab to famine-stricken Madras, and from start to finish of the story, they and Kipling alike seem to regard the disaster as a heaven-sent opportunity to vaunt the superiority of the Punjab:

'"One, two, three – eight districts go under the operations of the Famine Code *ek dum*. They've put Jimmy Hawkins in charge."

'"Good business!" said Scott, with the first sign of interest he had shown. "When in doubt hire a Punjabi. I worked under Jimmy when I first came out and he belonged to the Punjab. He has more *bundobust* than most men."

'"Jimmy's a Jubilee Knight now," said Martyn. "He was a good chap, even though he is a thrice-born civilian and went to the Benighted Presidency. What unholy names these Madras districts rejoice in – all *ungar* or *rungas* or *pillays* or *polliums*."'

Regimental loyalty represented a similar combination of sentiment and devotion to duty. Regimental traditions and accoutrements figure largely in Kipling's tales of officers' messes, and it is clear that, as one would expect of an enthusiastic Freemason, he hugely enjoyed the ritual toasts and the parade of regimental silver. But he was aware, too, that officers who stuck to their regiments were not following the easiest path of ambition. Staff officers had opted out; put their own careers before loyalty

46

to their men and their brother-officers of the regiment. Although Kipling came to know and admire some very senior staff officers, it was characteristic of him in his early days to prefer the less glamorous regimental officers; the men who actually had to do the fighting; the men whose authority had to be established on the spot (by illegal but honourable fisticuffs, if an Ortheris made this possible), and who could not shelter behind distant red tape, regulations, and posted orders, which were altogether too much like the remote law-making of legislators.

About this time, too, Kipling may have started to make the acquaintance of private soldiers. It was in keeping with the disreputable friendships he had formed in boyhood: the gipsy in Epping Forest; the old man at Westward Ho! known as 'Rabbit's eggs', because he believed that the pheasant's eggs he once found in a bush had actually been laid by the rabbit he had just scared off. Private soldiers were not simple heroes or rough diamonds to the Victorian public; they were drunken ruffians. It was exciting evidence that the independent-minded Gigger had not been completely stifled by Anglo-India that Kipling should delight in the company of coarse and criminal soldiers, and share their robust contempt for rules and restrictions.

He learned from them the kind of disreputable secrets that he loved: it was almost sheer joy to him when one of his soldier-friends was convicted of murder, and Kipling, who visited the man during his life imprisonment, knew better than the courts how justified the conviction was. A few years later the Lancashire Fusiliers were replaced by the East Surreys – a batch of accomplished cockney dog-stealers (like Ortheris). By this time Kipling was the devoted owner of a fox-terrier: he worked happily with his dog at his feet, while the editor of the *Gazette* who replaced Stephen Wheeler worked opposite with a similarly placed fox-terrier. One might have expected the future author of *Thy Servant, A Dog* to disapprove of dog-stealing with all the magisterial weight of that middle class respectability he could assume at will. In fact, he was just as happy learning their illicit secrets from the men as he was drinking regimental toasts among the 'domes of old tombs' or the 'marble-inlaid, empty apartments of dead Queens' with their officers in Fort Lahore.

The new editor of the *Gazette* felt that Kipling knew more about the state of the men's minds at Mian Mir than did their chaplain. He also noted that Kipling knew more of native society than any other man he met in India; remarked that there was a real Pathan horse-dealer called Mahbub Ali who used to bring unsalubrious information to the young reporter; and expressed surprise that Kipling even managed to win the confidence of some of the Eurasian community. (Indeed he did! A Junoesque Eurasian, involved in a divorce, offered Kipling the only bribe that could seriously appeal to him in his career – inside information!)

The change of editors heralded an exciting leap forward in Kipling's career. Kay Robinson was younger than Wheeler, and had already met Kipling. They had joked about their work being mistaken for each other's, as one wrote over the initials K.R. and the other as R.K. Robinson's direction from the proprietors was to brighten up the paper, and he set about this task with enthusiasm. One immediate consequence was that Kipling's literary fantasy was set free.

Through the dull, provincial pages of the *Civil and Military Gazette*, short pieces began to flash which signalled the arrival of a new and major talent. The literary productions of Anglo-India had hitherto

Lord Ripon, who succeeded Lord Lytton as Viceroy of India. A liberal reformer who knew nothing of Alice Kipling's artistic connections, he was not liked or admired by Rudyard.

been the output of busy men writing in their spare time. The standard normally achieved had been distinctly inferior to the weaker moments of *Punch*. Facetious Victorian verse was the principal ingredient, varied occasionally by vapid calendar-verses about Indian landscapes.

Kipling immediately adapted the style and matter of his versifying to the habits and tastes of his audience. The Swinburnian metres he had mastered at school were adapted to jolly narratives. A lightly cynical or merely facetious attitude pervaded his verses. If he had anything serious to say, he was likely to find he had written a hymn rather than a poem, for it was only in hymnody that Anglo-Indians were likely to recognise poetical spoutings which they ought to take seriously. These habits of poetic composition remained with Kipling for the rest of his life, so that, as he was aware, he wrote very

*A bronze cast of one of John Lockwood Kipling's
reliefs illustrating his son's work. Ortheris,
Mulvaney and Learoyd from* Soldiers Three.

48

few poems: very few metrical compositions, that is, in which the pleasure offered by the schemes of rhyme and rhythm were precisely harmonised with the pleasures offered by the other features of the work – diction, narrative, expression, and so on. Many of Kipling's most serious verses can be paraphrased without any striking loss of meaning or impact. But he was not a poetaster: these failures on his part are not the result of incompetence. He shows, too often, the ability to write successful individual lines and phrases; shows, also, the versifier's delight in deliberately mixing incongruous elements for a strikingly discordant (and comic) effect. He was a triumphantly successful writer of verses for an audience which did not like poetry. As his audience, whether in India or England, was post-Victorian British, he was far more widely read and enjoyed than any of the successful poets of his day.

In India his verses were enjoyed by the *Gazette's* readers. Some of them had a topicality that added spice to them. *Uriah*, for example, telling the tale of Jack Barrett, sent to work on an unhealthy station in the plains, so that his superior officer might marry his widow after he had died of fever, expressed the bitterness and frustration felt by several men who believed they knew who the originals of that little story were. *My Rival*, the plaint of a young girl who cannot distract the attention of any young men from the superior charms of a middle aged woman, must have delighted Alice Kipling and forced at least token amusement from Trix. For the ages proposed for the protagonists, seventeen and forty-nine, were precisely their own.

No Anglo-Indian writer had ever composed a phrase capable of passing into common usage. Kipling did so (for the first time) when he came to write verses on the snobbish exclusiveness of power that wished to reserve senior posts to college men and ex-officers:

> Wherefore the Little Tin Gods harried their
>   little tin souls,
> Seeing he came not from Chatham, jingled
>   no spur at his heel.

'Arithmetic on the Frontier', the best of the *Departmental Ditties*, found a cold, sardonic detachment that expressed Anglo-India's mixture of pride and discontent better than any heroics:

> A scrimmage in a Border Station –
>   A canter down some dark defile –
> Two thousand pounds of education
>   Drops to a ten-rupee jezail –
> The Crammer's boast, the Squadron's pride,
>   Shot like a rabbit in a ride.

The success of the first series of ten 'Ditties' in the *Gazette* encouraged Kipling to publish a volume. It came out in just such an amusingly jokey form as one might expect to emerge from a family conference. It was made up in the shape and form of a Civil Service envelope, containing official documentation from Rudyard Kipling to the reader. It was to pass through four more normal editions before Kipling left India, expanding each time to take in new verses that had appeared in the press. And the verses attracted more and more attention, until Kipling at last succeeded in offending both Lord Dufferin on his retirement – by presenting him ruminating over his achievements in a Browningesque monologue, and Lord Roberts, the commander-in-chief – by suggesting that some of his appointments had been nepotic. It was something of an achievement to sting with lampoons the two most senior figures who had approved the young man's rising career, but fortunately Kipling was, by then, soon to leave India.

Pieces that were more important for the future were short stories. One or two had been written before Kay Robinson's coming: dreamy passages painting pictures of exotic Lahore by night and day; the extraordinarily sympathetic, yet unsentimental, account of an opium den, *The Gate of a Hundred Sorrows*. And there were short stories of Poe-like mystery and imagination that appeared in the Kipling family's joint publication for Christmas, 1885, *Quartette*. But the repeated production of pieces to fill space in the *Gazette* was a valuable discipline, as the pieces had to be very short.

A family conference decided on a general title for the stories, punning on the two geographical areas of North India. *Plain Tales from the Hills*. Trix contributed one or two Plain Tales to the *Gazette*; not, of course, among those subsequently collected in Rudyard's volume.

The interests of ladies in Anglo-India were well represented in Rudyard's own stories: dangerous flirtations, broken engagements, nearly-broken marriages. The misty, muddy environment of Simla, with its dusty rides and furtive teas in Peliti's Grand Hotel while *affaires* flourished, and its dismal hired transport stations for greetings and farewells as lovers arrived from the plains, eloped to Europe, or deserted their helpless women, was tellingly evoked.

The men's world was predominantly one in which very young and callow men learned the ways of the world. The radical, intellectual nonsense was knocked out of young cubs or old politicians by harsh experience or violent practical jokes. Good chaps kept astonishingly stiff upper lips, with a dash of dry humour as relieving charm. Young men and women in love discovered all too often that unions outside the caste lines of race meant certain suffering for someone: a broken career for an officer who married a Eurasian girl, or loss of face for the Eurasian family that had hoped for such a marriage; a broken heart for the English girl whose planter sweetheart found that a Burmese wife was a good wife; nearly a broken neck for the young official who knew how to conduct an illicit love affair in the back alleys off the bazaar: a complete shattering of all respect for Europeans and Christianity on the part of an Indian 'Madame Butterfly'.

Peterhoff, the house in Simla that served as a viceregal residence. The Kiplings were frequent guests, and Rudyard made good use of his opportunity to observe Simla society.

For in these early stories Kipling was not consistent in his racial attitudes. He clearly recognised that any sort of union with a woman outside the racial caste-barrier would damage an official or military career irreparably, and he clearly saw no reason to reproach the authorities for their racism. Yet he felt considerable romantic sympathy for the lovers, who were likely to be enduring hostility from both sides of the race barriers. And he had nothing but respect for those who had the knowledge or craft to enable them to cross race barriers, whether as illicit lovers like Trejago *(Beyond the Pale)* and Holden *(Without Benefit of Clergy)*, or to learn the secrets of native criminals and magicians, like the wily police officer Strickland, introduced in several stories. And Kipling felt nothing but loathing for those who felt so superior to Indians that they ceased to respond to the human being within the brown skin.

In *The Story of Muhammad Din* he wrote one of the most economical and bitter attacks on British racism ever penned. He doesn't have to bother to tell us how utterly he detests a white doctor who can dismiss a dying child with, 'They have no stamina, these brats.' It says almost everything that could and should be said against the British in India by their conscious enemies. Kipling, taken as a whole, is a curious apologist for British imperialism.

A journalistic promotion led to a wider acquaintance with India. The proprietors transferred Kipling to the Allahabad *Pioneer,* the *Gazette's* big sister-paper. Allahabad meant a move into what is now the United Provinces, to the south and east of the Punjab. And the *Pioneer* quickly sent him on a trip through the Independent Principalities of Rajputana, from which he wrote his *Letters of Marque.* He was also to visit Calcutta, the seat of government in Bengal, at the *Pioneer's* behest.

His sympathies were not significantly broadened. In Calcutta, Kipling observed European-educated natives, and despised them. His generation made 'Bengali' almost a synonym for 'western-educated Indian', and always used the word with a touch of

A view of Simla, the hill station which was transformed into a complete Victorian town. The administration of India moved to Simla from Calcutta during the hot months. The scene of many of Kipling's Plain Tales from the Hills.

contempt. (In defence of his generation of Englishmen it should, perhaps, be observed that educated Punjabi Indians today may sound just as contemptuous when speaking of Bengalis). The British suspected that western education was wasted on Indians: that the 'babu', originally a term of respect for a learned man, was an incompetent clerk with half-digested ideas above his station.

Kipling was offended by the bad sanitation of Calcutta, and unaware that a mere twenty-five years earlier MPs at Westminster had carried on their political debates in just such a stench of sewage, he carried away the confused impression that no smell was so evil as to stop Indian politicians from discussing hifalutin theories, and so Indian self-government would mean inadequate health administration. Indian self-government, he concluded, must

The Viceroy's summer palace in Simla, built in the Scottish baronial style in 1889 to replace Peterhoff.

A company of Sikhs in 1880. Kipling had a great admiration for this fighting race.

never be allowed to come about. It was only desired by the *babus* in any case, and they were not representative of the people as a whole.

Astonishingly, one part of India Kipling never visited was Seeonee and the Waingunga River area in Central India. Although through *The Jungle Books* he made this the best known part of their overseas possessions to his fellow-citizens, he himself only knew it through a friend's holiday photograph-album. The one Mowgli location actually based on his own observation was Cold Lairs *(Kaa's Hunting)* which he modelled on the abandoned city of Amber. And the house occupied by Teddy in *Rikki-Tikki-Tavi* was the house owned by Professor Aleck and Mrs 'Teddy' (Edmonia) Hill, the friends who made the trip to Seeonee.

Writing for the *Pioneer* gave the opportunity for fiction of greater length. The editor proposed purchasing syndicated fiction by Bret Harte to fill 3,000 to 5,000 word spaces. Kipling volunteered to produce the goods on the spot. And so, in the second half of the 1880s, there appeared in India the stories that were to trigger the first Kipling 'boom', and enable the young man to return to London with a

well-established Indian reputation.

It was the Indian Railway Library collections which spread Kipling's work farthest. These little books were selected according to themes, and so demonstrated the sorts of subject that interested him.

Under the Deodars assembled stories of love, adultery and flirtation; the kind of writing that was suspiciously regarded as 'very French', and that, indeed, in Kipling's case, was and is popular in France. Equally popular across the Channel was *The Story of the Gadsbys*, a long series of dialogues about an officer whose marriage conflicts with his career, and whose innocent young wife ultimately wins game, set and match, without the author overtly commenting on the value of the husband who has left the army after her victory.

The Phantom Rickshaw contained four stories of horror and adventure. Anglo-India was a superstitious community: Theosophy was one of its rare contributions to the world. While his father robustly denounced Madame Blavatsky as 'one of the most interesting and unscrupulous impostors' he had ever met, Rudyard was landed with a Theosophist editor on the *Pioneer*. But although the table-tapping and teacup-turning aspects of drawing-room occultism always evoked Rudyard's lively scorn in his fiction, he displayed a less educated 'open-mindedness' about ghosts and psychic research otherwise, and may briefly and unhappily have dabbled in spiritualism. At any rate, he was always willing to write stories in which rather mysterious and ghostly forces came into play, without clearly committing himself to any final decision about the real or hallucinatory quality of the vision. A simple trick, which must by now be standard practice for fantasy writers, but which, in the 1880s, must have seemed a change from the certainties of a Poe or a Mrs Radcliffe, or the uncertainties of a Maturin or Monk Lewis.

One story in the collection was a masterpiece. *The Man Who Would be King* swept along with the superb narrative pace that the young Kipling gave his best work, and gave an unforgettable picture of the imperfect buccaneering spirit that gave birth to empires, contrasted with the suspicious, almost hostile, slightly overawed stabilities of primitive tribes and a modern newspaper office. Freemasonry provides an ironic, yet far from inappropriate link between the three disparate worlds.

An Indian attitude to Theosophy was put forward in *The Sending of Dana Da:* it was simply the means by which the unscrupulous, black or white, might make a profit out of the gullible. The whole collection in which this appears, *In Black and White*, establishes Kipling's attitude to racial differences at this time.

Kipling in India. 'Your poetry very good today sir, just coming out proper length!' From a drawing by A. S. Boyd in My First Book.

Winter on the North West Frontier, 1880.

53

The abandoned city of Amber in Jaipur, showing the palace and the fort. This was the original of Cold Lairs, in 'Kaa's Hunting', a story familiar to readers of The Jungle Books.

He did not think all races were equal. As policemen, the Pathans of *At Howli Thana* would never equal Englishmen in honesty and respect for duty. But the English would be hard put to it to find representatives who could equal the protagonists of *Dray Wara Yow Dee* and *In Flood Time* for their passionate and unashamed masculinity. 'You're a better *man* than I am', (my italics) are the significant words addressed to Gunga Din, and, at least by implication, not to him alone. The English, as we may infer from *On the City Wall*, have special talents which are destructive when adopted by Indians. The English are successful systematic thinkers, and therefore good administrators. Indians, by contrast, are better at spontaneous living. A prostitute in Amara is a respected representative of a great tradition: in England she is a social problem. English influence on Amara means that an old nationalist hero is no longer respected; the men of the city have become talkers rather than fighters. Wali Dad, a central character in the story, has become miserably dislocated from his own people by his western education. He is fit only to sneer elegantly at the world – and himself – until he reverts to the passionate religious fanaticism his education has weaned him away from.

Wee Willie Winkie is a collection of child stories. The two of interest are *Baa Baa, Black Sheep* and *The Drums of the Fore and Aft*. The autobiographical sketch of Southsea is powerful and controlled. It makes an appeal to Anglo-Indian sympathies by giving Punch instinctive Anglo-Indian attitudes which are affronted by the chilliness of England. It hints at acute psychological insight in constantly threatening the little boy's sense of identity: even his name, Punch, has obviously been given him to reduce him to a companion-piece for his younger sister, Judy. Thus, even in a happy family, Kipling seems to note, the child's personality may be the plaything of a carelessly affectionate adult world.

The Drums of the Fore and Aft offers a hearty corrective to any Victorian dreams of dear little orphans sent into the Queen's service. Jakin and Lew are reprobate gutter-snipes, and Kipling loves them for it. When they rally their demoralised regiment in battle, it is because they are drunk, and Kipling criticises no one for the presence of drunken children on the battlefield. When they die, they are heroes, and utterly unsentimentalised; indeed, by a master-stroke, the story abandons them, and wanders off into a detached consideration of the shame of the men of their regiment, who have been seen by Highlanders and Gurkhas to run from the enemy. Yet these, too, are not criticised; they were raw troops, and they have learned their business now.

It was soldier stories that really made Kipling's reputation. *Soldiers Three* brought together a number of the exploits of Ortheris, Learoyd and Mulvaney, whom, one suspects, Kipling created by thinking, 'There was an Englishman, an Irishman and a Scotchman. . . .'

The private soldier's morality appealed hugely to Kipling. Self-respect came from the group: the regiment was obviously bigger than the man. Yet the private soldier had no badges or external authority to boost his ego; his strength had to lie in his own personality and his capacity to serve the regiment well. Given that he was doing his job, and not letting the uniform down (by his own professional standards), he could disregard the rest of the world and its rules for ever. Fusspot officers might object to 'horrible drunkenness': the private soldier whose accoutrements were clean and tidy, whose health was good, and who took real orders, couldn't be broken to any rank lower than that he held, and didn't intend to let some one else's idea of virtue dictate how he used his spare time. Punishment fatigues might be accepted with resignation or with indignation: either way they were merely imposed by the greater strength of authority. But personal penitence was something the army could not and should not command, though it might go to the wife who suffered social reduction because her husband could not or would not stay out of scrapes.

In these stories, too, Kipling made a serious attempt to get away from proper 'literary' English, and to present the speech of an Irishman, a cockney, and a Yorkshireman, with all their own phonetic and syntactical idiosyncrasies. The attempt was not a success. Learoyd's Yorkshire cannot be spoken to resemble any sequence of sounds ever uttered within the Ridings; Mulvaney seems to owe more to music hall song-sheets than to Cork; Ortheris is much given to those sounds we all make, but which are supposed, magically, to represent a cockney accent when printed: 'wot', 'wen', 'sez'. But the attempt to offer common soldiers as serious literary figures is being made, and the accents that would glaringly offend genteel readers in daily life are firmly pushed forward as part of the personalities. Even their rough language is sketched in: the euphemistic 'bloomin'', 'beggar', 'sugar', even an occasional 'plucky', are sprinkled through Kipling's soldier writings.

It was these stories that attracted the favourable attention of the Commander-in-Chief, and it was a proud moment for Kipling when he was asked to ride in Simla Mall beside Lord Roberts of Kandahar, hero of the Second Afghan War, and explain to him what the ordinary men in barracks were thinking.

With the Viceroy and the Commander-in-Chief among his admirers, what more had Kipling to ask of India? He had served his seven years' apprenticeship as a newspaperman, and knew how to earn his living by his pen. He was twenty-three, and the best English writer India had ever seen. He had a literary personality, unique subject matter, and bright confidence. It was time to take Kay Robinson's advice, and go and dip his toes in the deep literary waters of London.

PRICE ONE SHILLING.

IN BLACK AND WHITE

BY RUDYARD KIPLING

A.H. WHEELER & Co's
No. 3
ONE RUPEE
INDIAN RAILWAY LIBRARY
LAHORE

LONDON:
SAMPSON LOW, MARSTON, SEARLE, & RIVINGTON,
Limited,
ST. DUNSTAN'S HOUSE, FETTER LANE, FLEET STREET, E.C.

Kipling's early stories were published in book form in the Indian Library Collections, a popular edition which could be bought all over India. One of the most notable volumes was In Black and White, *in which the stories examine the conflict of the Indian and Anglo-Saxon cultures.*

A Young Lion in London

In the spring of 1889 Rudyard Kipling sailed from Calcutta. He proposed to travel back to England via the Far East and America. He held a commission from the *Pioneer* to report his travels back to Allahabad. He had £200 savings in his pocket. He had Professor and Mrs Aleck Hill as his travelling companions.

The young Kipling was rather given to indeterminate dedications which could vaguely be offered to several people at once. *Plain Tales from the Hills* is dedicated to 'the wittiest woman in India'. The words met two of Kipling's requirements in the late 1880s: they excluded Flo Garrard, and they allowed Alice Kipling to accept them as a gracious compliment. Equally, Mrs F. C. Burton, the original of Mrs Hawksbee, was given to understand that they were intended for her. And Edmonia Hill, receiving a copy of *Plain Tales* with a verse inscription from its author, may have been permitted to think that she was the dedicatee.

Certainly, this pretty, lively, dark-haired young American from Beaver, Pennsylvania, was the married woman to whom young Rudyard paid the most assiduous attention during his last few years in India. And she determined the time of his leaving the country.

In October 1888 Mrs Hill nearly died of meningitis. When she had passed the crisis, she decided to return to America and visit her family, rather than convalesce in India. Rudyard immediately decided to go with her, even though his departure in the spring meant that he would miss Trix's wedding to John Fleming of the Indian Survey Department. And so, by the second week of March, he was with the Hills on board S.S. *Madura*, making for Rangoon.

Dufferin's annexation of Burma in the 1880s had met with Kipling's approval, and he had written one or two verse and prose pieces about the country, although he had never been there. Now he was to visit it, and take in such other places as would give him the secure feeling that he was a seasoned oriental traveller. Rangoon, Singapore, Penang, Hong Kong, Yokohama, Nagasaki: when he thought of places like these he felt wiser than any home-bound Englishman. Two years later, his mother suggested to him the line in which he conveyed this feeling of superiority to his contemporaries:

'And what should they know of England
who only England know?—'

Still, it was only as a globe-trotter that he knew these far-flung cities. And he showed himself to be a callow and inexperienced globe-trotter when he opened his visit to America by unleashing casual criticisms of the shibboleths of the republic on to the California press. Being at least as aggressive and almost as bumptious as Kipling himself, the American press was delighted to hit back, and held up its sleeve for years the recollection that Kipling had once made intemperate and under-informed comments on the country.

His letters back to the *Pioneer*, too, were studied appeals to British insularity. He moaned about American democracy, American manners, and, that habitual offence to the English throughout the nineteenth century, American spitting. Such Americans as were aware of him at this time thought of him as worse than Mrs Trollope and Dickens, the two most notable hostile critics of America from England in the previous generation.

But Rudyard was always a careless distributor of insult in his writing, and was actually thoroughly enjoying his passage through the States. He went fishing in the northwest, looking to the natives the very caricature of a tweed-suited Englishman. He made the usual trip across the country passing through Utah, where he made the usual observations on the Mormons; and Chicago, where he made the usual observations on the city. He visited Niagara Falls (which impressed him less than a grain elevator in Buffalo). He visited Boston, where the historical associations with the Revolutionary War impressed him. He went to Elmira, N.Y., crashed in upon the privacy of Mark Twain, and extracted an interview from him. And he wound up at Beaver, Pennsylvania, to stay with Mrs Hill and her family.

At this point, Mrs Hill neatly transferred her young admirer's attentions over to her unmarried younger sister, Caroline Taylor. The Taylor family

Opposite Contrasts in Calcutta in the nineteenth century. The crowded anchorage, and the Eden Gardens. The Gardens were the scene of popular evening drives by the British in Calcutta: the carriages proceeded along the Strand Road (foreground) and turned at the bandstand. Kipling and the Hills sailed from Calcutta in 1889, and Kipling never lived in India again.

were quiet, professional-class Methodists: Edmonia and Caroline's father was the President of a small college. For a short time Kipling seems to have felt that east-coast American Methodism was one of the most admirably stable creeds in the world, and to have half-deceived himself into imagining that he was in love with Caroline. Certainly he was delighted to have her company on the voyage to London, when Edmonia decided to return to India via Europe and take her sister with her.

On 5 October 1889 Rudyard Kipling landed in Liverpool. He was never to live in India again. His future lay in England; his essential reputation in literary London. After visiting his English relatives, and giving himself a short holiday in Paris, it was to London that he turned, and settled himself in rooms in Villiers Street off the Strand.

He was not rich. His £200 was almost exhausted, and he was too proud to borrow money from his aunts, or from the Misses Craik, who were still living in London. He may have been forced to the temporary expedient of pawning clothes while he looked for sympathetic publishers and editors. Certainly he claimed to have lived cheaply on sausage and mash, mild beer, and cheap tobacco.

Villiers Street was splendidly central. The Strand was the main London shopping thoroughfare of the time, and Villiers Street ran down to the Thames near Charing Cross. It brought its resident into contact with the sort of society he loved: outside the normal bourgeois stream; not perfectly respectable; possessed of unusual information and ever-so-slightly disreputable experience.

Not that London was like Lahore. The prostitute population of the West End pavements seemed to Kipling squalid and deplorable, quite unlike the charming Lalun. But barmaids, policemen, and music-hall artistes were thoroughly acceptable ac-quaintances. The drunken night-life of the poor around the West End was a pleasure to watch. The police constables of 'E' Division, who kept an old handcart ambulance behind St Clement Danes for carting away drunks, were willing to swap stories with the young gent from India, who also enjoyed their ribald exchanges with the 'real ladies' of the pavement. By now Kipling was pretty securely on the side of the police; they were respectful social inferiors, as the London harlots, one may assume, were not.

Gatti's Music Hall was just opposite Kipling's digs, and he could almost see in through its fanlight from his stairs. He found it fun to pay his fourpence, and go in for an evening, sometimes taking a respec-table barmaid as a companion. An old *lion comique* was willing to accept a drink from a young writer, and tell him how audiences were managed. Soldiers filled the pit and gallery, and the life of the private soldier continued to interest Kipling greatly. The tunes and rhythms of music hall songs provided bases on which Kipling's particular brand of light verse

Above *Kipling's sister Alice, always known as Trix. After her marriage to John Fleming.* Opposite *Mark Twain. Kipling called on the famous American writer unannounced at his home in Elmira, New York, and managed to interview him. Years later, both were awarded honorary degrees in the same ceremony at Oxford.*

could be composed. For practice, he even wrote a song for Gatti's, and enjoyed hearing singer and audience roaring the chorus to and fro:

At the back of the Knightsbridge Barracks
    When the fog's a-gatherin' dim,
The Lifeguard waits for the under-cook,
    But she won't wait for 'im.

London low-life contributed far less material for fiction than India had done. *The Record of Badalia Herodsfoot (Many Inventions)* is placed perhaps a couple of miles east of Kipling's digs, and in spite of its weepy, womanly ending, contains that common-sensical sympathy with the down-to-earth attitudes of people on the spot that Kipling always preferred to elevated theory. Indeed, Badalia, the slum girl who undertakes to distribute sensibly the charities which middle-class idealists were hopelessly mis-applying, is not unlike a cockney District Com-missioner, knowing 'her people' as well as any Orde

or Tallantyre. And Kipling put into her mouth one great classic phrase to answer those well-meaning progressive nuisances of the Charity Organisation Society, who objected that any relief above subsistence level (preferably in workhouses) would 'pauperise' the recipients: 'You can't pauperise them as 'asn't things to begin with. They're bloomin' well pauped.'

'Brugglesmith', in the same collection, gives a lovely picture of the innocently buccaneering nightlife of wild practical jokes, matey association with policemen, and yet mysteriously preserved middleclass respectability, that Kipling liked to imagine himself as living in London. The music hall contributes, through impresario Bat Masquerier and singer Vidal (Dal) Benzaguen to the discomfiture of *The Village that Voted the Earth was Flat*, and Dal Benzaguen's mother is recalled as an associate of young hack writers in the much later story, *Dayspring Mishandled*. Otherwise, Kipling's bachelor life in London leaves little trace on his work, outside the novel he wrote while it went on, *The Light that Failed*.

This self-revealing work took its main impetus from an accident that befell Kipling in London. Quite unexpectedly, he came across Flo Garrard in the street. It was an end of the belief that he felt anything for Caroline Taylor. An awkward letter to her, and the exploitation of his own agnosticism as incompatible with her Methodism helped Kipling wriggle out of that little entanglement.

Opposite *Charing Cross in the 1890s.*

Below *The building in Villiers Street, Charing Cross, where Kipling lived from 1889 to 1891. It is now called Kipling House.*

Then, all the young man's attention was back to his first love. Their relations since 1884 had been a little mysterious, and are hard to reconstruct now. Flo would appear to have given Rudyard manuscript notebooks as gifts; at any rate, she gave him one the Christmas before he left India. But she had not, it seems, been given such presents consequent upon their use as one might have expected. At any rate, she did not receive a copy of *Departmental Ditties* until the two had met again in London. It may, perhaps, be suspected that the 'accidental' quality of the street encounter does not mean that the two would not have met around this time in any case.

Flo was far less interested in Rudyard than in her own art. She had no intention of marrying her admirer, and simply envied him the success that his writing enjoyed, without ever understanding that she lacked the essential talent to command equivalent success herself. She hovered between London and a studio shared in Paris with a girl friend, and showed herself singularly unimpressed by the passion she was stirring.

Kipling suffered for months, and then wrote out his feelings and experiences in the form of *The Light that Failed*. He had wanted to risk the ambitious project of a novel for some time: a manuscript called *Mother Maturin* had been worked on in India, and ultimately cannibalized for the short stories. Now *Lippincott's Magazine*, which published a short complete novel in each number, and had enjoyed successes in 1890 with *Sherlock Holmes* and *Dorian Gray*, asked Kipling, of all people, to follow Wilde. They received Kipling's fictionalised account of his love and his enjoyment of success after a return from abroad.

The autobiographical element was sufficiently disguised by making Dick Heldar a painter, and adding his steadily encroaching blindness as a narrative point. The character of Dick was totally unlike the authorial persona assumed in the short stories, but its admixture of sentimentality, *amour propre*, bitterness and bounce, probably reflects accurately enough one side of Kipling's immature nature. When the novel's happy ending for the lovers made no impression on Flo, he altered it to the self-pitying tragedy that the book now is.

The lasting effects of Flo Garrard on Kipling's mind and art were probably twofold. Having encountered outright failure in his most consistent and impassioned experience of adolescent love, he retained for the rest of his life a suspicion that love was a tragic and renunciatory emotion. There had been evidence of a masochistic predisposition in this direction in the Indian stories: so many love affairs ending unhappily, with the humane freedom they brought to overleap caste barriers suffering destruction and oblivion. But the increasing tendency of Kipling's writing was to anaesthetise himself from the pain of love by presenting the suffering as all woman's. The classic Kipling formulation on love was, increasingly, to become a devoted but disregarded woman, willingly accepting suffering (or even, as in Badalia Herodsfoot's case, death) for a man who treated her badly. The sentimental poem with the sentimental title *Mary, Pity Women* captures its spirit neatly: at once lachrymose, religiose, and patronising. For some unknown reason, Kipling preferred the still more distancing device of making his wronged, loving women lower class.

A more positive outcome was his robust attitude to art. Flo had made an inordinate fuss over her trivial daubs. Although Kipling himself was a consummate artist, labouring for perfection in all his work, and conscious of a *daemon* that dictated its nature, he made no large pretentious claims. He liked to see himself as a craftsman or a workman, and he firmly rejected those who took their stand upon the holiness of Art. And this gave him a very clear literary-political place in the Aesthetic 1890s.

The setback in Kipling's personal life was not matched by any failure in his career. Before he reached England, Harper Brothers of New York had snootily refused to publish his stories, with the fatuous dismissal line, 'Young man, this house is devoted to the production of literature'. But less reputable American publishers were quite willing to take advantage of their country's refusal to join the international copyright convention, and published Kipling without either permission or any attempt to offer remuneration. This piracy started an interest in Kipling in America, which supported his Indian reputation as he arrived in London.

Two former colleagues were quick to lead him in the direction of work. Stephen Wheeler was writing for the *St James's Gazette*, and introduced Kipling to Sidney Low, its editor. Low had already passed a happy afternoon reading *Soldiers Three*, and wondered whether its author might not prove greater than Dickens. So he was delighted to meet Kipling, and willingly opened his columns to him.

Mowbray Morris, a former art editor of the Allahabad *Pioneer*, had also found success in England. He edited *Macmillan's Magazine*, and accepted as contributions two new poems. One of these, *The Ballad of East and West*, was the first major triumph Kipling published in London. Although, for some unknown reason, Kipling chose to dispense with the advantage of his overseas reputation, and published the *Ballad* over the pseudonym 'Yussuf', he was fortunate that the secret was not kept for a moment. Lord Tennyson and Professor Saintsbury were, perhaps, the most distinguished admirers this publication won him.

When Kipling turned back to prose fiction, Mowbray Morris again published his first new work, and gave him wise advice about his English audience. The delicious extravaganza *The Incarnation of Krishna Mulvaney*, with its preamble introducing the 'Soldiers Three' to their English audience, was

A drawing by Phil May of a nocturnal scene familiar to Londoners of the 1890s. A hopeful prostitute accosts a potential customer.

the first story Kipling wrote in London. Morris warned him that it contained about thirty lines more drunkenness than the English would tolerate, and Kipling obligingly excised them. Presumably it was his own innate anticipation of English squeamishness that led him to share, authorially, Mulvaney's outrage at the erotic carving on the Temple of Prithi-Devi at Benares. And perhaps it was the influence of living in London that led him to create a Mulvaney who was suddenly rather heavily respectful towards the authorial voice of the story.

The appearance of new short pieces in magazines reminded some readers that some of the other stories from the Indian Railway Library collections had appeared in London magazines the previous year. And a London publisher recalled that *Plain Tales from the Hills* had been lying on his shelves awaiting distribution in England for a year. Kipling in 1889 was a rising young author enjoying real recognition in London.

As such, it was almost inevitable that he should be introduced to the Savile Club: a fairly informal and lively assortment of authors and publishers who were waiting, according to one cynical clubland porter, to reach the almost senile state at which they would be fit for admission to the Athenaeum. Here Kipling met Andrew Lang, Rider Haggard, and Thomas A. Guthrie ('F. Anstey'). The author of multi-coloured 'Fairy Books', the author of *King Solomon's Mines* and the author of *Vice-Versa* were obviously not the literary heavyweights of the day, and they seemed to have hailed Kipling as one of themselves, urging him to give himself the supporting sympathies of a 'set'. But although he liked all three, and was to retain a close, lifelong friendship with Haggard, Kipling steered carefully clear of literary faction at first. He was advised to do this by Walter Besant, an elder statesman of the Savile:

> 'He advised me to "keep out of the dogfight". He said that if I were "in with one lot" I would have to be out with another; and that, at last, "things would get like a girls' school where they stick out their tongues at each other when they pass."'

Kipling naturally claimed to have followed this sage advice, and he did take it to the extent of refraining from personal criticism of any other named writer's work for the rest of his life. But from the outset he was a partisan little figure, even though he discreetly dissembled his attitudes in public for a year or so. Many of the members of the Savile Club would have been outraged if they knew how the twenty-three-year-old newcomer characterised them in a set of verses he sent back to Lahore:

> But I consort with long-haired things
> In velvet collar-rolls
> Who talk about the Aims of Art

Henry Rider Haggard at the age of forty-one. He and Rudyard Kipling were lifelong friends.

> And 'theories' and 'goals'
> And moo and coo with womenfolk
> About their blessed souls.
>
> But what they call 'psychology'
> Is lack of liver-pill,
> And all that blights their tender souls
> Is eating till they're ill,
> And their chief way of winning goals
> Consists of sitting still.

This sounds like a direct personal attack on Oscar Wilde, whose rolled velvet collars had been imitated by tailors and named 'the Oscar'; whose over-eating was becoming undisguised; and who called something rather more sinister than indigestion by the name of 'psychology'. Actually, Wilde was not a member of the Savile, and Kipling probably never met him. But he clearly refers to those influenced by him. Sidney Colvin, for example, art-critic and biographer of Keats, a friend of Wilde's whose appearance had been compared by Wilde with that of North American Plains Indians, was a guest at the Poynters one day. Colvin was a harmless butt to Wilde and Whistler. But Kipling loathed him:

> 'The same is an all-fired prig of immense water and suffers from all the nervo-hysterical diseases of the nineteenth century. . . . He recounted all his symptoms and made me sick. A queer beast with match-stick fingers and a dry unwholesome skin.'

But Kipling concealed his opinion, and Colvin's name figured prominently in support of Lang's nomination when 'Rudyard Kipling, author of *Plain*

A playbill for Gatti's, the famous music hall of the 1890s which stood across the road in Villiers Street under the railway arches.

Tales from the Hills, Departmental Ditties &c.', giving his Aunt Georgie's house in Fulham as his address, was put up for election to the Savile.

The list of supporters for this candidacy was almost a triumphal welcome from the successful names of the 1880s. Thomas Hardy, Henry James, Walter Besant, Edmund Gosse, George Saintsbury, Austin Dobson, Rider Haggard, Justin McCarthy and W. E. Henley were the best-known of the young man's sponsors.

Henley was, throughout 1890, Kipling's most important literary associate. The lame, vigorous poet, whose *Hospital Sketches* ('I am the master of my fate/I am the captain of my soul') remain his best-known work, had become editor of a small Edinburgh journal, the *Scots Observer*, and was violently transforming it into the *National Observer*, a platform for new writing and ideas he approved.

He might have seemed an unpromising friend. He had been very close to Robert Louis Stevenson, and then quarrelled bitterly with him. He had accepted sweetness and affection from Oscar Wilde, and was now in the process of shattering that friendship by his own prickliness and acerbity. But he had one quality that absolutely commended itself to Kipling: almost alone among the pillars of London literary society, he was a rugged individualist. He had suffered the amputation of his left leg when he was sixteen, and continuing tubercular infection constantly threatened his right foot. He had made his way up in the literary world without the help of influential friends – his father was a modest Gloucester bookseller – and he was not one of the self-important university aesthetes of literary London. A radical Tory, a romantic, an admirer of eighteenth-century England, of Dr Johnson, and especially of Fielding, Henley was willing to listen to Kipling's praise for the pioneers of empire. He was Kipling's first convert to imperialism.

It is even possible that it was Kipling who stimulated Henley's quarrel with Wilde: the young Anglo-Indian was far more disturbed by the narcissistic lassitude of aesthetic literateurs than was the lame editor who had grown up with them. It was with the almost simultaneous appearance of Kipling and *The Picture of Dorian Gray* that Henley and his would-be scholarly High Tory henchman, Charles Whibley, started their campaign of hostility towards decadent art.

Kipling submitted to Henley work that was as far removed as possible from the precious, erotic fragility of Wilde's school:

> 'What makes you look so white, so
> > white?' said Files-on-Parade.
> 'I'm dreadin' what I've got to watch,'
> > the Colour-Sergeant said.
> For they're hangin' Danny Deever,
> > you can hear the Dead March play,
> The Regiment's in 'ollow square –
> > they're hangin' him today;

Sidney Colvin, the literary and art critic. He supported Kipling's election to the Savile Club, unaware that Kipling disliked him intensely after a single meeting. From an engraving by Frederick Hollyer.

> They've taken of his buttons off an' cut
> > his stripes away,
> An' they're hangin' Danny Deever in the
> > mornin'.

Henley danced on his artificial leg in delight at receiving so original a contribution. Professor Masson in Edinburgh proved once again that scholarly academics are not necessarily the safest judges of new writing: 'Here's poetry at last!' he burst out to his lecture audience on the day 'Danny Deever' appeared. And Henley's audience received more *Barrack-Room Ballads* for their delight: 'Gunga Din', 'Fuzzy-Wuzzy', 'Loot'.

A confident Kipling cabled his parents, 'Genesis xlv.9.' The verse, when they looked it up, read:

> 'Haste ye, and go up to my father, and say
> unto him, Thus saith thy son Joseph, God
> hath made me lord of all Egypt: come
> down unto me; tarry not.'

Lockwood and Alice were, in fact, on their way home on leave in 1890. The 'Family Square' was reduced to a triangle by Trix's marriage but his parents remained Kipling's favourite audience, and he collaborated with his father on a political piece for the *Contemporary Review*. Wisely, Kipling never reprinted *The Enlightenments of Pagett M.P.*, for Lockwood was as politically short-sighted as his son, and their joint insistence on the folly and unimportance of the Indian National Congress did credit neither to their understanding nor their generosity.

But the excitement of success and the strain of living alone were doing Kipling's health no good. Trix, on a home visit with her husband, was shocked to find her brother unhappy and unwell in Villiers Street. He was still miserable over Flo Garrard, as he confessed when she asked about Caroline Taylor. The sudden death of Aleck Hill did not lead to the understanding that might have been anticipated between the widowed Edmonia and her English admirer. *The Light that Failed* was still pouring out his heartache to the world. And an attack of 'flu precipitated another of his breakdowns.

On recovering, he took a short trip to Italy, where Dufferin was now ambassador, and 'Mr Lockwood Kipling's son', as he modestly preferred to announce himself, was a welcome guest at the embassy.

The holiday did much to set him up again, but his easily aroused temper was agitated by Harper Brothers piratical publication in volume form of stories that had appeared in *Macmillan's*, and for which they had only negotiated for serial republication rights. It naturally offended a writer as cocky as Kipling when the hated firm that had once refused his work now calmly appropriated an extra story without any discussion, and paid him less than he

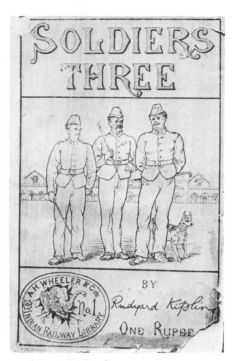

The cover of the **Indian Railway Library** *edition of* Soldiers Three.

The cover of the first edition of Departmental Ditties. *A spoof imitation of a civil service document.*

could command in England.

Kipling and his allies started a correspondence in the *Athenaeum* objecting to this American piracy, but it was a blow to the young hopeful when three senior writers whom he had regarded as personal mentors wrote a defence of Harpers' as an American firm that usually made *some* attempt to pay their debts. Thomas Hardy, Walter Besant and William Black were not men Kipling wished to mark down as enemies. He fired off a cheeky but disguised attack on them, in the form of *The Ballad of the Three Captains*; persuaded his friend Henry James to write an introduction to an authorised collection of short stories for America; instructed his agent, A. P. Watt, to pay close attention to American depradations for the future; and put the affair behind him.

By 1891 Kipling was an unqualified success. His work was enjoying a boom in London. His bank balance showed a credit in excess of £1,000. The demand for his work was sufficient to justify adding a lot of previously uncollected pieces from the Lahore *Civil and Military Gazette* and the Allahabad *Pioneer* to his new London work, and producing the really substantial collection *Life's Handicap*. He was so much in fashion that nobody seemed to worry about the fact that the volume contained a fair amount of thin and inferior work, pushed in to protect it from American piracy.

But he had a new plan for meeting the transatlantic threat. He was working ever more closely with a young American publisher, agent and writer, whom he expected to solve all his copyright problems: Wolcott Balestier.

A Friend and a Wife

WOLCOTT BALESTIER LEFT HIS NATIVE AMERICA in 1888 and came to London to make his fortune. He had a commission from J. W. Lovell & Co., the publishers, to make arrangements with British authors for cheap American reprints of their proven best-sellers. He intended to set up a publishing house of his own, once he had cultivated the best writers in England with his offers from Lovell's. He wanted to solve the Anglo-American copyright problem, caused by American publishers' refusal to accept international agreements. And he hoped, in the long run, to make a name for himself as a writer.

He set up an office in Dean's Yard, Westminster, and began to pursue Lovell's business with diligence and success. He cultivated Edmund Gosse and captivated Henry James. He secured rights in Mrs Humphry Ward's best-selling *Robert Ellesmere* for Lovell's. And he heard in literary conversation that Rudyard Kipling was coming to London from India.

'Rudyard Kipling? What is it?' he asked at once. 'Is it a real name? A man or a woman?'

He was exactly the kind of go-getting American publisher Kipling might have been expected to despise. But Edmund Gosse thought otherwise, and introduced the two at Mrs Humphry Ward's house. And Gosse's anticipation was correct; the two active, vigorous, young literary men liked each other from the outset.

Balestier subsequently called at Villiers Street, early in the evening, where, finding Kipling out, he sat waiting for him till midnight, and then plunged into proposals for a collaborative novel. It is astonishing evidence of his immediate hold over Kipling that he won agreement, and the novel came to be written.

A collaboration with Kipling seems, with hindsight, to have been a clear feather in Balestier's cap. But his attitude to his new friend was not solely that of a man on the make. As a would-be publisher, Balestier was capable of handling touchy writers with diplomacy. There seems no reason but good nature to account for his using this personal skill to reconcile Kipling with the New England realist novelist, William Dean Howells.

Howells had written an article referring casually to 'Mr Kipling's jaunty hat-cocked-on-one-side, wink-tipping sketches.' He had published it over the imprint of the never-to-be-forgiven Harpers, and Kipling had set Howells down as a devious enemy, while Howells accepted the not uncommon view that the young Englishman was spoiled by conceit. Balestier resolved this quarrel, assuring Howells that Kipling was totally free from vanity, and carrying back generous-minded messages to Kipling which turned what might have become a vendetta into a distant friendship.

It was probably Balestier's driving energy, combined with a number of common interests, that appealed to Kipling. The thinkers of London had led him to look longingly back to the do-ers of the Punjab, and a man who got on with settling the business side of writing, without scrupulously examining his own psyche, came as a welcome relief. Balestier was also concerned about the international copyright question, which had come to aggravate Kipling more than any writer since Dickens. No doubt Balestier spoke soothingly and sympathetically of the wrongs suffered by British authors. Furthermore, Balestier had practised as a journalist in America, and at this period, Kipling associated more freely and willingly with journalists than with any other class of men. 'Once a priest, always a priest,' he wrote; 'once a Mason, always a Mason; but once a journalist, always and for ever a journalist.'

The Light that Failed was handed over to Balestier for American distribution: Lovell's ran off a few copies of the original version at the same time as it appeared in *Lippincott's*, so that U.S. copyright was protected. Kipling was satisfied that he had, at last, thwarted pirates, though A. P. Watt, his agent, complained that he could have got him far better terms from America than Balestier and Lovell's offered.

Kipling cared nothing. He was already engaged on *The Naulahka, A Novel of East and West*. In this mis-spelled epic – (a naulakha would be something worth nine hundred thousand rupees, as is the jewel at the centre of the plot) – the fortunes of an American engineer are traced, as he proceeds from the Wild West to an Indian Native State, in pursuit of a fabulous jewel. Balestier was to write the American chapters and Kipling the Indian. In practice they collaborated more immediately than that. Balestier sat at a typewriter while Kipling paced around the room, and each threw out suggestions and sentences. The plot and character planning were probably strongly influenced by Kipling. (He was to work out ideas for and with Rider Haggard in a rather similar

Wolcott Balestier, the young American publisher.
The meeting of Balestier and Rudyard Kipling
was to have a strong influence on the latter's
life and career.

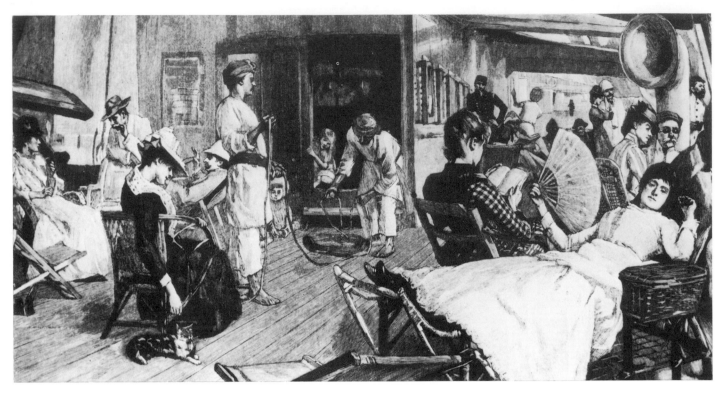

manner some years later, without going so far as to
offer the public a final collaborative effort.) The
writing of *The Naulahka* probably owes more to
Balestier.

While this work was in progress, Balestier, who
had prospered enough to command a cottage in the
Isle of Wight as well as his office and lodgings in
London, brought his family over from the States to
admire his success. His mother, two sisters, and
younger brother all came across to visit the young
man whose triumphs were so much admired in his
Vermont hometown.

The Balestiers were descended from a French
Huguenot family. They had always been adventur-
ous. One of them had married Paul Revere's
daughter, and later generations had owned property
in both East and West Indies, and made money in
New York and Chicago. In 1868, the reigning
Balestier had bought a big farmhouse in Brattleboro,
Vermont, and here in the 1880s and '90s, his widow,
Caroline Starr Wolcott Balestier, reigned supreme.

The Wolcotts were an old-established Connecticut
family. In their past history they traced three State
Governors, and one signatory of the Declaration of
Independence. Old Grandmother Wolcott Balestier
was a dominant figure in Brattleboro, where she and
her husband had established their superiority over
the town by dressing for dinner and drinking impor-
ted French wines. She did not get on easily with her

descendants, and seems to have enjoyed seeing traces
of her husband's wild Balestier ancestry, rather
than her own sedate Wolcott blood, emerging in the
younger generation.

Of these, Wolcott was the most successful and
polished: the most Wolcott. He had enjoyed a
glowing student career at Cornell; had prospered as
a journalist in the West; and attracted the attention
and admiration of Brattleboro's upper crust when
he was known to be thriving in London. His sisters –
severe, intelligent Caroline, and proper, pretty
Josephine – admired him unreservedly, and were
immensely proud of his rise.

Not so Madam Balestier, his grandmother. She
preferred the scapegrace younger son, Beatty.
Wolcott might make friends across the world, but it
was Beatty who had Brattleboro eating out of his
hand. He swore more vehemently than most
Brattleboro citizens, and drank more than was
common in Vermont. He drove his sleigh and his
trap at a constant gallop, and raced through life at
the same rate, standing anyone who crossed his path
a drink, spending freely and open-handedly, and
borrowing without a moment's hesitation when he
ran out of cash. Both the Balestier boys had charm,
but Wolcott's was a sophisticated cosmopolitan
unction, whereas Beatty's was the rough, tough,
parochial good-nature of a handsome local sportsman
and bad boy.

When he came to visit his brother in London, in
1890, Beatty enjoyed the bright lights so unreservedly, and went the big city pace so fast, that his
serious elder brother had no alternative but to pack
him off to his grandmother in Brattleboro as soon as
possible.

Caroline, Josephine, and Wolcott's mother, on the

other hand, were welcome to stay on as long as they liked. Mrs Balestier was suffering from some disappointment. She had hoped that her son's conquest of London meant that she would be made free of European High Society. Weekly 'At Homes' for the most distinguished intellectuals did not compare with the rounds of Lords and Ladies she had anticipated. But Caroline and Josephine were delighted with everything their brother did, and Caroline set about cleaning up the cottage on the Isle of Wight, and ordering the Dean's Yard office. It was while she was wandering through Dean's Yard with a pile of housekeeping books under her arm that she first met Rudyard Kipling.

Lockwood and Alice were in London on home leave at the time. They were introduced to Wolcott, and to his sister. Alice immediately recognised in Caroline, three years older than Ruddy and unusually strong-minded, a serious threat to the 'Family Square'. 'That woman is going to marry our Ruddy,' she declared, and did her best to prevent her from succeeding. Rudyard's health offered the first opportunity to throw some hindrance in the way of the understanding that had grown up between himself and his friend's sister. The English winters

Olive Schreiner, the South African novelist, was another admirer of Kipling's work. She met him on his visit to Cape Town in 1891.

did not seem good for him, and the overwork of 1890 was paid for in ill health. His family and his doctor urged him to go abroad.

To their solicitation was added that of his critics. His work was starting to show signs of hurry. The novelty of tales about life in India was wearing off. Edmund Gosse was a friend and an admirer but he warned Kipling that he was publishing too much, and admonished him, in a critique in the *Century Magazine*, to go back to the Far East, returning in ten years with 'another precious and admirable budget of loot out of wonderland'.

Kipling prepared to take a break. Early in 1891 he set off for America with his uncle Fred Macdonald, the Methodist minister. The two intended to pay a visit to Fred and Alice's eldest brother Henry, the American exile. They were, alas, forestalled by Henry's death while they were still at sea, so that Rudyard returned immediately to England, and spent the summer on the Isle of Wight with Wolcott, Caroline and Josephine. As autumn approached, he boarded a liner for South Africa, leaving little more indication of his intentions than a statement that before his return he would visit the doyen of English letters, Robert Louis Stevenson, who was living on Samoa as 'Tusitala, the Teller of Tales'.

This voyage really initiated another facet of Kipling's literary persona. He was to be the poet of the passenger liner; the creative voice from the first-class saloon. He was a more habitual traveller than most Englishmen of his generation. He was to have children who, before they passed puberty, expected to meet stewards they knew on their annual liner voyage to South Africa. In the *Just So Stories*, the epigraph verses to *The Crab that Played with the Sea* comprise a kind of riddle, introducing by name or initial no less than nineteen steamship lines.

Kipling respected steam as the power at the heart of all modern romance. He respected engineers as men who worked themselves and their engines and their freight or passengers around the world. He approved of his own acquaintance with the wide world. But he was not a pioneering explorer. After he had left India, he never visited any of the hard-won frontiers of western civilisation, except Rhodesia. He toured the seven seas from the security of polished mahogany deck-rails, and braved the elements from the comfort of heavy travelling-rugs. He reflected a moment in the life of late Victorian and Edwardian Britain: a moment of comfortable middle-class life, when luxury travel was easily available and offered the possibility of undemanding adventure. He seized the opportunity, and recorded the experience.

He spent September in Cape Town. It was, then, a peaceful little town with none of the bustle of a modern city, and no real tension to give warning of a war with the Boers at the end of the decade. Olive Schreiner, the South African novelist, became a friend and admirer. She tackled Kipling on the subject of Maisie in *The Light that Failed*, and he promised, with slightly patronising flirtatiousness, to show her the truth about Maisie in a year's time. Events in England were to move too fast for him to keep this tantalising promise.

He met naval people for the first time at Simonstown. He was struck by the comfort in which the Admiral of the Cape Station lived: there were live turtles tied to the end of his private jetty, waiting to be fished out and turned into soup. The junior officers were boisterous fun: they undertook splendid rags, in the course of which rooms might be turned upside down. And one of them had taken a small gun-boat in the direction of Portuguese East Africa, and leaned a little on the Portuguese. Individual militaristic horseplay as a substitute for frock-coated diplomacy delighted Kipling, and he embellished the incident in *Judson and the Empire*.

After a month in South Africa he sailed on to New Zealand, where his ship was accompanied in to Wellington Harbour by 'Pelorus Jack', a famous shark that convoyed shipping in those parts. Kipling went out in the same harbour on a moonlight picnic in a huge canoe with ten beautiful girls. He visited one of the old masters from Westward Ho! who had become a professor at Christchurch. He ate kiwi. And he left New Zealand, sailing to Australia in company with General Booth, the founder of the Salvation Army, who was mightily sea-sick.

At Melbourne, Kipling fell into the company of local journalists. They invited him to report the Melbourne Cup for a local paper, but he had done enough race meeting reports in India. He and his hosts were amused by the fact that *Plain Tales* offended against local standards of propriety so much as to be banned from the public library.

A visit to a Labour Congress hardened Kipling's right-wing tendencies. The purchase of English lifeboats was under debate, and was rejected in favour of the construction of similar boats by Australian labour in Australia. Kipling took this to be a selfish interference with the freedom and safety of the community as a whole. For ever after he was to see organised Labour as irresponsible and indolent. He took the conservative view that a self-respecting working man who performed his work to the best of his ability was bound to command his just reward in a free market, whereas a unionised working man would be compelled to work as incompetently as the weakest member of his union, and his remuneration would bear no relation to honest effort. It was apparent to Kipling that no sensible employer could fail to make life as comfortable as possible for a loyal and hard-working employee, so that any uionisation at all constituted a vicious restrictive practice.

After three weeks in Australia, Kipling should

Wellington, New Zealand, from a Victorian engraving.

General William Booth, the founder of the Salvation Army. 'Young feller,' he said to Rudyard Kipling, who had criticised his method of preaching, 'if I thought I could win one more soul to the Lord by walking on my head and playing the tambourine with my toes . . . I'd learn how!'

have gone to Samoa if he were to make it at all. In fact, he decided to sail straight to Ceylon and India, and he never did meet Stevenson.

He did meet Booth again, as the evangelist was a fellow-passenger to Colombo. At Adelaide, a vast fleet of little boats came to see the General off, and he delivered a holy harangue from the liner's upper deck. One of his gestures puzzled Kipling: it was an abrupt downward sweep of the hand and arm that seemed quite unrelated to the salvationist's rhetoric. Then his eye followed the movement forward, and he noted that a woman in a little paddle-boat had accidentally caught her skirts up to her knees, and the General's arm was vehemently enjoining her to cover up the inflammatory vision of ankle and calf.

Kipling became quite friendly with Booth. He taxed him with having made a spectacle of himself in New Zealand, when he came aboard their boat walking backward, playing a tambourine, and letting the wind blow his cloak up over his head so that he looked like a giant tulip. 'Young feller,' was the General's reply, 'if I thought I could win *one* more soul to the Lord by walking on my head and playing the tambourine with my toes, I'd – I'd learn how.' Kipling admitted the logic of the argument, given Booth's premisses, and thenceforth decided that St Paul and Muhammed must have been just such single-minded tyrants over themselves and their flocks.

From Ceylon, he passed quickly through South India, which he had never before seen, and was never

to write about in any detail. Four days and nights on a train took him out of the unfamiliar country, and he joined his parents in Lahore just before Christmas. Before he could settle down to being lionised locally, a cable came from Caroline Balestier bearing the startling news that Wolcott was dead.

Wolcott had gone to Dresden on business. He had started a new firm, in partnership with William Heinemann, intending to produce a general library of cheap reprints, modelled on the German *Tauchnitz* editions. In Dresden he collapsed with typhoid fever, and his mother and sisters came out to Germany to find him dying. Caroline took charge immediately.

She cabled Rudyard. She sent for Henry James, who came at once, like a character in one of his own novels, to see what he could do to help. There was little. Wolcott was dead within eight days. Caroline coped with almost everything, and prepared to take her prostrate mother and sister back to America, once Wolcott's European affairs were cleared up. 'A little person of extraordinary capacity – who will float them successfully home,' Henry James called her. Beatty offered to come over to England to take charge of things, but Caroline firmly and prudently refused. She sold the house on the Isle of Wight. She transferred Wolcott's business commitments and assets to William Heinemann. And she settled down to wait for Rudyard in London.

She did not have long to wait. Within a fortnight of receiving her cable, Kipling was in England; a remarkably fast journey for the period. He was never to see India again.

But he wasted no time in looking back over the past. He immediately turned to the future. He took out a special licence, and eight days after his arrival, he married Caroline at a gloomy little ceremony in All Souls', Langham Place. Henry James gave the bride away. Rudyard's cousin 'Ambo' Poynter was the best man. Edmund Gosse and William Heinemann were the congregation. Everyone else had 'flu, and the couple had to part on the steps of the church, in order for Carrie to go back and nurse her mother and Josephine. In the circumstances, it is hardly surprising that the bride wore plain brown wool.

Kipling had taken his final major step. He had married a strong woman. 'Caroline Balestier was a good man spoiled,' in Lockwood Kipling's good-humoured opinion. And Henry James, who suffered the gravest doubts as to the advisability of the match, spoke of the 'almost manly nature of her emotion'. It seems possible that both Rudyard and Carrie were consciously acting in a way that accorded with Wolcott's known wishes, in marrying so promptly. They shared a devotion to his memory, and Carrie seems to have accepted from her brother a charge to further Rudyard's career as lovingly as she had supported his own. There were to be many satisfactions for Rudyard in life with a competent, capable, determined wife.

*Henry James, from Lehmann's pencil drawing
of 1892. He was a devoted friend of Wolcott
Balestier's, and an admirer of Kipling's early
work. Kipling, for his part, saw James as the
true literary successor of Jane Austen.*

In and out of Vermont

MRS BALESTIER AND JOSEPHINE SOON recovered, and off went the newlyweds on their honeymoon journey at last. The newspapers were willing to pay Rudyard for his general impressions of the countries he visited. He was a happy and successful man, who could finance his travels by sharing his experiences with the readers of *The Times* and the New York *Sun*.

The first stop was America. There were still relatives in Brattleboro for Rudyard to meet. And so the young couple travelled by liner to New York; by train to Vermont; and off in Beatty's sledge from the railway station to Brattleboro itself. 'Thirty below freezing!' Rudyard reported to those readers who, perhaps unwittingly, were accompanying him on what was an essentially private journey.

> 'It was inconceivable till one stepped into it at midnight, and the first shock of that clear, still air took away the breath as does a plunge into sea-water. A walrus sitting on a woolpack was our host in his sleigh, and he wrapped us in hairy goatskin coats, caps that came down over the ears, buffalo robes and blankets.'

The 'walrus on a woolpack' was Beatty Balestier. Himself the proud husband of a pretty young wife, Mai, he was happy to welcome his elder sister back with her new husband, and hear their admiration of his baby daughter Marjorie. Rudyard and Carrie enjoyed Beatty and Mai's hospitality, adored Marjorie, and were delighted by the land Beatty was farming.

It faced Mount Monadnock, a favourite peak of the New England poet Ralph Waldo Emerson. Rudyard had first heard its name when, as a boy, he read a parody of Emerson, without in the least knowing what it was all about:

> I am crowned coeval
> With Monadnock's crest,
> And my wings extended
> Touch the East and West.

Later he had discovered the New England transcendentalist's actual writing on the mountain, which he admired, although characteristically it was even mistier and more confused than the parody:

> High over the river intervals,
> Above the ploughman's highest line,
> Over the owners' farthest walls!
> Up where the airy citadel

> O'erlooks the surging landscape's swell!
> Youth, for a moment free as they,
> Teach thy feet to feel the ground,
> Ere yet arrives the wintry day
> When Time thy feet has bound.

But Kipling was an admirer of Emerson, and he longed to own a view over the transcendentally sacred mountain. Beatty, always open-handed, was willing to oblige, and offered a plot of land as a gift. Carrie, who was, as Henry James noted, 'a hard devoted capable little person', saw in this offer an opportunity to take Beatty's somewhat entangled affairs into her own hands. She suggested that the Kiplings should buy the farm in its entirety, and allow Beatty a fixed income to manage it for them. After some discussion with lawyers, Beatty finally transferred ten acres of well-placed land to the Kiplings, in return for a small payment and perpetual rights to farm a part of the plot where the Kiplings would not wish to build. Beatty's haymaking, in fact, was to protect Rudyard's view. It was an amicable agreement between four young people who wanted to live near each other. At the time it was drawn up it did not seem certain that Rudyard would wish to start building in the face of Mount Monadnock for quite some time.

After the family meetings, and hasty introductions through old Madam Balestier to some of the notables of Brattleboro, the Kiplings moved on for the remainder of their wedding holiday. They crossed America and Canada, and sailed to Japan, with plans to cruise in the Pacific and make Rudyard's previously deferred visit to R. L. Stevenson on Samoa. In the end they got no further than Yokohama, where they encountered a setback that might have utterly disheartened a less robust young writer than Rudyard.

On 8 June 1892 there was a slight earth tremor in Yokohama. Prophetic, Kipling called it later. The next day he went down to his bank to draw some cash. The manager urged him to take more while he was travelling, but Kipling contented himself with £10. By the afternoon, when he decided that he could after all use a little more, the Oriental Banking Company, holding all his savings – a total of at least £2,000 – had closed its doors and ceased payment. From a comfortably prosperous young success, Kipling was reduced in a moment to a man who owned about $100 in New York, and a ticket for an

*Main Street, Brattleboro, Vermont, in the
1890s. Looking north.*

elaborate Cook's Tour. 'So all the work that won the money must be done over again,' he wrote, immediately adding his humane concern for other, less fortunate losers, 'but some of the people are old, and more are tired, and all are disheartened.'

He proceeded, forthwith, to entertain his newspaper audience with an account of the way the news was received at the Overseas Club in Yokohama.

'The manager of a bank which had *not* failed was explaining how, in his opinion, the crash had come about. This was also very human. It helped none. Entered a lean American, throwing back his waterproof all dripping with rain; his face was calm and peaceful. "Boy, whisky and soda," he said.

'"How much haf you losd?" said a Teuton bluntly. "Eight-fifty," replied the son of George Washington sweetly. "Don't see how that prevents me having a drink. My glass, sirr." . . . If there is anything that one loves an American for it is the way he stands certain kinds of punishment. An Englishman and a heavy loser was being chaffed by a Scotchman whose account at the Japan end of the line had been a trifle overdrawn. True, he would lose in England, but the thought of the few dollars saved here cheered him.

'The curious thing in the talk was that there was no abuse of the bank. The men were in the Eastern trade themselves and they knew. It was the Yokohama manager and the clerks thrown out of employment (connection with a broken bank, by the way, goes far to ruin a young man's prospects) for whom they were sorry.'

The stiff upper lip, of course, inhibited Kipling from sharing with his readers the fact that he was one of the victims of the crash. Modesty forbade him to tell them that he had efficiently organised a meeting of the bank's Yokohama creditors at which they accepted deferred shares, in order to allow the bank to try to recover. He could not know that, as a result of this generous policy, he would recover his deposit with interest some years later.

Cook's behaved well, and refunded the money from the unused portion of the Kiplings' trip. Once again, Stevenson was unvisited. And the young couple returned to Brattleboro, poor, but characteristically independent and unafraid.

Carrie's young man was, now, not quite what the town expected for a daughter of the rather superior Balestier family. The Kiplings settled into a small hired-man's house, which they called Bliss Cottage, and here their first daughter was born on 29 December. Rudyard's birthday was on the 30th and Carrie's the 31st, so they were delighted by the timing, regardless of three feet of snow around the house. They named the little girl Josephine, deftly complimenting Carrie's sister at the same time as naming Rudyard's daughter for himself. And with a child of his own, Rudyard was idyllically happy.

His belief in the necessity of children to human contentment found clear expression in an important story in the volume he was seeing through the press at that time. *Many Inventions* brought together the stories of his bachelor years in London and his earliest settlement in Vermont, and, taken as a whole, forms the most even and satisfying of all his collections. The knowingness and thrusting mannerisms of his earliest work are tamed in these stories, and the anti-liberalism of his maturity lacks the snarling illiberalism which was yet to become a recurrent blemish on his work. For example, to have a war-like Pathan emissary in London write home in colourful language, gloating over the spoils of Hindustan that will become available if the European madness of Liberal Democracy is transported to India (*One View of the Question*), is high-spirited, far from ill-natured, and, most important of all, points centrally to the kind of vital question about the exercise of power that liberals are too often willing to stifle.

Many of the stories were about India. *The Lost Legion*, not being an actual ghost or horror story, is the most satisfyingly adult piece Kipling wrote in this vein. The stories of 'The Soldiers Three' continue a tendency to develop Mulvaney and Ortheris, in particular, as men with characters rather than as representative privates. *The Finest Story in the World*, a speculation on the transmigration of souls as a form of extra-sensory perception – a subject that interested Kipling as it did Henley ('I was a King in Babylon/When you were a Christian slave') – exemplifies Kipling's early loneliness in London, in that it finds a welcome companion from the familiar land in Grish Chunder the Bengali. Only a strong stimulus could permit Kipling to enjoy the idea of a Babu as a companion.

The first published Mowgli story appeared in *Many Inventions*. *Mowgli's Brothers*, as yet unpublished, had been the first written. It developed, according to its author, from a not very distinguished passage in Rider Haggard, supplemented

Josephine, Carrie and Rudyard's first child. She was born at Bliss Cottage, Brattleboro, on 29 December 1892.

Yokohama, looking strangely occidental, a photograph taken at the end of the nineteenth century. It was here that Kipling learned that his bank had failed, and that his savings were wiped out.

by stories known to Lockwood Kipling about babies in India nursed by wolves. But, as the story of Romulus and Remus shows, the idea was almost as old as western civilisation, and none the worse for that. *In the Rukh* did not pursue the very personal myth that Kipling was to unfold in *The Jungle Books*, but presented the faun-like figure of an adult Mowgli adapting himself to contact with white civilisation in the forests of the Doon country, and finding a working place as a ranger in the remarkably flexible and unbureaucratic British Empire of Kipling's ideal vision.

The Disturber of Traffic was the first of his stories to deal with mental breakdown. His handling of the lighthouse keeper in the Java Straits who becomes obsessed with the wash left by passing ships, and gradually loses more and more touch with reality as he tries to interfere with the passage of the world's merchant marines, was sensitive and sympathetic. There is nothing to indicate to the reader that the writer might have a personal interest in the subject: it has all the air of a traveller's tale, saved from being an unfeeling account of a lonely man's distress by 'the author', whose presence tempers the potential contempt of the old Trinity House man telling the story.

The most revealing of the stories in the book is *Children of the Zodiac*. This enigmatic myth is extremely important, because it is virtually the only place where Kipling makes an outright declaration of the value he set on art. 'The children' are demi-gods, who represent qualities or types essential to the

Naulakha, the house built by the Kiplings on the land they bought from Carrie's brother, Beatty Balestier.

only escape terror by serving and delighting men. They have to humble themselves: the twins are ordered about as well as adored; the Bull is enslaved. Leo, the artist, observes the experiences of his fellows before discovering his own function, and, indeed, it is part of that function to share experience. He must abandon his demi-divinity, because, 'the Immortals know nothing worth laughter or tears', and he will have to evoke these. Making songs gives him nothing but pain, for the driving force in his creative power is knowledge of the fact of death. Yet the effect of the songs is to make men braver, more industrious, and more loving: less concerned about death, and fitter for living well and usefully. It is a practical Punjabi administrator's view of art: by no means for art's sake; entirely for the sake of human well-being. Art must be inspiring, though Kipling does not suggest that it should be consciously didactic.

well-being of mankind. The Bull is work; the Girl is love; the Twins are childhood; Leo, the central figure, is the artist. The Ram is exemplary excellence of a surprisingly eighteen-ninety-ish aesthetic kind: it has only to be seen and admired by mankind for them to try to produce sheep of equal splendour: unlike the other 'children' it *does* nothing.

All these demi-gods are perfectly happy as long as they exist independently of mankind. Their troubles come, when they learn from the Houses of Death (the Crab, the Scorpion, the Fishes) that they are not immortal. Then, one by one, they find that they can

And the artist must expect abuse from toilers who have enjoyed his creations, and taken spiritual sustenance from him, but who do not believe that the act of creation costs any real effort. Even this is better than receiving praise, pence and decorations, which may corrupt the art as well as the artist. Art must be Work. Then it may be Work for Work's sake.

Work was, in fact, quick to bring Kipling rewards in excess of those he had lost. Royalties from *Barrack-Room Ballads* and *The Naulahka* soon made him a prosperous man, and he prepared to build a house fit for a Balestier of Brattleboro'.

On the site he had received from Beatty he erected Naulakha, a long, lovely house, faced with wood shingles. Domestic engineering always delighted Rudyard and Carrie. They drove a deep water shaft, and erected a wind-pump over it. When this proved

Kipling's study at Naulakha. a photograph taken in 1895. The inscription above the fire-place was carved by John Lockwood Kipling when he and Alice visited their son in 1894.

inadequate, they replaced it with a low-power atmospheric pump. In addition they had a stable, a drive, an avenue and a tennis-court established outside.

Beatty oversaw all this work, and the Kiplings paid him well for it. Arranging contracts for them, hiring labourers and ox-teams, and carrying out their wishes, added several thousand dollars to Beatty's shaky farming income over the next few years. The only warning sign that this might not prove an everlastingly idyllic relationship lay in Carrie's habit of paying him in dribs and drabs; making him come up to the house to receive small amounts; scarcely ever entrusting him with large sums; and delegating authority to him only when she was quite sure that she had dictated everything down to the last detail. No doubt she meant well. She was, after all, a good, managing woman, entrusted by Rudyard with total control over their business affairs, and Beatty was a representative Vermont small-farming financial disaster. But it was tactless of big sister not to allow little brother more freedom. And she took still graver risks in enquiring censoriously about his private affairs and growing indebtedness.

Indoors, Carrie's guardianship over Rudyard was symbolically demonstrated by the position of her sitting-room. It commanded the door of his study, and prevented anyone from seeing him without first confronting her. Only close friends or genuinely desirable business acquaintances were allowed through. Kipling's old habit of sitting up late, swapping tall stories with fellow-journalists, was a thing of the past. Carrie had stopped it even before their truncated honeymoon was over. Brattleboro reporters were forbidden to invade the privacy of their distinguished colleague, and like all good newspapermen bilked of a story they resented it. The Balestier girl and her celebrated English husband were thought to be stand-offish; above themselves even by Balestier standards.

Kipling was quite unaware of this silent division growing up between himself and his neighbours. He only knew that he loved the quiet and solitude of his New England home. He was willing to do anything that did not intrude upon his privacy, for any one – even strangers. When he was out walking in the hills, and met a woman whose distant house looked across at his, he cheerfully agreed to her request that he should never shutter his windows at nights, as the friendly sight of his lights had come to mean so much to her. This was the kind of unobtrusive, uninterfering solidarity with his fellow-men that Kipling the married man understood best. Since Carrie kept such visitors as she believed to be unwelcome quite away from him, he had no idea that he had a single ill-wisher in Vermont.

There were wonderful outdoor parties and barn dances at Beatty's. Mai produced homemade cakes and homebrewed cider, and the dancing would last

A familiar illustration from The First Jungle Book, *by W. H. Drake. Bagheera lies out on a branch and calls to Mowgli, while Baloo watches from the ground.*

until the small hours of the morning. Kipling loved looking in at such festivities, and probably took it that he participated, by familial right, in Beatty's local popularity.

In fact, the Kiplings were liked by very few people. The local Episcopalian and Presbyterian ministers were friendly, although the Kiplings were not church-goers, and a mysterious local tradition credited Rudyard with staying at home to write hymns on Sunday mornings, instead of going to worship with other people. The would-be exclusive denizens of Brattleboro and its environs were willing to allow the Kiplings to be the most exclusive of them all. An ex-governor of the state who lived nearby regarded himself as a friend. And Kipling spent three happy years at Naulakha, during which time he saw himself as a prospective resident of the USA for the remainder of his life. 'I love this country' was his simple summary.

Peaceful family events took place in Vermont. Lockwood and Alice retired in 1894, and an immediate visit from his father was one satisfaction for Rudyard. Lockwood carved an inscription above the fireplace in Rudyard's library: 'The Night Cometh when No Man can Work'. And he helped his son with *The Jungle Books* which were being written at this time. Lockwood's knowledge of India provided some details in the Mowgli stories. His critical eye lent caution to other stories so that *The Miracle of Purun Bagat* became the masterly little account of a life dividing neatly between two cultures that it is.

The Jungle Books have been best-selling volumes since their first publication, and deservedly so. Rudyard was in full command of his power by the mid-1890s. The Mowgli stories, as a sequence of fables, perfectly embody attitudes and expectations which have proved abidingly attractive to middle-class England. A responsible, active life in a stable hierarchical society is advocated. The reader is invited to identify with Mowgli, whose status as a man is at the peak of the hierarchy, but whose age as a child sends him back, almost to the bottom. Mowgli first obeys, and then wields authority. A 'training in leadership', after the manner of the Public Schools is thus excitingly transformed into a jungle childhood.

But Kipling's passion for 'outsiders' is also respected in Mowgli's estrangement from human society, and ultimate alienation from the wolf pack. He stands on his own feet, knowing that he has always respected the Jungle Law, but avoiding the temptation to shallow conformity which lies as a pitfall for the law-abiding.

Intellectuals are consciously attacked as the *bandar-log*: chattering monkey-people who play with

ideas – particularly ideas which offend other people – but achieve nothing themselves. The unflattering picture has, naturally, offended many serious adult readers, and attracted for Kipling the unfortunate vocal admiration of anti-intellectual philistines. Yet as a comment on the parlour-pink aesthetes, who valued their skill in the expression of supercilious malice without making any very obvious contribution to the quality of life around them, it should have been usefully provocative in 1894. In an age of 'celebrities' it is important to question the quality of those who are fashionably offered as great minds, and *Kaa's Hunting* is not really any more philistine a work than Frisch's *The Fire-Raisers*, with its equally scathing mockery of the impotent self-importance of a theorising intelligentsia.

That Kipling was as great a 'lord of language' as any of his more hifalutin contemporaries was shown in *The Second Jungle Book* in particular. *The Undertakers*, a curiously undervalued story, makes brilliant use of the 'talking animal' convention, in its depiction of the sycophancy and effusiveness among three loathsome parasites. The empty courtesies and artificial pretension to great civilisation provides a perfect satire on corrupt and cruel power such as may then have existed in the courts of some independent princes, and today must be found among the world's more distasteful military juntas and dictatorships.

In *The King's Ankus*, Kipling stole his plot shamelessly from Chaucer's *Pardoner's Tale*, and created an object lesson in the use of familiar secondhand material. His frame, with Mowgli and

Rikki-Tikki-Tavi confronted by Nag, the cobra.

Bagheera tracking the thieves of the ankus, provides new dimensions of interest, structural, narrative and moral, to the original. And he compliments his reader by assuming that Chaucer will be recognised and the plot need not be totally recounted: he does not explicitly name the means by which the last three holders of the ankus die.

The gold stamped figure of the cobra holding the ankus on the royal blue cover made *The Second Jungle Book* as pleasing a physical object as any of the lush aesthetic publications of the 1890s. *The Jungle Book*, with its elephants and mahouts, was equally beautiful. And Lockwood Kipling's decorations and illustrations to the books are, by now, his best-known work, even if many readers have not realised that the J L K who drew Mowgli was the author's father.

In 1895 the Kiplings' American dream started to turn sour. At the beginning of the year, Carrie scorched her face badly in opening the oven door. Convalescence from this quite severe accident took her and her husband to Washington, D.C., where Kipling found President Cleveland's entourage despicable. A political dispute over the borders of Venezuela and British Guiana was being used for somewhat demagogic purposes in the USA, and anti-British feeling was starting to run high enough to threaten actual war. Dr Jameson's abortive attempt to seize the Afrikaaner capital in the Transvaal also offended Americans, always quick to oppose grandiose British expansionist imperialism. Curiously, the one close political friend Kipling made in America was of Dutch stock, and opened the acquaintance by loudly thanking God that he hadn't a drop of 'damned British blood' in his veins.

Theodore Roosevelt was the leading American politician who wished to see the USA itself become an imperial power in the 1890s. Like Kipling, he was a myopic intellectual with an admiration for powerful men of action. Unlike Kipling, he set out to make himself just such a man. Shooting, riding, fishing, and ultimately, in the Spanish-American War, leading a tactically ridiculous but historically successful charge up San Juan Hill in Cuba, he was almost a portly American parody of a Kipling hero. There was something endearingly comic about him. On his political rallies, he was always greeted with bands playing 'A Hot Time in the Old Town Tonight'. It was somehow appropriate that his refusal to shoot bear-cubs while they were still growing should have attached his name to the nursery 'Teddy Bear'.

He had a bluff openness that delighted Kipling. And he enjoyed Kipling's sly returns. For Kipling *knew* South Africa and knew that in the eyes of their Boer uncles and aunties (or *'ooms'* and *'tanties'*) the New York Roosevelts were nothing but damn Dutchmen (or *verdomder Hollanders*)! The two men became admiring friends. Both were fervent patriots. Each would have liked to see the other's skills and energies devoted to the service of his own country.

Neither, when they met, could have foreseen a 'special relationship' through which they might have worked in English-speaking union. For, as Roosevelt proudly and bluntly told Kipling, he intended to squeeze the money for a larger navy out of Congress by threatening them with the might of the Royal Navy as a potential enemy. And neither could have foreseen that within thirty years the radical imperialism they espoused would look out of date, and they would seem politically comic figures to most of the men in their countries who wielded real power.

Back in Vermont, trouble came from Beatty. Once Naulakha was finished he had only his farm to live on. And, slowly but surely, his farm failed. The worse his financial condition became, the more he drank. The poorer the Balestiers grew, the more the Kiplings prospered. Mai began to resent what she took to be Carrie's superior attitude. Carrie was concerned in her own way about Beatty, and strained relations further by trying to organise his affairs. Beatty's drunkenness made him an unwelcome visitor. He became unreliable when looking after the Kipling's affairs while they holidayed in England, and ran their household accounts into temporary debt. Even his grandmother lost patience with him, and her wealth was no longer at his disposal. Finally, with bankruptcy staring him in the face, he quarrelled absolutely with the Kiplings over Carrie's decision to build a formal garden on part of the land he felt entitled to farm under the terms of their original agreement.

The quarrel was inconvenient for the Kiplings. They stopped seeing the Balestiers, and corresponded by note. Beatty was no longer available to carry mail down to the Post Office for them. Rudyard had to take his own letters in through the townsfolk of Brattleboro, and he felt that he was stared at. When the Kiplings' pump broke down, they were unable to get water from the obvious source, the Balestier farm.

John Lockwood Kipling's tailpiece for The Second Jungle Book. *'Mowgli's song against people.'*

Stephen Grover Cleveland in 1895. He was twice President of the United States, and contributed to the growing anti-British feeling abroad by his strong resistance to the use of force by the British in a border dispute with Venezuela.

Theodore Roosevelt as President. In spite of the climate of opinion in America he succeeded in increasing the status of the United States as a world power. He and Kipling understood each other and became firm friends.

Finally the crash came for Beatty. He was bankrupted. This provoked local gossip, and Rudyard was silly and indiscreet enough to join in. He told a neighbour that he had been compelled 'to carry Beatty for the last year – to hold him up by the seat of his breeches'. He had, of course, never been ungenerous to his brother-in-law, and Carrie had offered to relieve the Balestiers of some financial strain by bringing up Marjorie in Naulakha. But this proposal had only angered and upset Mai, and when Rudyard's patronising insult was thoughtfully passed on to Beatty, a storm was unavoidable.

On 6 May 1896 Rudyard went out for a gentle spin on his bicycle. At the foot of a hill, not far from Madam Balestier's property, Beatty appeared, driving a team of horses at his usual breakneck speed. Rudyard fell off his bicycle, and picked himself up to find a furiously drunken Beatty blocking his way, and menacing him with a whip.

'See here!' shouted Beatty, 'I want to talk to you.'

'If you have anything to say, you can say it to my lawyer,' answered Rudyard, who was obviously at a momentary disadvantage.

'By Jesus, this is no case for lawyers!' roared Beatty, and broke into a tirade of abuse.

Kipling was uneasy when confronted by the threat of actual violence. His tempestuous farcical stories were created in the study; his life was one of cushioned security. He had been protected from any breath of criticism since living with Carrie, and was hardly capable of dealing with an angry Vermont farmer, yelling, 'If you won't retract the lies you've been telling about me within a week, I'll blow out your goddam brains!'

'If I don't do certain things, you'll kill me?' Rudyard asked, with infuriating English primness and literal-mindedness.

'By Jesus, I will!' (What else *could* Beatty say?)

'Then,' said Rudyard, like a well-trained nanny, 'remember you will only have yourself to blame for the consequences.'

'Do you dare to threaten me, you little bastard?' shouted Beatty, and drove violently away to a friend's house, where he fell into maudlin regret over having kicked up an excessive row.

Rudyard went home and talked the scene over with Carrie. And from that moment he was caught in the cross-fire of the quarrel between brother and sister. He went earnestly down to Brattleboro the next morning, and laid charges against Beatty for 'assault with indecent and opprobrious names and epithets and threatening to kill'. Two days later, Beatty was arrested, and Kipling's hopes of a peaceful life in Vermont were ended.

By the standards of his own stories he had behaved preposterously. He had reacted to violence with prissiness. He had taken a tongue-lashing to heart, and run to the law for help – *he*, Rudyard Kipling, who in story after story had claimed to admire and respond to vigorous insult! He was making a fool of

*The end of Dr Leander Starr Jameson's
ill-advised Raid. He is taken prisoner by P. A.
Cronje, the Boer commandant, after his band
was surrounded on 2 January 1896. This
overture to the Boer War increased American
resentment of British imperialism.*

himself and a martyr of Beatty. He tried, further, to pour oil on troubled flames, by offering to stand bail for Beatty!

Beatty knew exactly how to profit from the situation. The sympathy of the town was with him, and the Brattleboro press was only too pleased to have ammunition against aloof Mr Kipling. Beatty paid his own bail, and negotiated with the newspapers for the highest bidder to print his story.

His day in court was an occasion he thoroughly enjoyed, with examining lawyers extracting all his bluff good nature. To Rudyard, the witness-box was an ordeal, and it seemed to him that the lawyers were deliberately prolonging his cross-examination for the benefit of the gutter press. His privacy was trampled over. His inability to live at peace with his brother-in-law was shouted to the world. His assailant was bound over – what more could have been expected after such a trivial incident? And Rudyard was left to feel that the majesty of the law of America regarded him as a man with no proper sense of proportion.

It was more than he could bear. He gathered up Carrie, Josephine, and his second daughter, Elsie, who had been born at Naulakha, and fled to England. The stately house facing Mount Monadnock was simply abandoned. Mr Kipling came back to England, where, he hoped, a gentleman who had the misfortune to be set upon – or at least sworn at – by a ruffian, would not himself be treated like a criminal.

*Kipling, at thirty-two, was the youngest member
of the Athenaeum. Two of the distinguished men
he dined with upon his election were Alfred
Milner (left), and Cecil Rhodes.*

The Imperial Zenith of Reputation

'THIS ENGLAND IS STUFFY,' COMPLAINED LITTLE Josephine. Her father laughed, and called her a little American. But in large part he agreed with her, and missed the familiar comfort of Naulakha: the reliable heating of American houses; the regular and distinct seasons, where autumn was crisp and clear, and not a moist and misty anticipation of a wet and muddy winter. England was not a country where Kipling could easily experiment with new crazes, as he loved to do: trying out skis before any one else in Vermont had seen them, or playing golf on the snow with scarlet balls. These things would be eccentricity in England. They might lead to social ostracism.

The story *An Error in the Fourth Dimension*, written soon after Kipling's flight from Vermont, has often been taken as a vicious slap at the country which had rejected him. It tells of a millionaire who has settled in England, and, for his own convenience upon an unimportant occasion, flags down an express-train from the end of his garden, expecting to be able to board it and travel quickly to London. The railway company tries to persuade him to accept a legally binding commitment never to interfere with their traffic; he assumes that he need only have a private word with their president to sort everything out, and, by his insistence that he is rich enough to buy the entire company, persuades them that he is mad. When it is revealed that he is an American . . . what had seemed to be insanity is instantly recognised as a typical national foible.

Now, this story does contain a few moments of black bile, in which Kipling clearly expresses his feelings about the dreadful spring and summer of 1896. There is a nasty description of Wilton Sargent, the millionaire, as unmistably American:

> 'It was a lawful son of the Youngest People, whose predecessors were the Red Indian. His voice had risen to the high, throaty crow of his breed when they labour under excitement. His close-set eyes showed by turns unnecessary fear, annoyance beyond reason, rapid and purposeless flight of thoughts, the child's lust for immediate revenge, and the child's pathetic bewilderment, who knocks his head against the bad wicked table.'

Thus, evidently, had Beatty Balestier appeared in a lane in Vermont.

There is a silly suggestion that all Americans like cheap cigars, and smoke them in lurid dives. There is a deeply-felt reference to the screaming headlines of the New York press, and their merciless treatment of the famous.

But the total impression created by the story is not anti-American. Quite the contrary; it is the work of a man who perceives, understands and admires aspects of both British and American society, but feels that they are, as it were dimensionally, incapable of appreciating each other. It is the work of an Anglo-Indian with an American wife who has spent more perfectly contented years of adult life in Vermont than anywhere else.

Wilton Sargent is – and it is an essential point – a millionaire's son and heir, not a self-made man. He represents a group which reasonably alarmed Kipling: men of immense wealth, who had not earned their own position, yet believed that they were fully entitled to all its privileges. And Kipling knew full well that America was even more suspicious of such men than England, and on better grounds. England wondered about the unsettling effect of quite so much wealth: America challenged their enjoyment of indolence. Wilton Sargent's 'country wanted to know why he did not go to the office daily, as his father had done before him'. He behaves rather like Kipling in America, shutting himself up in a private country house, and keeping himself to himself. And Kipling shows himself in sympathy with the ordinary Americans who expect their rich men to work for their money. Wilton learns his lesson; stops trying to use his money to buy class in England, and goes back to work in America. Kipling can understand his view that England is hidebound and parochial, and quite approves of him once he goes back to being a useful businessman. The historical certitude with which the English treat their own *mores* as divine laws amuses Kipling quite as much as does American brashness. The narrator of the story retains Wilton's friendship; but takes a rise out of the doctor who has come to certify the man who stopped the train.

The books Kipling published in 1897 and 1898 set out the effects of American life upon him. *Captains Courageous* idealises the way of life of small fishermen in Massachusetts. Kipling had gone out with the fishing fleet for material, and his descriptions of life at sea and the work of the fleet are alive and fresh. The best aspects of the New England puritan ethic were easily assimilated into his own moral outlook.

Hard work and rugged independence are key virtues; clean living and due respect for legitimate (and only legitimate) authority are important; true kindness and humanity will never be found to be in conflict with these priorities. It is this final over-simplification, of course, which makes his general ethic slightly suspect. But it is entirely suitable to a boy's morality story like *Captains Courageous*.

Kipling often seems to be trying to correct his own potential faults through the stereotyped adolescents his fiction attacks. In the early Indian *Tales*, the young men in need of correction were usually intellectuals who thought that their book-learning meant that they knew more than the men around them. Had the youthful 'Gigger' initially shared their error? By the mid-1890s Kipling was a rich man, and *Captains Courageous* is structured around a sermon on the dangers of unearned riches. Kipling still believed that early training held the means of salvation. Harvey Cheyne is thrown on to Disco Troop's fishing smack before his soft, spoiled life has utterly ruined him. Cheyne's father, on the other hand, a man who has earned his millions, is treated with respect, by Kipling as by Troop. Having *made* the money, the elder Cheyne is entitled to wield its power as he wishes, even for such personal objects as racing his neurotic wife across the continent faster than any one has ever travelled before.

Kipling had no objection to self-made men indulging their whims. He asked the railway magnate, F. M. Finney, to tell him how long it would take to run a train from California to Massachusetts using the quickest possible routes, and cutting corners whenever the opportunity arose. He took the details of Mr and Mrs Cheyne's journey from Finney's information, and felt that he had been involved in a technological adventure when Finney subsequently, for his private amusement, ran a train across the route, and beat the record claimed in the book.

But in England such high spirits were not to be found. The Kiplings rented Rock House, at Maidencombe, near Torquay, where Rudyard's study commanded a view straight over the sea, looking almost directly down on to the decks of the little Devonshire crabbers. It gave him far too little pleasure. It was not like the view of the Vermont mountains he had loved. A violent storm on his arrival swept away the back gate and tore down trees all over the property, and it seemed an ill omen. Although he would not say or do anything to remind himself of the previous year's unhappiness, Carrie felt that he was longing to return to Brattleboro, if only Beatty were not there.

The Seven Seas, a volume of poems which were more seriously philosophic than the *Barrack-Room Ballads,* raised his literary prestige. Charles Eliot Norton, luminary of Harvard, wrote a long, eulogistic review in the *Atlantic Monthly*, praising Kipling's 'passionate, moral, imperial patriotism.' Kipling was surprised and delighted to be taken so seriously. Norton had been a friend in America, but Kipling had modestly assumed that his own limited education must place his work beneath the serious notice of this intellectuals' intellectual. He confessed, in a letter to Norton, that he had been disinclined to take his own versification too seriously: partly because he expected that a greater poet of steam and empire would soon emerge (none did); and partly because he feared the vitiating effect of being self-consciously 'A Poet'.

A poet in the high aesthetic line he may not have been, but he certainly was, in the established British mould, 'A Man of Letters.' At thirty-two he was elected to membership of the Athenaeum as a person eminent in public life. He was far and away the youngest member, and celebrated his election at a dinner with three much older men: the editor of *The Times*, Alfred Milner, and Cecil Rhodes, who had been an awe-inspiring figure lunching a few tables away from him in Cape Town when he visited South Africa.

He began to make friendly contact with the academic establishment, one of the few official groups from which he was willing to accept honours. He dined at High Table in Balliol, under the slightly misty impression that Oxford was a city full of 'four hundred year-old universities'. The under-graduates cheered him so loudly that the Master was unable to say grace.

After a visit to a theatre in the West End, he met Balliol's most effortlessly superior alumnus: George Nathaniel Curzon, the Conservative politician who was shortly to become the most Kiplingesque of Indian Viceroys, and some years later, to lose the leadership of the Conservative party to cousin Stanley Baldwin.

But metropolitan excitements were offset by the tedium of Torquay. Kipling complained to Norton about the 'Bloody British' weather, and went on to object to the 'rummy' British breed. 'Torquay,' he said, 'is such a place as I do desire to upset by dancing through it with nothing on but my spec-tacles. Villas, clipped hedges and shaven lawns; fat old ladies with respirators and obese landaus.'

To compensate for all this pomp and circumstance there was a new area of active life to be explored: the Royal Navy. Captain E.H. Bayly, whom Kipling had met at Simonstown, invited him to come on a cruiser for manoeuvres in the Channel. He accepted with alacrity.

He refused an even more grand offer, to sail with the Mediterranean fleet, and watch the hostilities that were taking place between the Turks and the Cretans. Actual naval warfare was not something he ever wished to experience at first hand. But manoeuvres were a splendid opportunity for ir-responsible schoolboy anti-heroics, and whether he ever saw any such curious nautical behaviour or not, he continued to visit the Channel Fleet as often as possible, until he was celebrating its peacetime

A still from the film of Captains Courageous *(1937), which enjoyed great success. Kipling's novel was published in 1897, and gave a vivid picture of the life of small fishermen of the Massachusetts coast. The author went out with the fishing fleet to gain material at first hand.*

A torpedo boat destroyer – they were later called simply destroyers – on manoeuvres with the battle fleet.

doings in the unlikely adventures of Petty Officer Emmanuel Pyecroft.

On trials in a new destroyer, he was almost shaken to pieces by the vibrations she set up when running flat out. But he was thrilled and impressed by the practical example of the romance of steam, and delighted to discover that all the engineers knew his poem *McAndrew's Hymn*.

Once he even managed to get Lockwood Kipling invited with him. The old man was, in truth, rather more adventurous than his famous son. Knocking about the world in tramp steamers was a way in which he would have liked to pass his retirement, and it was in character that he should take advantage of Rudyard's celebrity to see the sea from a new deck, rather than try to wangle invitations to the Athenaeum or Balliol.

Rudyard's writing remained material for his father's illustrative skills. Lockwood and Alice had settled at Tisbury in Wiltshire, but 'the Pater' came down to Torquay and set up a studio to work on a new project for illustrating an American edition of his son's writings. The novel idea was that Lockwood should mould low reliefs of principal characters and incidents, and a photographer should be called in to take carefully lit pictures of them. How well the project succeeded will be familiar to readers of the standard edition of *Kim*. What is not apparent from the book illustrations is the considerable size of the originals: splendid objects, about two feet across, from some of which the Kiplings took bronze casts.

This artistic plaster-work travelled with Rudyard and Carrie when they abandoned Torquay in despair, and moved to Sussex. The Burne-Joneses had a summer home called North End House on the village green at Rottingdean. Stanley Baldwin had married a girl called Cissie Ridsdale, whose people owned another large house on the green, and the wedding had taken place in the village. Earlier, Meg Burne-Jones had married Jack Mackail there, and many offshoots of the Macdonald tribe spent holidays in the quiet little place, away from the train routes and so free from day-trippers. The publican remembered Ruddy spending holidays there as a schoolboy. So that when a house called The Elms fell vacant on the green, the Kiplings were moving back into Rudyard's family sphere by renting it.

Time had not weakened Rud's strong ties as nephew and cousin. In 1897, both Cissie Baldwin and Carrie Kipling were pregnant, and Rudyard's friendship with Stan was intensified. In that year Phil Burne-Jones had a sensational success with a very bad painting, and Rudyard contributed support with a very bad poem. The painting was called *The Vampire*, and was a piece of vulgar late-Victorian, pseudo-profound sexiness. It depicted a demonically triumphant woman standing over a prostrate young man on a bed. It meant nothing, but all manner of sado-masochistic fantasies might be read into it.

Rudyard's verses, printed in the catalogue to his cousin's exhibition, contributed their piece to the currency the word 'vampire' was acquiring. They reverted to the callow knowingness of his earliest work; dismissed the young man in love as a fool, and his woman as 'a rag and a bone and a hank of hair,' and finished up with what might have been a last vicious kick at self-contained Flo Garrard:

the woman who did not know
(And now we know that she never could know)
And did not understand!

It is possible that Kipling resumed contact with Flo in 1900, and as late as 1912 a notebook of his appears to have found its way into her hands. Although there could be no question of any resumption of romantic interest, the adolescent wound Flo inflicted remained the strongest (or most intense) amatory experience of Kipling's life: no one has ever suggested that he felt for Carrie anything of the soupy and sentimental love he was celebrating in *The Brushwood Boy* at this period.

A more charitable explanation for a very bad poem, that temporarily damaged Kipling's reputation, lies in the suggestion that he was trying to warn Phil off playing around with Mrs Patrick Campbell, who was certainly more capable of looking after her toughly theatrical emotions in flirtation than any young man. If this is so the warning was ill-calculated, being overheated enough to intensify the dramatic passion it may have been intended to assuage.

At North End House, just before the Kiplings moved into The Elms, Carrie's third child was born. To their great delight it was a boy, and they named him John for Rudyard's father. Although The Elms proved not entirely satisfactory, and Rudyard was soon unsuccessfully house-hunting in a desultory way, the happiness of his nuclear family was complete. Beyond, in the old 'Family Square', things were more troubled.

Tisbury was really too cold and damp for Alice after the years in India. She lost weight alarmingly; she suffered from periods of intense insomnia, and she was the victim of sudden spasms of nervous pain. She took to wearing a sandy toupee, and although she enjoyed a reasonably high social position in the village, her dancing days were over. The witty, worldly centre of attraction that Alice Macdonald had been was faded.

Trix spent a good deal of time with her parents, but her presence was not consolatory. To all appearances, she continued as she had been, a smart, elegant young lady, with the family capacity to turn her ideas into print. 1897 saw the publication of her first novel, *The Pinchbeck Goddess*, a sprightly social romance with the Simla setting her brother had so early made his own. She was to publish one further novel, and a volume of verses in collaboration with Alice coyly named *Hand-in-Hand: Verses by A Mother and Daughter*.

One of John Lockwood Kipling's plaques illustrating his son's work. A scene from In the Presence.

But behind the cool exterior of print, Trix's mind was disturbed. She had been dabbling with crystal-gazing and automatic writing since the early 1890s, and while in India engaged in a curious correspondence with an English lady who practised 'psychical research'. Years later, when Rudyard was asked if he thought there was anything in spiritualism, he replied very earnestly, 'There is. I know. Have nothing to do with it.'

Was this because he knew that Trix's mind slowly gave way? The first hint of incompatability between herself and her husband came in 1890, when Fleming was home on leave and spent all his time in Edinburgh being treated for insomnia, while Trix stayed with his sister. As time went on, it became increasingly clear that Fleming could not give Trix whatever the extraordinary sympathy and devotion was that she needed. He was a kind, patient man, but 'psychic' activities and irrational behaviour were beyond his comprehension. Trix began to react against him. Sometimes she withdrew completely into herself for unnaturally long periods, and could not be recalled into the real world. At other times she would evince violent hostility to her husband. Doctors told him that he was on no account to try to communicate with her when she was in either of these states. And so the couple came to spend more and more time apart.

At last, in 1898, Trix suffered a complete break-down, and went to live with her mother in Tisbury. She entered upon a period of intensified 'psychic' activity; was rarely able to spend short periods with her husband; and did not fully recover until the 1920s, when she moved to Edinburgh. She lived to the age of eighty, ending her life as a mildly eccentric old lady, noted for going to the zoo and talking to the animals in Hindustani.

Rudyard was kept fairly busy offering support to Trix whenever possible. He was one of the few people whose presence she could stand in her worst moments. Then, in the summer of 1898, Uncle Ned Burne-Jones died. Now there was a bereaved Aunt Georgie living across the green and needing comfort. Rudyard was unfailingly kind and sympathetic, and gave his aunt advice about her plans for a life of Burne-Jones.

Children remained one of his great delights. In addition to three of his own, he had little cousins to play with when the Mackail children were staying at North End House, and he founded a Boys' Club in the village. Private though he kept his personal life, odd flashes in his verse reveal the confident, loving, conspiratorial relationship he had with his daughters; particularly, at this time, Josephine, the elder and more imaginatively playful:

Let's – oh, *anything*, daddy, so long as
 it's you and me,
And going truly exploring, and not being
 in till tea!
Here's your boots (I've brought 'em), and
 here's your cap and stick,
And here's your pipe and tobacco. Oh,
 come along out of it – quick!

He enjoyed playing the threatening ogre to a houseful of children, and, typically, dressed up the game in patriotic historical robes for them. His children and the Mackails were Cavaliers at Rottingdean: he was a wicked Roundhead, and waged furious and delightful war against Josephine and her cousin Angela.

In the evening he told them stories which, when polished and published, would be known to millions as the *Just So Stories*. With the daughter of 'the daughter of my uncle', he perfected the ritual tone and address – 'O, best beloved,' – which was to add so much to the ultimate children's book.

The adult volume, *The Day's Work*, brought together stories written in Vermont and after. It marked a definite darkening in Kipling's outlook. The Indian stories were long, and concentrated heavily on work and duty. Animal stories took up the same theme: *The Maltese Cat* celebrated the little polo Kipling had played in India, and his indebtedness to his pony's professionalism: *A Walking Delegate* re-created perfectly the horses Kipling had owned in Vermont, all presented by their actual names, with anthropomorphised personalities, in a vivid description of their pasture.

Their conversation instructs a lazy, would-be revolutionary visitor in the virtues of work and the respect due to man.

From animals, Kipling went on to write about machines. *The Ship that Found Herself* is a simple technical experiment, presenting the parts of a ship coming together on her maiden voyage, as an allegory on co-operative work. *·007* is a simple technical disaster: a story of a steam-engine working and winning acceptance in the freemasonry of other engines in the shed. It signally fails to rise above the allegorical level of commonplace children's books about anthropomorphised talking trains.

The title of the collection is well chosen. Lockwood's inscription over the library fireplace at Naulakha had suggested it. But it points to the uneasy concern that was developing in Kipling: a need to justify the wealth of his class by claiming that their work was more difficult, demanding, sophisticated and useful than that of others, and therefore they deserved higher rewards. Kipling was no defender of the Idle Rich, but he was never acutely aware of the problems of the Industrious Poor. In this volume he began, especially in *A Walking Delegate*, to suggest that Labour organisation was an obvious product of the malicious hatred of the idle poor for the industrious rich.

The love stories, *The Brushwood Boy* and *William the Conqueror*, were about as emotionally enthralling as announcements in *The Times* engagement column. The best parts of the book were the hilarious farces *My Sunday at Home* and *Bread Upon the Waters*, and the pictures of India.

The two years 1897 and 1898 were years in which Kipling's imperialism matched that of his fellow-countrymen precisely. He had indicated that he was not willing to be created Poet Laureate when Salisbury's Conservative administration wished to fill the vacancy left by Tennyson's death. Apart from being the mantle of such wretched poetasters as Pye and Cibber, it was the sort of honour Kipling believed to be both dangerous and, as his own 'True Thomas' expressed it, insulting to a writer:

I ha' harpit ye up to the Throne o' God,
 I ha' harpit your midmost soul in three.
I ha' harpit ye down to the Hinges o' Hell,
 And – ye – would – make – a Knight o' me!

But he was in the habit of sending, *gratis*, verses on public events to be printed in *The Times*, and these were far more highly regarded than the turgid offerings of the absurd hack, Alfred Austin, to whom Salisbury eventually gave the laureateship. In the 1890s Kipling grew increasingly anxious about England's lack of concern for its colonies. He sent *The Times* a colonial's plea to *The Native-Born* in 1895, and a stately comment on Canadian Preferential Tariff, *Our Lady of the Snows*, in 1897.

It was Queen Victoria's Diamond Jubilee, in 1897, however, that really brought Kipling to the forefront of patriotic appeal. It seemed appropriate that he

*'The Capture of a Spirit', an exposure of a
dubious seance which took place in Great Russell
Street. Kipling took no comfort from such
exposures: his sister Trix became involved in
'psychical research' to a degree that ruined her
marriage and led to a complete breakdown
in 1898.*

should write something for the occasion, but, with
his intense dislike of 'jelly-bellied flag-flapping', he
found it extremely difficult to compose a suitable
paean of praise to Britannia. A visitor to North End
House noticed in a waste paper basket some rejected
draft verses in which Kipling expressed his doubts
about the 'tumult and the shouting'. She urged him
to preserve them, and Aunt Georgie concurred. The
verses were polished, and sent to Rider Haggard for
his opinion. He approved. A final section was excised; the poem, which had originally been headed
After was given the more sonorous title *Recessional*,
and with publication in *The Times*, Kipling had a

major success on his hands.

The verses struck exactly the note of unease that
overtakes an Englishman who suspects that the
proud claims he has just made may be a bit exaggerated. It was the modest apology for the strained
boasting of the Jubilee that the nation wished to
hear. Its sonorities were those of *Hymns Ancient
and Modern;* its very metre was consciously based on
'Eternal Father, strong to save'; so the most unpoetic
reader could instantly recognise it as reverential
verse. The only stanza to call down adverse criticism
(for the crudely racist sentiment of its fourth line)
crystallizes the effect of the whole:

If, drunk with sight of power, we loose
   Wild tongues that have not Thee in awe,
Such boastings as the Gentiles use,
   Or lesser breeds without the Law –
Lord God of Hosts, be with us yet,
Lest we forget – lest we forget!

The reiterated last line is satisfyingly vague; every reader could interpret for himself whether it meant that the nation was to bear in mind its failings, or its awesome responsibilities and greatness. The modesty which apologises for the excesses of the Jubilee carefully refrains from suggesting that the nation actually *could* sink essentially to the level of 'Gentiles' or 'lesser breeds without the Law'. The humility, in short, is false and spiritually complacent, and the entire piece catches a tone which the English are likely to feel subjectively as deep sincerity, and all other races perceive as bafflingly impermeable hypocrisy.

The poem satisfied conservative and liberal minds alike. Congratulations poured in from all sides. The idea of the vulgar, jingling balladeer was put aside and Kipling was, for the time being, accepted nationally as a serious and inspiring poet. There might have been more reservations had it been realised that the published verses only expressed half of Kipling's intention; that he had destroyed a section advising the nation to go out and smite the ungodly wherever they threatened the national interest. He told Haggard that he was afraid the published stanzas might be taken as an encouragement to a pacific foreign policy. 'What I wanted to say,' he explained, 'was:– "Don't gas but be ready to give people snuff" – and I only covered the first

The celebration of the event that inspired Rudyard Kipling's most famous poem. Queen Victoria's Diamond Jubilee 1897 procession leaves Buckingham Palace. The Queen sits facing her daughter Princess Beatrice, and Alexandra, Princess of Wales.

part of the notion. Obviously, his message was identical with Teddy Roosevelt's famous slogan, "Speak softly and carry a big stick."

Kipling was coming to feel closer and closer to Roosevelt. And the drift of politics seemed to be making conscious American imperialism a practical possibility. The Spanish–American War left the United States with Cuba and the Philippines to administer, both wrested from the power of a European nation which had proved itself incapable of competently ruling its imperially held territory. In South Africa, Britain seemed to be squaring up to a similar problem. The South African Dutch were careless about city sanitation; were not prepared to give the rights of full citizens to non-Afrikaaner residents in their territory, nor many human rights to native Africans; were making no industrial progress; were, in short, not colonising after the manner and under the auspices of Cecil Rhodes.

The Kipling family wintered in South Africa in 1897–8. Rider Haggard, the popular *romancier* of the land, as Kipling was of India, gave advice. Kipling was shown around by Rhodes and Milner, the practical imperialists, and went on a bicycle tour of Rhodes's newly-won colony around Bulawayo. He came home to spread Rhodes's message of expansion

The procession passing along King William Street. Indian princes and high-ranking officers were a notable feature of the procession.

in Africa, calmly recommending restraint and the easing of tension between British and Dutch in English-held territories, but leaving wide open the question of violence in the Transvaal.

He started work on an imperialist poem for America, *The White Man's Burden*. It drew upon his recollection of the Indian administrators' sense of exile, and described empire-building as an utterly thankless task, undertaken for the good of humanity. The only reward offered in the poem was that of conscious racial superiority. The economic advantages of imperialism were never a real consideration to Kipling; he may not even have been aware of them. He was economically naive enough to believe that Cecil Rhodes's vast personal fortune was simply the inevitable outcome of a dynamic and virtuous personality, coupled with very hard work. He was, though he did not know it – hence his plausible sincerity – inviting Americans to play at imperialism

with British blinkers: 'Take up the White Man's burden': take up, that is, considerable national economic advantages, only after you have thoroughly persuaded yourself that you are actually undertaking some unrewarded drudgery through motives of the purest *noblesse oblige*.

Teddy Roosevelt, who received the first copy of the completed verses, had no high opinion of them as poetry, but recognised that they might be very useful to him politically. Joint Anglo-American imperialism – a rule of the world by technologically efficient English-speaking Protestants – was now Kipling's dream. On an impulse, he decided to spend the winter of 1898–1899 in America.

The three Kipling children. Left to right:
Elsie, John and Josephine.

Tragedy

THERE WERE BUSINESS AFFAIRS TO BE DEALT with in the USA. Scribner's, whose representative, Frank Doubleday, was the one American publisher Kipling trusted, were moving slowly with their *Outward Bound* edition of his works. Apart from any other considerations, Lockwood was not to be hurried with his plaster reliefs.

But while this dragged on, another supposedly respectable firm, Putnam's proposed sailing close to the wind by bringing out a *Brushwood Boy* edition of as much of Kipling's writing as could be squeezed around America's elastic copyright restrictions. This was to be stopped, and Kipling intended to be on the spot at the legal proceedings to put down the piracy.

There was also Naulakha to consider. The house ought either to be sold or put in order in case the Kiplings should wish to use it again. At any rate, it seemed impossible to go on leaving it standing empty. This, too, Kipling proposed dealing with in person rather than through agents.

The North Atlantic crossing is always likely to be rough in December and January. The Kiplings met a gale which made the children and their nanny very sea-sick. It was not to be one of the serenely comfortable first-class liner journeys that studded Rudyard's life. When they arrived in New York, Josephine and Elsie had bad colds, and they all felt very miserable as they stood around in the freezing customs-shed for two hours, while reporters badgered Rudyard for a statement, and he refused to say anything.

The newspapers, in fact, were full of *The White Man's Burden*. Kipling had arrived in America at the point when his influence in that country was at its peak. He was the poet who had said something relevant about American politics. His American wife and three years' residence in Vermont excused the impertinence of an Englishman preaching to Uncle Sam. And he was news.

His brother-in-law in Brattleboro recognised this truth. For Beatty, any sort of publicity, even nation-wide notoriety, was likely to prove more profitable than New England obscurity. Carrie and Rudyard might choose to freeze-off the press, but Beatty had experience of the useful friendship of reporters and the ease with which a story might purchase it. He announced to the New York papers that he intended to sue Rudyard for 'malicious prosecution' three years previously. He was claiming $50,000 damages, he said.

Rudyard and Carrie had no time to pay any attention to Beatty's posturings. In the Hotel Grenoble on West 56th Street, where they were staying, the little girls' colds had worsened, and were now diagnosed as whooping-cough. Doctors were called in – one of them Theo Dunham, who had married Carrie's sister Josephine – and pronounced that there were 'complications' to the whooping-cough.

The anxiety of nursing sick children in a hotel during the hard New York winter was a terrible strain for their parents, and six days after landing, Carrie herself succumbed to a feverish temperature. But she was always strong-willed. Within five days she had pulled herself out of bed, and a week later she was driving around New York with Rudyard, and discovering the technological wonders of an 'electric cab'. By 20 February, the children were well enough to be taken out for a walk in Central Park in the afternoon.

That night, when Rudyard came home from the Century Club, Carrie saw that he was far from well. He had been the fit member of the family while sickness raged around him: now, in the sudden calm after the storm, he was dull and listless, and his temperature was high. The next day Theo Dunham examined him, and described his condition as 'inflammation in one lung'. Whatever this meant, precisely, the illness was serious, and Carrie was compelled to call in a specialist and engage a night-nurse.

Two days later, little Josephine suffered a relapse. Like her father, she had a feverish high temperature; like him, too, she now had something more serious than whooping-cough. Carrie decided that she could not cope with two invalids in the hotel, and made the difficult decision to have Josephine sent to stay with friends on Long Island. She then turned her full attention to Rudyard, who now needed a day nurse as well as a night nurse. A third nurse was engaged for Elsie, who showed some of her sister's symptoms, and was suspected of developing pneumonia. And John, the baby, added to the catastrophic multiplicity of invalids by catching bronchitis. Fortunately, both the younger children recovered fast.

Not so Rudyard. Carrie, always more stiff-upper-lipped than the traditional Englishman, sent a laconic and inaccurate report to Charles Eliot

93

Norton: 'Rud is rather ill. I trust the papers will not exaggerate it.' The papers did not exaggerate: once they had, perforce, been told, and a group of reporters settled permanently in the hotel lobby, they charted the course of Rud's very serious illness as it was revealed to them.

Frank Doubleday took charge of relations with the press. He was more tactful than Carrie, and understood that any attempt to withhold information would only provoke hostility without diminishing curiosity. He passed on the doctors' reports, and the whole world followed Rudyard's progress. The inflammation spread across to his other lung, and suffused the upper as well as the lower lobes. His condition was 'serious'; his breathing was 'alarmingly difficult'; the 'greatest apprehension' about his recovery was admitted; the most the doctors would say was that they were 'not without hope'. At last, on 4 March, he was out of danger, and messages of congratulation poured in.

It was fortuitous that no major world events took place during the last weeks of February 1899. Normally the illness of a writer of Kipling's stature would have received notice in a paragraph. As it was, his illness was more newsworthy than anything else at the time, except for the illness of Pope Leo XIII. In consequence, the readers of the world's press, especially the readers of England and America, responded with the intensity that headline news seemed to demand.

Prayers were said in the churches for Kipling's recovery. Crowds around the Hotel Grenoble impeded traffic, and people were to be seen praying on their knees on the pavement outside the hotel. On his recovery, Kipling received messages of congratulation from the Kaiser, from the editor of *The Times*, from Cecil Rhodes, from Mark Twain, from Theodore Roosevelt, from actors, painters, writers and politicians in England and America; from the Suffolk Regiment Sergeants' Mess, and the crew of H.M.S. *Pelorus*; from the Allahabad Soldiers' Institute and from St Edmund's School, Canterbury. There were many, many more. It was one of the greatest demonstrations of popular sympathy ever accorded a writer. Fortunately, Kipling was still too ill to take it in.

Fortunately, because 5 March was not a time for rejoicing. Josephine's condition had worsened progressively, like her father's, and suffered the additional complication that she could not retain solid food. On Sunday, 5 March, Carrie went over to Long Island to visit her. As she left, at ten o'clock in the evening, Josephine sent her love to 'Daddy and all.' It was her last recorded message. The next day she died.

The job of nursing and protecting Rudyard, and finally breaking the news to him, fell on Carrie. The doctors declared that in his weakened state he must not be told of the loss of his adored daughter. Frank Doubleday's relations with the press were so good that reporters agreed almost to suppress the story, giving it so little space that it might not come accidentally to Rudyard's notice. When Carrie went to Josephine's funeral, she threw on a red scarf before entering her husband's room, in order that he might not see that she was in mourning. But in the end he had to be told.

Caroline Kipling has often been criticised. She

Central Park in the 1890s. The Esplanade and the Bethesda fountain.

An early electric automobile. Rudyard and Carrie enjoyed riding in New York in an electric cab

lacked the warmth and friendliness that many people detected in her husband. She seemed to cut him off from social relaxation with the barriers of her own coldness, severity and possessive jealousy. She would hurry him off to bed if he started drinking and talking freely in company after dinner. She encouraged the extreme and extraordinary secretiveness with which he tried to protect his personal life from any outside gaze. She seemed to impose her own will on him and the rest of the family. In this particular winter of 1899, when Alice Kipling had objected that a hard Atlantic crossing would be dangerous for the children, it was Carrie who had swept her mother-in-law's objections aside, and insisted that the family were going.

But Carrie had her signal virtues, and was almost bound to conceal them in reticence. Her husband was a sensitive man, who had learned to protect himself with a boisterous verbal exterior. Ever since the House of Desolation he had cultivated, as a hard shell, an appearance of jocular social confidence. He avoided and disliked the company of consciously sensitive introverts unless, like Henry James, they wrapped their sensitivity decently under a covering of the formal etiquette of the day. He feared any pressure that might make him peer into the workings of his own personality; his writings show how much he feared that over-strained emotions might lead him to Trix's condition of recurrent breakdown. And in those days, when Sigmund Freud was an obscure 'nerve-doctor' in Vienna, the condition of temporary breakdown was not widely recognised. Kipling was afraid that he might 'go mad'.

All this will have been known to Carrie. She knew, too, that whenever real threats to his personality appeared, the blustering Rudyard retreated. He had taken diplomatic evasive action to avoid corporal punishment at Westward Ho! He had 'called a cop'

when confronted with Beatty's loud-mouthed idle threats. He was all things to all men when he met them socially; a much more shy, adaptable little figure than his vehement platform and literary assertiveness would suggest.

He preferred to avoid strange people. He was at his best with children, who accepted, enjoyed and loved the sparkling surface of personality he assumed with them. He had probably been happier with Josephine than with any one else in the world.

Carrie made it her business to give Rudyard the protection he needed. She kept him in her company because he felt secure in the privacy of the family. She put the security he had built up with her to its strongest test when she broke the news of Josephine's death to him. And, convalescent though he was, he weathered it. The shock was traumatic. It left permanent scars. But his reason did not give way. He was able to appear before friends, and had recovered a little occasional watery cheerfulness by June. He was able to go on working. And he owed this to Carrie: to her constant ministration to his needs; to her careful selection of the people he met and the places he visited; and to the manner in which, quite properly privately, they shared their grief.

At Easter, notice was served on the world that Rudyard was strong enough to confirm the recovery his doctors had announced in March. He sent a message to Reuter's which was published in many of the world's newspapers:

> 'Will you allow me through your columns to attempt some acknowledgement of the wonderful sympathy, affection and kindness shown towards me in my recent illness, as well as of the unfailing courtesy that controlled its expression? I am not strong enough to answer letters in detail, so must take this means of thanking, as humbly as sincerely, the countless people of goodwill throughout the world, who have put me under a debt I can never hope to repay.'

It was, doubtless, kept from him that there had been one grave failing in courteous consideration. In April, when Frank Doubleday moved him to a private hotel in Lakewood, the Grenoble took the opportunity to throw out Carrie, Elsie, John and the nanny. Illness is notoriously bad for business in hotels.

In May, the doctors told Rudyard that his lung had healed. But they ordered six months' rest, and insisted that he must never again spend winter in England. By June, the family was just about fit to return home.

The business that had brought Rudyard to America was incomplete. The lawsuit against Putnam's was started, but it reached no final decision until 1901, when Rudyard lost on appeal. Fortunately, by that time Putnam's had abandoned the idea of *The Brushwood Boy Edition*.

Above The Elms, Rottingdean, which became the Kiplings' home when they left Torquay, and where they returned after their tragic visit to America. Their neighbours were all part of the family circle: the Burne-Jones, the Mackails, and the Baldwins.

Right The Times, 27 February 1899. The report, with its careful time-marking, gives some idea of the remarkable interest the public took in the progress of Kipling's illness.

Naulakha stayed empty until 1902. Then, with a final home established in England, Rudyard brought himself to get rid of that last remnant of the dream of living in America; the dream that had become a nightmare. He had the oriental rugs he wanted shipped over to England, and invited one of the doctors who had tended him in 1899 to help himself to rods and guns. With the house almost empty, he sold the whole estate for considerably less than it had cost him to build and lay out the house and grounds. Beatty's last, vindictive action was to remind the town that he felt he had some sort of title to the ground. The rumour of this possible legal incumbrance may have kept the price of Naulakha artificially low.

The loss of Josephine left two tangible marks in Rudyard's writing. One came in the *Just So Stories*. *The First Letter* and *How the Alphabet was Made* are transparently the work of a man who has been very close to his little daughter. But the relationship by then might owe as much to Rudyard's love for Elsie as to his memories of Josephine. It is in the attached poems, *Merrow Down I and II* that Josephine is recalled. They are ballads of time passing from Neolithic man's tribal occupation of Surrey. The ancient tribes are not very strongly realised in the first: the shade of Taffimai 'In mocassins and deer-skin cloak' sounds more like a Red Indian in the second. Their most interesting technical feature is the use of triple-rhymes in the second and fourth

recommendation of the British Government.

MR. RUDYARD KIPLING.

(FROM OUR OWN CORRESPONDENT.)

NEW YORK, FEB. 26.

The following bulletin was issued at 9 o'clock this morning :—

" Mr. Kipling remains in a critical condition and the disease continues.

" E. J. JANEWAY.

" THEODORE DUNHAM."

The disease is now admitted to be pneumonia. The same doctors said at 9 o'clock last evening :—

" Mr. Kipling has been in a serious condition throughout the afternoon and evening. His condition is one which occasions anxiety, but is not without hope."

Both lungs are known to be involved, the fever runs high, delirium is frequent, and the patient's strength is ebbing fast, but Mr. Kipling's courage is unfailing and his will power is unshaken. In his resolve to live is thought to lie perhaps his best chance.

It is said that the seeds of his malady were sown while he was compelled to wait on the dock till his luggage was pried into by the Customs officers under the surveillance of tradesmen's spies. American sympathies are universal.

(THROUGH LAFFAN'S AGENCY.)

NEW YORK, FEB. 26.

Mr. Doubleday, one of Mr. Kipling's publishers, passed the night with the patient. He left the room looking anxious, and said that Mr. Kipling had spent a fairly comfortable night. During the first part he was alarmingly weak. He realizes the great seriousness of his case, but remains cheerful and confident that he will pull through. He asked brightly if all the steamers had weathered the blizzard, and smiled pleasantly when he was told of the Bulgaria. He ate with relish the beef extracts prepared for him, and remarked that they were good and that he felt better. In obedience to her husband's wishes, Mrs. Kipling has ceased keeping constant watch by her husband's side. She comes to see him at short intervals, and cannot rest herself, being always in tears and looking very careworn. Dr. Dunham, whose wife is Mrs. Kipling's sister, has taken up his residence in the hotel.

The public interest in every bulletin is unprecedented. No foreigner in this generation struck by disease while visiting here has been watched with such sincere anxiety. Many of the telegrams have been read by Mr. Kipling, who is greatly cheered by the inquiries.

3 30 P.M.

The following bulletin has just been issued :—
" Mr. Kipling remains in a very critical condition."

LATER.

A bulletin issued at 7 o'clock this evening, signed by Dr. Janeway and Dr. Dunham, says :—
" Mr. Kipling's condition has been very serious to-day, giving rise to the gravest apprehension of the outcome."

(THROUGH REUTER'S AGENCY.)

NEW YORK, FEB. 26.

The demeanour of the physicians at 7 o'clock this evening indicated that a very critical stage had been reached. The patient is delirious, and oxygen is constantly used.

THE LINER BULGARIA.

(FROM OUR OWN CORRESPONDENT.)

BERLIN, FEB. 26.

The following is the text of the message

"A gentleman in kharki."

Above *The centre pages of* The Absent-minded
Beggar, *showing Kipling's neat handwriting.
He wrote the verses and Sir Arthur Sullivan set
them to music to raise contributions to a welfare
fund for soldiers of the Boer War and their
dependants. The total realised came to a quarter
of a million pounds.*

Top *Joseph Chamberlain as an Ancient Mariner
with his own particular albatross. The Boer War
was by no means a high-minded adventure, as
many people with wider views took pains to point
out. A cartoon from* Truth, *December 1901.*

97

The Kaiser, Wilhelm II, was one of the many distinguished people who sent a message of congratulation to Kipling when he recovered from his illness in New York in 1899.

lines of each stanza, utilising identical syllables for the second and third part of each rhyme. This gives an effect of naive simplicity without that touch of comedy that fully differentiated multiple-rhymes usually invite.

Two stanzas discreetly indicate Kipling's sense of loss:

> In mocassins and deer-skin cloak,
>   Unfearing, free and fair she flits,
> And lights her little damp-wood smoke
>   To show her Daddy where she flits.

> For far – oh, very far behind,
>   So far she cannot call to him,
> Comes Tegumai alone to find
>   The daughter that was all to him!

It is not unusual for verses by Kipling to suggest that there is some personal motive underlying them; that a resonance deeper than the whole poem justifies is being sounded in odd lines. This poem suggests that it may be right to suspect that something more than uncertain taste dictated the curious

hinting at unrealised profundities to be found in, say, *Rahere* or *The Nursing Sister*. If we did not know the circumstance of Josephine's death, it would be impossible to deduce why the homely Ancient British 'Daddy' – himself a shade – should be given such a disturbing sense of anguished distance from his ghostly daughter. Here, Kipling's half-exposure of private feelings disturbs a public poem. (Readers who like it would probably feel that a 'haunting' note has been added to the simple verses.)

They, a celebrated story from the collection *Traffics and Discoveries*, is Kipling's other treatment of the theme of paternal bereavement. It is more overt, and therefore more satisfactory. It describes a blind lady whose beautiful Sussex house is filled with the spirits of dead children. The narrator drives on to her property accidentally – the story is constantly and effectively being brought down to earth by his monstrously material motor-car – and is puzzled by the ubiquitous presence of children who never quite come out of hiding. Repeated visits intensify the mystery, until an unseen child's hand takes his and, to his amazement, gives him a recognisable (quasi-Masonic) secret signal that his lost daughter used to give him when he was busy with other grown-ups.

The story is intensely personal. The blind lady's 'House beautiful' is very like Bateman's, the house Kipling owned when he wrote it. The narrator shares Kipling's deep love of the Sussex countryside, and his contrasting love of the mechanical pleasures of motoring. The blind lady, like Trix, possesses strange psychic powers.

And, as in so many of Kipling's 'personal' pieces, some key points are omitted or left unexplained. The climax of the story lies in the narrator's recognition that it would be 'wrong' for him to come back to the house, although it is 'right' for the blind lady to maintain her contact with the dead children. This 'wrongness' is given no universal validity in the story's own terms: most of the lady's servants and many of her tenants have settled there specifically to retain contact with their lost children, who are attracted back to the house. The narrator's personality, then, remains slightly enigmatic, and the story is a bit of a puzzle. It seems most likely that the narrator is moved by the childlessness of the blind lady, who cries, 'Oh, you *must* bear or lose [children]. There is no other way – and yet they love me.' Kipling's sensitive and almost laboured treatment of the subject appears to lead him to the conclusion that bereaved parents must balance their loss against the fact that they have actually been privileged to have children: the narrator, in his mind, returns to 'my sorrow and my joy'.

They was written five years after Josephine's death. The sorrow remained strong for Rudyard. The joy was too far in retrospect. In 1889 the return to The Elms was a return to a house that was distressingly full of memories.

'A bit of a war'

THE TROUBLE WITH THE DUTCH IN SOUTH Africa was that they had been there too long. As the earliest stable European settlers in the area, Afrikaaners had 'gone native': the Boers had abandoned their colonial affiliation (taking the name of Dutch as all their own, and dismissing their European fatherlanders as 'verdomder Hollanders'); but instead of adopting nationhood in the new land, they had accepted the custom of the continent and adopted tribalism.

Tribalism means refusing to live with neighbours who cannot be dominated. It means putting the paramountcy of the tribe above the ideals of efficient and harmonious administration. It means that an attachment to tribal kin must outweigh attachment to any geographical region (strong though the passion for the tribe's traditional lands may be). Tribalism is inferior to nationalism because in the long run it is less humane, just as nationalism is less humane than internationalism.

The Boer tribe succeeded in suppressing or driving out their black neighbours – but were then confronted with strong British settlement in the Cape. The British offered them association in racist nationalism: white Europeans should join together as the dominant race to administer the territory efficiently, and although the resident black population was not to be accorded power, it should be granted certain rights of inferior citizenship, in order to preserve the peace of the nation.

The proposal was British. The weight of British numbers ensured that it was likely to come about in Cape Colony. And so the Afrikaaners practised the obvious tribal solution when confronted with an invading tribe too strong for physical resistance. They evacuated the territory. In the Great Trek they marched up into the Transvaal where they could isolate themselves from the distasteful folk-ways of the British, and see nothing but good wholesome Boer customs around them. And no one could affront them by the absurd proposition that they treat Englanders as equals, and Kaffirs as free humans. It is a common premise of tribalism that all other tribes being inferior, conquered tribes may be enslaved at the behest of the conqueror.

The problem that the Boer republics of the Transvaal and the Orange Free State then faced was a steady influx of British settlers, and a rise in British numbers that their own birth-rate could not match.

Before long, even in their own territories, the Afrikaaners could no longer claim numerical supremacy. But they clung to the imposition of fiercely tribalist laws, refusing certain basic rights of citizenship to *uitlanders* (outsiders), and successfully presenting themselves to the liberal world at large as beleaguered little states, threatened by the greedy, imperialist British neighbour.

There were, of course, conscious British expansionist imperialists in South Africa. Cecil Rhodes, from somewhat inarticulate but hazily idealistic motives, wanted to see Africa British from the Cape to the Zambesi, with British rail and telegraph services running from the Cape to Cairo. Alfred Milner wanted the benefits of British administration – enlightened and efficient, as he saw it – extended beyond the limitations of the Cape area. Both men saw Afrikaaner treatment of *uitlanders* as a deplorable affront to civilised Britons. Both had been humiliated by the failure of the Jameson Raid: an abortive attack on the Boer settlement by Rhodes' henchman Dr Jameson. That had only succeeded in making the British look irresponsible and incompetent. Jameson had cooled his heels in a Boer prison, to the general satisfaction of the whole world, except for Britain's imperial dreamers in South Africa. And 'Uncle' Paul Kruger, the Afrikaaner leader, had gained an effective piece of propaganda support from his enemies, which won him open sympathy from the Great Powers of Europe.

But by the time Rudyard Kipling came to obey his doctors, and winter in South Africa for 1899–1900, Oom Paul was confronting a consciously imperial colonial secretary in Westminster. Joseph Chamberlain bristled at Kruger, and made threatening noises. Kruger overplayed his hand in laying down that British troops must be removed from the territories surrounding his tribal republic, and backing his demand with the threat of war. When his ultimatum expired, the consequent state of war gave Chamberlain the opportunity to do what he and his friends were itching to do: move more troops into South Africa, and prepare to overrun the Dutch republics.

Before Kipling left England the war had begun, and the British army, under the command of Sir Redvers Buller, had suffered several humiliating defeats at the hands of brave and determined Boer

Below *An episode from the Boer War, 13 February 1900*. The Advance to Relieve Kimberley, *from a painting by G. D. Giles. National Army Museum, Sandhurst.*

Above *Two views of Bateman's, the Jacobean ironmaster's house at Burwash in Sussex which Rudyard and Carrie decided, at first sight, was going to be their home.*

Below *Kipling embraced the coming of the car with delight, and after two years with a 'locomobile' steam carriage bought a car from Mr Lanchester himself. An early Lanchester, of 1909, is shown here.*

generals, whose khaki-clad volunteer commandoes galloped lightly over the veldt and ambushed the awkward, slow-moving Tommies in their conspicuous red tunics.

Kipling believed in approaching national and international politics from village level, and at the outbreak of war, set himself to raise a volunteer company from Rottingdean. He sent a political poem to *The Times*, arguing that the war was a return to *The Old Issue*: freedom from such arbitrary tyranny as had been overthrown with the Divine Right of Kings. The *uitlanders* were Englishmen, suffering, at Kruger's hands, a curtailment of the hard-won freedoms of England:

> He shall mark our goings, question
> whence we came,
> Set his guards about us, as in Freedom's
> name.
>
> He shall take a tribute; toll of all our
> ware;
> He shall take our gold for arms – arms
> we may not bear.
>
> He shall break his Judges if they cross
> his word;
> He shall rule above the Law calling on
> the Lord.
>
> He shall peep and mutter; and the night
> shall bring
> Watchers 'neath our window, lest we
> mock the King.

The question Kipling left unanswered was what all this had to do with the English living in England. A solidarity of all English-descended settlers with the mother-country was taken for granted by imperialists, and the South African War was the first occasion on which it was put to the test. Volunteers flew to the colours in Australia and New Zealand, as well as in England. Yet it was at home that questions began to be asked. Liberals wondered whether foreign wars to establish the might and right of England were, as a matter of course, a good thing. 'Pro-Boers', who opposed the war either for political reasons, or on the simple moral ground that war itself was a bad thing, sprang up. Within three years of the universal appeal of *Recessional*, Kipling had become the voice of a party within the nation, albeit a majority party. The break extended to close areas of his family: deeply beloved Aunt Georgie could not bear to read Rudyard's South African War writings.

A rather less controversial piece was *The Absent-Minded Beggar,* written to raise contributions to a welfare fund for soldiers and their dependents. Alfred Harmsworth was campaigning in the *Daily Mail* for soldiers' comforts: tobacco was particularly in demand. Kipling was more concerned with the

Dr Jameson and some of the officers who took part in the abortive Raid of 1896 returning to England. After their surrender to Cronje they spent some time in a Boer prison. Jameson is fourth from the left.

Joseph Chamberlain, the Colonial Secretary who conducted the negotiations with Kruger. Attempts to reach agreement were abandoned when Kruger demanded the removal of British troops from the territories surrounding the Boer republics.

dependents, and the rollicking 'Barrack Room Ballad' he wrote was widely publicised in the *Mail*.

There are families by thousands, far too
   proud to beg or speak,
And they'll put their sticks and
   bedding up the spout,
And they'll live on half o' nothing, paid
   'em punctual once a week,
'Cause the man that earns the wage is
   ordered out.
He's an absent-minded beggar, but he
   heard his country's call,
And his reg'ment didn't need to send
   to find him!
He chucked his job and joined it – so
   the job before us all
Is to help the home that Tommy's
   left behind him!

Sir Arthur Sullivan set it to music, and all rights went to The Absent-Minded Beggar Fund, which ultimately raised a quarter of a million pounds. For this undoubted public service, Kipling was offered a knighthood. He was gratified, but convinced that any such public honour would at least appear to compromise his independence, he refused.

In January 1900 the Kiplings sailed for Cape Town, and arrived to hear of yet another British disaster, at Spion Kop. But successive defeat stirred the War Office to act, and Buller was relieved of his command. Kipling's old Indian hero and admirer, Lord Roberts, was sent out to use the overwhelming odds in Britain's favour more effectively. Before departing for the field he sent for Kipling, and spent an evening talking things over with him. Roberts was well aware that armies needed favourable publicity as much as any other group, and he had enjoyed the flattering references to himself in Kipling's writings. He briefed journalists carefully on his movements, and when he enjoyed his first South African success, the relief of the Siege of Kimberley, Kipling was able to hurry to the scene to greet Cecil Rhodes, who had been among the besieged.

The Orange Free State was quickly taken, and in its capital, Bloemfontein, Roberts set up an army newspaper called *The Friend*. Four war correspondents travelled up from Cape Town to produce it, at his request, and one of them, Perceval Landon, *The Times*'s man in South Africa, asked Kipling for an immediate contribution. Before long, Roberts had followed this with a request that he join the four in Bloemfontein, and once again Kipling found himself back at newspaper office work: sub-editing, correcting proofs, meeting deadlines.

Paul Kruger, the president of the Boer republic of the Transvaal.

Overleaf *Kipling's study at Bateman's. The house and grounds are now in the care of the National Trust.*

and the *Daily Telegraph's* correspondent jogged leisurely up to the front together in a little Cape cart. A Guards officer came with them, and pointed out careful rows of trenches as they passed. These were strategically placed, but the Boers had abandoned them, preferring the open veldt with its opportunities for rapid retreat by pony.

They passed up through lines of British infantry, Rudyard distributing tobacco all the way, until they came to a ridge from which the Boers were firing sporadically. Stranded between the two armies was an unhappy farmhouse flying *five* white flags. Here four Afrikaaner civilians – two men and two women – met them without enthusiasm, and there they tried to leave their cart and its driver. But he refused to stay, averring that the occupants of the farmhouse would quietly shoot him, in spite of their tokens of neutrality. Indeed, he seemed to take a white flag on a Dutch farmhouse as a guarantee that treacherous bullets would fly from its windows as soon as attention wavered. Kipling did not forget this accusation when, later, he had cause to remember this particular farmhouse.

The battle was inconclusive. Roberts had hoped that cavalry would surround the Boers, and then infantry could attack them head-on. In fact, the cavalry moved too slowly; the Boer force contented itself with some desultory firing in the direction of the infantry (and Kipling), and then withdrew before they could be cut off. Infantry and artillery pursued them ineffectively. The war correspondents were given the impression that an enemy force had been 'dislodged'. But the whole day's work was really pretty pointless.

Two things of interest emerged. One was the way in which Kipling actually described such shooting as he saw. His writing was rather surprisingly remote from *Gunga Din's* 'bullets kickin' dust-spots on the green', or *The 'Eathen's* hugly bullets come peckin' through the dust'. The *Barrack-Room Ballads* had used imagination to simulate realism. With reality in front of his eyes, Kipling abandoned the attempt to describe fear and discomfort, and produced some altogether more aesthetic and mannered stylistics. He aimed at the cool, level-headed artist's account of something so interesting that its danger could be almost dismissed. And so the rifle-fire became 'a single bullet' that 'now and again . . . sang to himself'. The enemy's pom-poms were interesting for the differing effects of their shells upon earth (where

It was fun to be back in the familiar job without feeling the pressure of building a career on it. The colleagues were delightful. The pressure of work created unity of purpose. Rudyard thought there would never be such a paper again, and 'Never such fine larks'. That first winter in South Africa, he told an American friend, 'there happened to be a bit of a war on, and I had the time of my life'.

Part of this marvellous time was his first view of actual battle. He had described physical warfare often enough, in prose and verse. His descriptions were regarded as masterpieces of realism. Fighting soldiers recognised their own fear and stress in the rage of battle, and Kipling's perpetual capacity to capture the technical essence of any group of men talking their own shop made his accounts of fighting sound convincingly full of military professionalism. But apart from the one pot-shot fired at him when he strayed into the Khyber Pass, he never saw a bullet fired in anger until he came to Karee Siding.

This was the sort of remote, unimportant battle wherein victory seems a foregone conclusion, defeat is impossible, and generals are happy to allow war correspondents to come and smell cordite. Kipling

Kipling in 1920. A cartoon from The World,
by Bert Thomas.

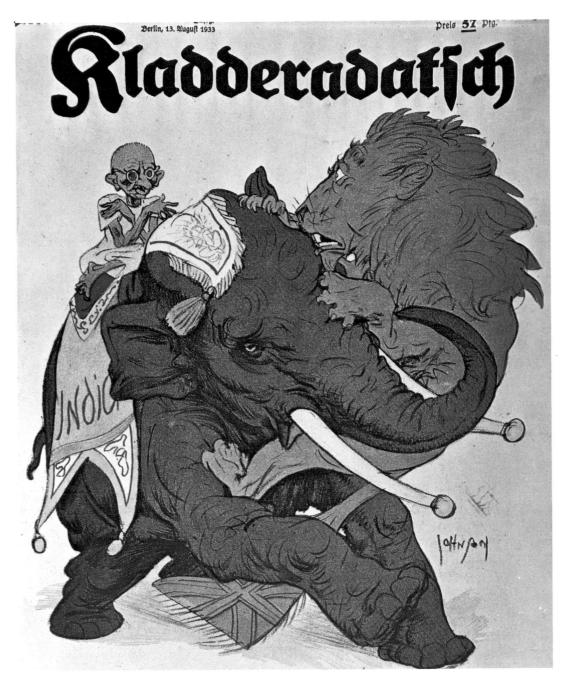

*The massacre of unarmed citizens by General
Dyer at Amritsar in 1919 brought Gandhi into
active politics. By 1933, as this German cartoon
suggests, the Indian elephant, guided by the
Mahatma, was giving the British lion a
remarkable amount of trouble.*

Boer soldiers posing for the camera at Spion Kop, the scene of a humiliating defeat for the British.

they thudded) and rock-face (where they broke up and yowled like cats). And British pom-pom fire evoked an interesting, but quite unpredictable piece of description:

> 'Then to the left, almost under us, a small piece of hanging woodland filled and fumed with our shrapnel much as a man's moustache fills with cigarette-smoke. It was most impressive and lasted for quite twenty minutes.'

The other noteworthy feature of the day was that Kipling himself became the victim of an atrocity story. It was reported in the American press, on information from Geneva, that Kipling and his associates had gone to the farmhouse with the five white flags (and the place and date and their names were correctly given), where they were said to have found two Afrikaaner women hiding under beds. They had entertained themselves, it was reported, by giving them a hundred yards start, and then shooting them down for sport. Kipling pretended to be amused by the naivety which believed that any Afrikaaner woman of the period was slim enough to fit under a bed. But obviously the report was deeply wounding to a man of his sensibility, and he retaliated, first by writing viciously hostile fiction about the treachery of Dutch civilian farmers, and subsequently by attributing the *canard* to pro-Dutch Germans, and suggesting that, except for the generosity of the hundred-yard start, it obviously represented what Germans would *expect* anyone to do to

unarmed enemy civilians. The incident did not teach him to mistrust atrocity stories.

In Bloemfontein there came news of another defeat, just as though no Roberts had been sent to the country. At an unimportant point named Sanna's Post, a column had been ambushed on its way to secure the Bloemfontein water supply. Six guns and five hundred men were lost. Junior officers, it seemed, had behaved with great gallantry and courage. Their attitude, on their return, was one of sheer professional admiration for the Dutch. But they had been 'sugared about by the old men', in one of Kipling's useful phrases, and for a short time it was even feared that Bloemfontein itself might fall. When that panic abated, Rudyard returned to Cape Town, where Carrie had been sick and worried about him. And the whole family returned to England.

At home, Kipling plunged into war propaganda. He dined with Joseph Chamberlain, the country's most influential statesman. He started a branch of the Navy League in Rottingdean, and practised rifle-shooting, since the Boers had turned out to have a humiliating edge over the British in marksmanship. He had a drill-hall built in Rottingdean, and complained that the local contractor took five times as long over it as an American would have done. When he visited his parents at Tisbury, he made patriotic speeches in support of the Conservative candidate at an election meeting.

Altogether he had moved a long way from the position of Beetle and M'Turk (*Stalky & Co.* had been published just before the outbreak of the war), who despised cadets playing at soldiers. Kipling now lived as if he wanted nothing more of life than an endless game of soldiering, and he would have liked to compel everyone else to play, too. As he started

*Field Marshal Lord Roberts in his tent before
the surrender of Bloemfontein. He gave Kipling
his first opportunity of seeing war actually in
progress, at the inconclusive battle of
Karee Siding.*

A Labour party poster of 1924. Kipling was an unashamed reactionary and detested most of the changes he saw around him after the First World War. Of the true condition of life for two million unemployed he knew nothing — but socialists were one of the groups he blamed for the changes.

"WORKLESS"

PUBLISHED BY THE LABOUR PARTY 33, Eccleston Square, London, S.W. & PRINTED BY VINCENT BROOKS, DAY & SON, Ltd. 48, Parker St. Kingsway, London W.C.2

back for South Africa at Christmas, he was engaged upon a horrifying 'story', subsequently published as a pamphlet, called *The Army of a Dream*. It enthusiastically envisaged the entire male population of Britain, from infants to dotards, enrolled in various forms of militia, and devoting all their spare time, and a good deal of their working hours, to endless drilling, war games and manoeuvres. This militaristic vision did in fact represent Kipling's desire for the nation, and back in Cape Town in 1901 he met the man who was to come near to realising a modified part of it.

Colonel Robert Baden-Powell was having a very good war. He had been given a mobile command, with orders to defend the borders of Rhodesia against the Boers, but had committed the elementary strategic error of collecting such extensive supplies for his troops that they were too valuable to dump under a light guard. His men were immobilised in Mafeking, defending and living off the stores that should have been supporting them in a roving defence of railway lines and border country.

The Boers immediately cut the railway that Baden-Powell was to have kept open, and besieged Mafeking. Baden-Powell had no objection. He had enough stores to sit tight until relief seemed likely to come, and, with many South African towns under siege, the fact that he had enough troops to break out if he were really determined was overlooked.

Baden-Powell's immense success and prestige derived, essentially, from his literary skills. He had written a number of army manuals, and commanded a style that was sprightly and readable, if sometimes a little *too* carefree and inconsequential. When he sent bright, plucky despatches from Mafeking to the effect that a day's Boer shelling seemed to have killed a dog, the war correspondents in Cape Town were overjoyed. He made good copy. His despatches could be sent direct to the press in London, where, reprinted verbatim, they suggested modest but indomitable courage. It appealed to the British imagination that Mafeking should be defended by amateur contrivances and schoolboy japes: a biscuit-tin searchlamp, and imaginary barbed wire.

By the time Mafeking was relieved, Baden-Powell was a national hero. The extraordinary outburst of popular celebration that greeted the lifting of the siege exceeded even that which was to come at the ending of the war. It was also the first indication of the form taken by expressions of essentially traditional popular patriotic feeling in essentially modern, overcrowded cities.

Baden-Powell found being besieged so comfortable that he had to be issued with quite strong and specific orders to prevent him from settling down in another town, taking with him another large and potentially useful body of men.

He was a man after Kipling's own heart. A man whose gentlemanly polish did not conceal the fact that he believed in simple, boyish kickings and duckings to maintain order. The sort of right-wing Conservative who believes that his own rigid defence of the *status quo* of his adolescence is quite non-political, and derives from a higher morality, quite independent of the factious bickering of right, left and centre. A remarkable all-rounder who wrote, acted, sketched and sculpted, always with some success, and had exhibited a bust at the Royal Academy on one occasion. A man with the very British capacity (perfected later by Lawrence of Arabia) to distract attention from his recapitulation of his own achievements by loudly expressing his own modest astonishment at them, or else laughingly refusing to take them as seriously as everyone else seemed to. He shared Kipling's enthusiasm for fly-fishing. He had a fund of stories to tell and experiences to recount. He was a man of great boyish energy and charm. And his Boy Scout Movement would fulfill at least a part of Rudyard's dream of a universal army in training in England, although Baden-Powell had the sense and military experience to cut out the drilling and formal manoeuvres that Kipling proposed, and substitute for them simple patriotic rituals and manly, exciting 'wide games'.

The war itself was foundering again. Roberts had saved the British from immediate defeat, but had not left them in a clearly winning position. The Boers avoided direct confrontation and relied upon dashing guerilla skirmishes. Kitchener replaced Roberts, and inherited his distressing policy of concentration camps for women and children from disaffected areas. Thousands of innocent civilians died in these, because the authorities, unable to keep fever at bay even in their own armies, were quite incapable of running hygienic and healthy camps. Kipling fumed at their incompetence, and was galled by the fact that it was the Dutch who were fighting the adventurous, crafty campaigns that he had hoped to see conducted by Stalky-like Britons.

For relief, he turned his mind to planning for the post-war empire. Rhodes, on his release from Kimberley, took the Kiplings out to his estate at Groote Schuur. Here he proposed building a house which was to be made available to writers and artists of the empire. And who better, as its first occupant, than Rudyard Kipling, ordered by his doctors to winter abroad? The Woolsack, on the Groote Schuur estate, was to be the Kipling's regular winter home until 1908. Carrie discussed its plans with the architect, and there was no home she ever liked better.

Here Rudyard and Rhodes talked with Milner and Jameson about the future of the colony. British rule over the former Dutch republics was taken for granted. There was no question in the minds of the imperialists but that the conquered Boers would, however, be given equal rights of citizenship; equal rights for all white men was what all the fighting had been about. In any case, they all respected the Boer

Colonel Robert Baden-Powell enjoying the secure and comfortable siege of Mafeking, 1899. With Lord Edward Cecil he takes observations from a housetop.

fighting men, although Rudyard, like many British Tommies, loathed the Dutch civilians who made no secret of their impotent disaffection while living in Cape Colony.

But Rhodes had a new dream. He wanted to link his new country with his old university. He was saving money, during the last years of his enormously wealthy life, to endow scholarships to Oxford, where young men could acquire that knowledge, articulacy and polish which he now felt to be as essential to a life of power as money. Rhodes scholars were to be healthy young patriots: character and physical fitness were to be as important as academic aptitude. Their years in the mother country would strengthen the ties of empire with bonds of affection. They would gain strength of character through living frugal student lives. Carrie Kipling made one decisive alteration to the men's plans here: she knew that the £250 *per annum* Rhodes proposed meant a life nearer to poverty than frugality, and on her advice Rhodes raised the original sum to £300.

A year later he was dead. Rudyard was unable to join Jameson and his other lieutenants at the burial in the Matoppo Hills. But the course of his life had been affected by the awkward, inarticulate empire builder, and he sent tributary verses. He was consulted by Jameson on the execution of Rhodes' will, and some years later became a Rhodes trustee, taking his duties very seriously. And he clung to the vision of white men in the dominions, working together for the freedom and prosperity of the empire.

Before the war ended, Rudyard sent one more political poem to *The Times*. Whatever his dreams for a peacetime army, he had no doubt that in time of war conscription was essential. Roberts agreed with him, and Kipling saw it as his duty to arouse a nation that he believed to be growing increasingly

slack. *The Islanders* was a long, rhetorical attack on a sleeping England, busily following its peacetime pursuits in blinkered confidence, while in South Africa a war was almost being lost. It seems remarkable today that many readers should have struggled through the verses to the end. But enough did to be seriously outraged by Kipling's attack on sportsmen. 'The flannelled fools at the wicket or the muddied oafs at the goal' was not a phrase the moderate conservative middle classes had expected to hear from the man they took to be their bard. Nor had they anticipated that the creator of M'Turk would one day turn and rend them for making the cock-pheasant 'master of many a shire'. But, to their credit, Kipling's admirers swallowed the insults. After a few, dignified letters to *The Times* pointing out the number of first-class cricketers who had given their lives in South Africa, the editor and readers agreed that perhaps Test Matches *were* commanding too much attention at a time when a war was being waged. Kipling was forgiven. It was the last time he was to make a really effective attack upon the Establishment.

When the war finally ended, the Kiplings were in England. This was just as well, for poor, brave Aunt Georgie was so disgusted by the abuse of her country's might to trample on two little republics that she hung a black banner on her house, reading, 'We have killed and also taken possession.' This anti-patriotic demonstration aroused the villagers, and an angry crowd gathered. Rudyard had to hurry over from The Elms to North End House, and use his great personal prestige as a patriotic ballad-monger to restore order. But, as Georgie had written to Crom Price, for all their political differences, she and her nephew went on 'caring more for each other personally, quite steadily'.

Peace induced a philosophical mood in Rudyard's verse. In spite of occasional lines of sheer rubbish, like *Boots* and *Ubique*, his Boer War ballads had, on the whole, reached a higher standard than the earlier soldier songs. *Stellenbosch* achieved a milder form of the junior officers' satire that a later and bloodier war would associate with the name of Siegfried Sassoon:

> The General 'ad 'produced a great
> effect',
> The General 'ad the country cleared –
> almost;
> The General ''ad no reason to expect',
> And the Boers 'ad us bloomin' well on
> toast!

Lichtenberg exploited a line he had overheard uttered by an Australian soldier:

> And I smelt wattle by Lichtenberg
> Riding in, in the rain!

The whole poem, unusually in Kipling, anticipates the straightforward, unmannered writing of descriptive Georgian poets, when they found themselves at war in a strange landscape in 1914.

Wilful-Missing represented a quite extraordinary exercise of imaginative generosity on Kipling's part. In a war about which his own feelings were simple to the point of jingoism, he managed to produce a poem that was sympathetic toward unhappy deserters. Likewise, at the end of the war, he made an unusual reflection on the feelings of the working man confronted with the unshakeable class hierarchy of England. *Chant-Pagan* expresses a dissatisfaction that Kipling would normally have dismissed as selfish and sulky socialism.

> Me that 'ave rode through the dark
> Forty mile, often, on end,
> Along the Ma'ollisberg Range,
> With only the stars for my mark
> An' only the night for my friend,
> An' things runnin' off as you pass,
> An' things jumpin' up in the grass,
> An' the silence, the shine an' the size
> Of the 'igh unexpressible skies –
> I am takin' some letters almost
> As much as a mile to the post,
> An' 'mind you come back with the change!'
> > Me!

It is hard to believe that the same writer produced the silly patriotic reverie, *The Return*, in which the soldier back in ''Ackneystadt' claims to have learned philosophical maturity, and proceeds to express it in the wooden declaration:

> *If England was what England seems,*
> *An' not the England of our dreams*
> *But only putty, brass, an' paint,*
> *'Ow quick we'd drop 'er! But she aint!*

Life for the Kiplings was prosperous and climatically idyllic. Every summer in England: every winter in the sun of South Africa, with the beautiful beaches of Cape Town for John and Elsie to swim and play on. Cecil Rhodes had built a private zoo at Groote Schuur, where the children discovered a llama that spat if you made rude noises at it. So they took their little friends up to meet the friendly beast . . . and the prank was just such as their father delighted in.

Carrie made herself responsible for a baby lion, called Sullivan, that seemed to be wasting away in the hands of Rhodes' staff. She took it down to The Woolsack, and fed it herself, on milk. After a while it seemed to be losing strength again, and the vet said it was time the little creature took some fresh mutton broth. It refused to drink this novel liquid, so Carrie tried to give it some to lick from her hand. It licked the skin off her finger! So it was cuffed to teach it manners, and left overnight in its den to consider a bowl of broth, and by the morning it had satisfactorily weaned itself to a meat diet. It was very disappointing when the family went home for the summer, and Rhodes's keepers again proved incompetent, feeding it on gritty, frozen meat, so that it did not survive the season.

Groote Schuur itself was bequeathed by Rhodes to the nation, as a Prime Ministerial residence. In the first elections after the war, Dr Jameson became Prime Minister, so the occupants of The Woolsack still had a friend up at the big house. Each year this continued until, in 1908, to the Kiplings' surprise and horror, Jameson was unseated. A Boer Prime Minister, J. X. Merriman, was to profane Rhodes' imperial home! British writers were no longer comfortable intimates of the cabinet. Kipling spitefully observed that the *Bond*, the Afrikaaner secret society which controlled Dutch Nationalist extremist politics, would rather have had their own man, Malan, in power. He added a crudely tribalist lament at the handing over of power from what he termed a higher civilisation to what he termed a lower. He refused to give up his right to live in The Woolsack whenever he so desired. But he left South Africa, never to return.

Groote Schuur, the house in Cecil Rhodes'
estate at the Cape which he bequeathed to the
nation as a residence for the Prime Minister of
South Africa. Rhodes also built a house, The Woolsack,
on the estate in which the Kiplings
made their winter home for eight years.

*Rudyard Kipling in 1907, when he was awarded
the Nobel Prize for Literature.*

A Home in Sussex

In 1897, THE YEAR BEFORE HIS DEATH, UNCLE Ned Burne-Jones wrote to Rudyard one of the facetious letters that were characteristic of the family, though unexpected in bearded, knighted Victorian painters.

> Sir,
>
> I should like to caution you against the new-fangled bicycle you mention. I knew a gentleman most respectable on the Stock Exchange and connected by marriage with the Pocklington family who stand very high in the county as had a fatal injury in his *latissimus dorsi* in consequence of one of these bicycles. My advice would be if I might presume, Sir, stick to books.

As long as the bicycle was the latest 'new-fangled' means of locomotion, Kipling, of course, stuck to it. But in 1899 the proprietor of the *Daily Mail* came to Rottingdean to see Kipling, and a friend called through the Kiplings' door, 'Mr Harmsworth has just brought round one of those motor-car things. Come and try it!'

The words could hardly have been more fateful if uttered to Toad himself. Rudyard came, and saw, and the motor-car conquered. He hired an eight-mile-an-hour top-speed, belt-driven motorised victoria, and drove it for the remainder of that season in England. The next year he bought a Locomobile: an American motor-car that ran on steam power.

This was an era when all motoring was pioneering excitement; when there were no petrol pumps or service stations along the roads; when the driver and chauffeur might have to act as their own untutored mechanics at a moment's notice. The harnessing of steam power to an unreliable petrol burner (with a flame that always went out in cross-winds, and never lit with the same explosion twice running) was an interesting creation of hazard. Not surprisingly, the steam motor-car did not survive into the second motoring generation. But the steam Locomobile gave Kipling two happy years' unfaithful service.

It was followed by an early Lanchester. Delivered to the door by the original Mr Lanchester. Stripped down completely over a small Sussex pavement by the same gentleman when it broke down unexpectedly. Named by the family 'Jane Cakebread Lanchester', and evidently loved.

Early motoring put Kipling into just such a posture of danger-free adventure as he had come to enjoy. He had a swashbuckling, buccaneering feeling, as he challenged the patient pony-carts, and threw dust in the faces of panting cyclists. Policemen, once rather *outré* acquaintances for a young writer, now became dangerous enemies, who might charge the unwary with speeding. The Automobile Association, a little band of prosperous burghers, who fondly imagined themselves to be daring outlaws, provided 'mustard-coloured scouts', who were just as deferential to 'the quality' as the old-time policemen, and supplied shock-troops with stop-watches against the endless guile and hostility of bobbies and magistrates. Kipling made such a fuss about motoring, both in and out of print, that it sometimes surprised his friends to discover that he did not drive himself, but always relied upon a chauffeur.

The main use Kipling made of the car in the years at the turn of the century was in travelling over Sussex and Kent to look for a suitable home to settle in. The Elms was quite unsatisfactory. Apart from memories of Josephine, there was an increasing incursion of trippers into Rottingdean, and the slow spread of hideous suburbia from Brighton, covering the downs. Kipling wanted a remote house; a beautiful house; a house with enough land of its own to let him put down roots.

He found it just outside Burwash, a village in East Sussex, a couple of miles from the Etchingham railway station. A very steep narrow lane ran down from one end of the village, through woods into an open valley. There, on the right, stood an old Jacobean ironmaster's house, with minimal eighteenth century additions and a double oast-house bulging from the back. It was utterly secluded, utterly peaceful, and, lying in gardens that the current owner was setting in delightful order, utterly beautiful. Without a moment's hesitation, Rudyard and Carrie exclaimed, 'That's her!' There was only one snag about Bateman's. It was already let.

Deeply disappointed, Rudyard and Carrie returned to Rottingdean, and spent another year driving around the countryside in search of something suitable. Aunt Georgie, who thoroughly enjoyed coming with them on these adventurous runs, was probably less sorry than they that they

The scene in Belfast City Hall in 1912 when thousands of Ulstermen rushed to sign the Anti-Home Rule pledge. Kipling found the years before the First World War disturbing, threatening as they did the order and – for many – the prosperity founded on imperial authority.

could not yet move. But within a year Bateman's was back on the market, and the Kiplings obtained it. As soon as the contracts were exchanged, the retiring owner revealed the house's major snag as he saw it: the steepness of the hill literally killed carriage-horses. Rudyard optimistically pointed to Jane Cakebread. 'Oh! *Those* things haven't come to stay,' was the vendor's response. But of course, they had, and the hill gave motors no difficulty. Years later Kipling discovered that his confidence in the future of mechanical travel had won him his house at half the purchase price that would have been demanded if the owner had suspected that steep inclines were a drawback of the past.

The Kiplings set about furnishing and decorating Bateman's with almost perfect taste. Hostile critics of the 1930s, and bright young modernists who wanted everything made up-to-date, have sometimes supported Elsie's feeling that the place was rather dark and gloomy. It was not, and it was bequeathed to the National Trust by Carrie, and has been maintained almost unaltered to this day, so that the assertion may be tested.

It was solid, square-built, mullioned, heavy-beamed seventeenth-century English domestic architecture. And so, with excellent sense, the Kiplings filled it with solid, traditional, English wood furniture, and kept the walls and floors in natural colours and materials as far as possible. Touches of richness, like the Cordova leather with which they covered the dining-room walls, were not out of keeping with the character of the house. Kipling's Indian pieces – mainly fine rugs, silver and brasswork – were such as adapt themselves easily to any setting.

Two small Art Nouveau gilt looking-glasses in the drawing-room indicated Kipling's capacity to ingest well-chosen examples of high modernity. An Elizabethan four-poster bed was surmounted with a charming canopy in which the initials RK and CK were worked into a blazon. Rudyard's study was a long, low-ceilinged room, surrounded by his books, with a settee for him to rest on, and a desk, ten feet long, to hold his mass of papers, paper-weights, pen-wipers and other working equipment. A pewter inkpot that he had bought when living in Villiers Street had the names of stories and books he had completed from it scratched around its base.

The first major piece of writing to emerge from Bateman's was *Kim*. Here, a mature Kipling produced his final thoughts on India, and the role of the British in the subcontinent.

He had been working on his Indian novel for a number of years. The last of his early scheme for a sensational novel, to be called *Mother Maturin*, was incorporated. But Kim's wanderings from the Lahore bazaar, through the British army, and up the Himalayas, were far removed from that original plan for a study of the seamy side of poor Indian and Eurasian life. Kipling's design had become grander and grander in discussions with his father: only a tenth of their great vision of Indian life from top to bottom could finally be incorporated in the book.

Such splendidly broad coverage seemed to Kipling to dictate a picaresque treatment: a hero wandering from place to place, and encountering different people and different adventures as he went. He remarked, rather grandly, that what was good enough for Cervantes was good enough for him. But Alice Kipling had some idea of her son's strengths and weaknesses, and snapped, 'Don't you stand in your wool-boots hiding behind Cervantes with *me*! You *know* you couldn't make a plot to save your soul.'

Kim is obviously a masterpiece of descriptive writing. Oscar Wilde had described the *Plain Tales* as giving the effect of sitting under a palm-tree, watching life by flashes of inspired vulgarity. Now George Moore, who may have been jealous, accused Kipling of describing an oriental sunset by following the evening around like a detective in a divorce suit. But ordinary readers have never been troubled by any feeling that *Kim* is over-written. They have, rather, enjoyed the immediate impression of the sights and sounds and smells of India, all described with certainty and with love.

The book is an idealisation of imperial rule. But it represents the truth as Kipling saw it. And it places the highest human values among the Indians. The Europeans are either shadowy, like Colonel Creighton; transitory, like the young officer who was

The film industry, again, found a work of Kipling's irresistible. Kim, *after many false starts, was finally filmed and released in 1950. The casting of Errol Flynn as Mahbub Ali pleased no one, though the exotic setting made the film a commercial success.*

born in India and is seen once only; or even downright silly, like Bennett the Protestant chaplain, and the English drummer-boys. Only the Lahore museum-keeper – an effective portrait of Lockwood Kipling – and Father Victor the Catholic chaplain are decisively shown to have maturity and depth. And even Father Victor is only allowed to exhibit his depth by admitting his frequent mystification before the wonders of the eastern personality.

By contrast, even such a minor oriental as Lurgan, the Eurasian or Levantine 'healer of sick pearls' is a man from whom Kim instantly perceives he has much to learn.

Writing about India gave Rudyard the opportunity to express parts of his nature that Alice, and probably Carrie, might have preferred to see suppressed. He took his love of disreputability to astonishing lengths (for the time) in hinting, without any disapprobation, that Kim's arrival provokes a moment of vicious jealousy in the pederastic love existing between Lurgan and his boy. And in passing from Lurgan to Huneefa and her sleazily exotic magic, Kipling is passing back into *Mother Maturin* territory, whereas his previous few books had suggested an increase in respectability.

Much of *Kim* recaptures the faintly vulgar, knowing *machismo* of the younger Kipling. The 'Woman of Shamlegh' episode invites us to be impressed by 'lands where women make the love'. Mahbub Ali's assertive masculinity ('I had shot my man and begot my man . . .') can become a little wearing. But only a little. For Kipling is now presenting these things as part of a much wider

A 'locomobile' steam carriage.

Lord Curzon as Viceroy of India, and (opposite)
*a scene from the Durbar of 1903. Kipling was
invited to attend this grand occasion but declined:
he also declined public honours, refusing a
knighthood on two occasions.*

diversity. Lispeth and Mahbub Ali coexist with simpler and less obviously exciting folk, like the Ressaldar and the Jat farmer.

All India had to be related to British rule. It is historically unfortunate that Kipling emblemised that rule through 'The Great Game'; a fatuous counter-espionage exercise, resting on the assumption that Tsarist Russia was always likely to invade from the steppes. But the folly was not originally Kipling's. Fear of Russia had dominated the Indian Government's foreign policy throughout the nineteenth century: hence all the fuss about the North West frontier, the Khyber Pass, and the buffer state of Afghanistan. As late as Curzon's Viceroyalty, while *Kim* was being published, the question of Russian access to the Persian Gulf still exercised the minds of the Council in Simla. And, artistically, Kipling demonstrated in other ways the stability and security that were associated with British rule.

The Indians divided into two groups: those who were unwittingly protected by the British Raj, and those who recognised the advantages to their own people, and willingly co-operated with the Secret Service. Kipling forced himself to swallow his own prejudices, and recognise that all India must mean *all* India. The despised Bengali Babus had to be integrated with the picture. And so Hurree Chunder Mookerjee is shown to be a brave and resourceful agent, deserving the respect of Kim as of Creighton Sahib. (Babu politics and the Indian National Congress were discreetly ignored: a safer strategy than direct attack).

The most important 'protected' figure is, of course, the lama. One of Kipling's major artistic triumphs, he is the most successful representative of holiness in English literature since nineteenth century evangelicalism introduced a note of priggishness to the concept. And his great spiritual qualities are established in the values of the book, which are demonstrated to us through Kim's love and respect for the people he meets, as being finer and more important than the virtues of other characters. European spirituality, by contrast, is either the arid Protestantism of Mr Bennett, or the 'Darkness and Devils!' Catholicism of Father Victor: something rather lower than Mahbub Ali's vigorous, bigoted Muhammedanism.

But by virtue of his very moral stature, the lama demonstrates the absolute necessity of British rule. Spirituality alone cannot defend itself. The lama would be swindled on every hand had he not Kim to look after him – Kim, who we remember is a secret *sahib:* an emblem of the watchful, invisible protection of England. His worldliness is vital to the lama's very survival, and the old Ressaldar draws the wider parallel: 'If evil man were not now and then slain it would not be a good world for weaponless dreamers.'

A more remarkable stroke still is Kipling's demonstration that it would not be a good world if it were ruled by the 'weaponless dreamers' of the clergy. Holiness such as the lama's is not acquired congenitally, and an elevation of the priesthood to power on the grounds that some of them attain supreme spiritual wisdom overlooks the fact that most of them do not, and that power is corrupting. It is the lama himself who recalls the monastery wars in which he once participated, regretting, characteristically, the sins of pride and anger, rather than the instance of maladministration:

> 'I did not seek truth in those days, but the talk of doctrine. An illusion! I drank the beer and ate the bread of Guru Ch'wan. Next day one said: "We go out to fight Sangor Gutok down the valley to discover (mark again how Lust is tied to Anger!) which abbot shall bear rule in the valley, and take the profit of the prayers they print at Sangor Gutok." I went, and we fought a day. . . . With our long pencases as I could have shown. . . . I say, we fought under the poplars, both abbots and all the monks, and one laid my forehead open to the bone.'

The book's weakness lies where Alice Kipling might have predicted, she proving, in this instance, more perceptive than Lockwood. When Rudyard reported *Kim* finished, his father asked, 'Did *it* stop, or you?' and commented that it ought not to be too bad when Kipling replied that *it* had stopped itself. But the consequence of this spontaneity is an awkward failure in the structure, which might have been avoided had Kipling been capable of plotting.

The course of the book demonstrates perfectly Kipling's vision of the best in India (the lama) protected by the best in British rule (Kim) journeying together to their mutual advantage. They have, as they early acknowledge, parallel quests: the lama's for spiritual perfection (the River of the Arrow), and Kim's for his own identity (an interpretation of his birth certificate and his father's regimental discharge and Masonic papers). When Kim finds his father's old regiment, and his legal identity is established, he finds that his search is not completed. He must travel on with the lama, and the two in harmony benefit each other and every one they meet.

When the lama finds his river, his quest ends, and the book ends too. Yet it is not clear where Kim has been left. Is he first and foremost the lama's *chela*, whose salvation has been won by his master's attainment of perfection? This is what the book's last sentence suggests. But the lama is going to die soon, and Kim clearly is not. Nor does he seem likely to abandon his status as a *sahib*, and his role in the Secret Service; the latter, at least, completely incompatible with the lama's type of spirituality. And so his identity is even more indeterminate at the end of the book than it was at the beginning, when he symbolically controlled a Punjab wrested from Hindus and Muslims. This is not a betrayal of India by British Imperialist Kipling, as some critics have maintained. It is simply a failure to note the technical impossibility of structuring a book around *two* linked journeys, and ending it by completing *one* of them.

Lockwood Kipling moulded some of his finest plaster reliefs for the book's illustrations, and carved for Rudyard little figures of Kim and the lama as personal cribbage pegs. Lockwood at least, had no doubt that his son had created the finest novel by an Englishman about British India, and paternal bias did not mislead him. *Kim* remains the outstanding English artistic achievement to emerge from the Indian episode in Britain's history.

But the novel did not enjoy the popular success it deserved. It came out at the wrong time to arouse great interest. India was neither the novelty it had been in the 1880s, nor the focus of political attention it was to become after 1920. *Kim* was a late Victorian masterpiece published as the Edwardian era opened.

Edwardianism was Victorianism grown middle aged, and stout, and self-satisfied. It was heavy port and sickly sweets after the solid meal of the nineteenth century. The empire, which had meant romance to Disraeli, and duty to Kipling, became a complacent boast. Social conscience which had manifested itself in shocking government reports stimulating the vast human sympathy of Dickens and revolutionary outrage of Marx, became tame statistics collected by the Webbs and inviting the technological suburban paradise envisioned by H. G. Wells.

Inferior writers were knighted: J. M. Barrie, Conan Doyle; ultimately Kipling's imitator, Henry Newbolt. Superior writers were not so honoured: Joseph Conrad, Henry James, Thomas Hardy. Kipling was once again offered the opportunity to become Sir Rudyard, and in once again refusing the

121

honour, noted sourly that the offer had slipped from the Order of the Bath to the Order of St Michael and St George. Shaw joined him in refusing any title, giving the whimsical explanation that only a dukedom was worth acceptance, and the Order of Merit was believed by most people to mean 'Old Man'.

It was a period of which, in some respects, Kipling seemed the perfect representative, as has been recognised in recent years by the confectioners who adopted his name for a range of slightly expensive cakes, hoping thereby to create an impression of security and modest luxury. Yet it was not a time into which Rudyard, the half-suppressed rebel against convention, could easily fit. His most admired poem was '*If–*' which he had based on his impression of the personality of Dr Jameson. He became almost as sick of its repetitious insertion in anthologies as Elgar became sick of *Land of Hope and Glory*. Three collections of stories represent the bulk of Kipling's writing for adult readers in the years between the death of Queen Victoria and the outbreak of the Great War. They establish a gloomily negative view of life, relieved by flashes of boisterousness and a tough attempt to fit into conventional upper-class English society.

Traffics and Discoveries is, perhaps, Kipling's most depressing book. It includes his three Boer War stories, all shot through with venom against the peaceful Dutch farmers who are accused of

Thomas Hardy, Kipling's great contemporary, and possibly the model for Eustace Cleever in A Conference of the Powers (Many Inventions). *Hardy's literary traditionalism and insularity were regretted by Kipling and Arnold Bennett, who felt that English fiction had much to learn from the French.*

Kipling's daughter, Elsie. She worked with her father on a dramatization of the Petty Officer Pyecroft stories in Traffics and Discoveries *(1904) which was produced in London in 1913.*

self-righteous treachery. The writing shows no comprehension of the fact that the sporting Afrikaaner horsemen, admired as honourable foes, had more in common with their own people than with the jolly British officers they were fighting. Kipling's account makes it hard to see why the two armies did not settle their accounts over a football match, before joining in a massacre of Dutch farmers. The worst offence of the Dutch seemed to be their ability to arouse other 'lesser breeds' (perhaps specifically, Eurasians) to doubt the inexorable rightness of universal British rule.

The naval stories about Petty Officer Pyecroft never won wide popular favour. Pyecroft was too much of an eccentric to be a representative sailor, as Mulvaney had been a representative soldier. But the desire to use the stories to extol the navy hindered Pyecroft's eccentricity from flowering to the fullest farce. The character remained popular with the family. In 1913, Elsie, by then a young woman, collaborated with her father in writing a one-act play about Pyecroft. It was performed in the West End, but found little favour with the theatre-going public, and Kipling made no further attempt to write for the stage.

The Army of a Dream came as close as Kipling ever reached to recommending dictatorial authoritarianism in England: with characteristic British 'hypocrisy' he proposed that universal military service should not be made compulsory . . . only any man who did not belong to a military unit should lose the right to vote.

The best stories were melancholy. *They* expressed his personal grief. *Wireless*, a return to the transmigration of souls theme, compared the discovery of Marconi's telegraph with flashes of Keatsian inspiration in an unhappy, consumptive chemist's assistant. And *Mrs Bathurst* developed from the praise he had once heard lavished on a woman in New Zealand, who was not obviously good-looking, yet could not be forgotten by any man who saw her. Her mysterious appeal is matched by the mystery of her love. Mrs Bathurst and her lover, Vickery, are in some unexplained way harried by their passion, and are finally struck dead by lightning in a remote teak forest, though their reason for being there is never explained. Kipling's habit of revision by excision was practised so severely on this story that it remains a sequence of impressions rather than a comprehensible narrative.

The final story, *Below the Mill Dam*, turns to the one area of his life that was entirely satisfactory. Bateman's seemed too large and dark to be lit by candles, and so Kipling had an old mill on the River Dudwell harnessed to generate electricity, and carried the power up to the house on a rejected deep

Kipling wrote, and illustrated, the Just So Stories, *which was published in 1902 and became a perennial favourite. The influence of Aubrey Beardsley, whom Kipling had met in the 1890s is apparent in the use of black and white line and mass. 'The Cat that Walked by Himself.'*

sea cable, laid underground. The mill was mentioned in Domesday Book, and it delighted Kipling to create around it a little fable in which complacent nostalgia for English history was thrown out in the interest of modern technical progress.

Life at Bateman's provided the motive force for the most positive stories in his next two collections also. *An Habitation Enforced (Actions and Reactions)* and *My Son's Wife (A Diversity of Creatures)* deal respectively with an American couple, and a world-weary London intellectual, settling cosily into the life of village and county in houses very like Kipling's. The minor landed gentry tone predominated, for although Rudyard wrote respectfully of the skills of the labouring men of Sussex – hedgers, tree-surgeons, water-diviners and well-sinkers – he did not mix with them as easily as he had done with the Indians and soldiers of the Punjab. He made no friends in Burwash apart from Colonel Feilden, who owned a smart William and Mary house. His other 'neighbours' were the owners of other country houses and small estates: Lady Edward Cecil, wife of one of Baden-Powell's principal Mafeking lieutenants; Perceval Landon of *The Times*, Rudyard's closest friend at this period, as Lady Edward was Carrie's; the Baden-Powells themselves, who found the house they finally bought in 1913 while motoring across Sussex with the Kiplings.

For the rest, Rudyard preferred to associate with colonials from the new dominions. Jameson came to stay at Bateman's after his fall from office. It would be pleasing to think that he lay behind the far from '*If*–'-like Penfentenyou, a colonial provincial Prime Minister featured in some of Kipling's most hilarious farces.

The idea of breakdown found its way back into stories. The cheerful cover of a tale about a haunted house cannot disguise the knowledge and fear underlying the powerful re-creation of an extreme depressive anxiety in *The House Surgeon*. Two futuristic tales about the 'Aerial Board of Control' look hopefully forward to a time when all-powerful transport administrators should rule the world dictatorially, and benignly dispel the dangerous nonsense of democracy.

All around, the family seemed to be enjoying success. Uncle Fred Macdonald became President of the Methodist Conference in 1901. Uncle Alfred Baldwin became chairman of the Great Western Railway. Cousin Stan, first an ironmaster like his father, at last followed him into Parliament.

Rudyard himself was the most successful of all. Arnold Bennett, who cared more about such things than most men of letters, noted that Kipling was the best paid man in literary London by an immense distance: he could, in fact, command any figure he chose per 1,000 words.

The establishment longed to honour him. He and Carrie were invited to the coronation of Edward VII, but in the end decided against going. They were invited to go to India for the Delhi Durbar, with the future George V, but declined. They were invited to the coronation of George V, but again left their seats in the Abbey empty.

But where there was no apparent compromise with temporal power, Rudyard accepted honours. Oxford offered him an honorary doctorate, and he accepted with alacrity. Similarly honoured at the ceremony was Mark Twain, whose disgust with 'the damned human race' emphatically included a loathing of Anglo-American imperialism in general – and the late Cecil Rhodes in particular. He can have had little to say to the younger writer who had once interviewed him. But General Booth was also accepting an honorary degree, and he immediately marched over to his former fellow-passenger, and asked him, in ringing tones, 'How's your soul?'

The greatest honour came in 1907. The Nobel Prize for Literature was offered to Kipling, the first Englishman to be so honoured. He and Carrie travelled to Stockholm through the snow, and found the city in mourning as the King of Sweden had just died. Official court mourning was evening dress, which, Rudyard noted, looked most impressive. But the unexciting journey through a rather drab winter landscape could not detract from the immense gratification the honour gave him. Recognition abroad always delighted Kipling. As a spokesman for England he loved to have his message heard abroad.

A time of success was also a time of bereavement. Aunt Aggie Poynter died first, of cancer, in 1906: brave to the last. Alfred Baldwin died soon after reaching his pinnacle at the G.W.R. Aunt Louie stayed at Bateman's, warmed by all the hospitality and consolation it lay in her nephew's power to offer. Cormell Price died, and his colleague Crofts.

In 1910 Alice Kipling died at Tisbury. Shortly after, Lockwood followed her. Trix was quite incapacitated by grief, and all the funeral arrangements devolved upon Rudyard. They had been the critics he most valued. There would never be anyone with whom he could talk over a piece of writing as confidently and affectionately as with his father. No one else would pick up his manuscript, and quietly add a couple of paragraphs of local colour, which Kipling would allow to stand. The strongest link with India and the past was broken.

But the deaths did not plunge Rudyard into despair. There remained the future: John and Elsie. Throughout the Edwardian period, Rudyard's love of children in general (he was delighted to become one of the first Commissioners of the Boy Scouts Association), and his own pair in particular, evoked the positive note that kept Rudyard Kipling, perky, ebullient, fervently patriotic, the continuing voice of the positive aspirations of his class and country.

His first children's book of the decade was the *Just So Stories*: perfect prose for reading aloud, perfectly illustrated by the author, with a Beardsleyan sense of the Art nouveau possibilities in black and white.

Puck of Pook's Hill and *Rewards and Fairies* were specifically for John and Elsie. Dan and Una, the children who meet Puck, and through him the old denizens of Sussex, were based on Kipling's own children. Pook's Hill was a real hill, visible from Bateman's, and under its slopes, John and Elsie had enacted what they could remember of *A Midsummer Night's Dream*, with Rudyard as Bottom in a paper ass's head. There was an old Iron Age forge nearby. And so, with quite a lot of hope for the future, Kipling gave his children tales of the past, showing them the characteristics of discipline, courage, independence and hard work that he believed had gone to building the nation.

He worked carefully on the stories, using all his skill to ensure that the simple narratives were not lost on children, while hinting at layers of deeper political meaning for adults. His suspicions of Trade Unions; his certainty that it was vital to prepare for war in order to preserve peace; his fear of Irish Home Rule agitation; his anxiety that imperial authority not be abnegated, even while it avoided pomposity and self-importance; all these were conveyed to adult readers of his children's books.

He had become a Conservative of the extreme right wing. Max Aitken (later Lord Beaverbrook) and Andrew Bonar Law, two Canadians who were influential younger Conservative politicians, were among his close friends. But he embarrassed them and the Conservative party when he addressed a crowd of cheering Unionists in Tunbridge Wells. For he was too vitriolic; he aroused as much Liberal indignation as Conservative enthusiasm. His 1880 Indian views, when applied to the present-day situation, were becoming out-of-date and unwanted.

As a conservative with a deep passion for the armed forces he bore one great disappointment. John's weak eyesight meant that he would be unable to take up the naval cadetship long promised him by no less a sailor than Sir John Fisher, the First Sea Lord. Worse, his eyes might prove too weak to be acceptable to the army. Wellington School, a firmly military institution, found him a pleasant, straightforward lad, quite good at games. But he was less good at work, and his masters could not even guarantee that he would pass the Army Exams which the old United Services College (now defunct) had been established to overcome. John had to be moved to one of the crammers despised by Stalky & Co. And Kipling entered 1914 a worried parent, unsure what career might be found for the son he adored.

Opposite King George V and Queen Mary in 1910, upon their accession to the throne. King George and Rudyard Kipling were to become close friends, though Kipling's dislike of great public occasions led him to decline an invitation to attend the coronation.

*Bernard Partridge's famous cartoon on the
violation of Belgium's neutrality.*

The Great War

THREE MAIN AREAS OF POLITICAL CONFLICT
engaged Kipling in the years immediately before the
War. The militant suffragettes were an inevitable
public concern. Their extravagant activities; tying
themselves to railings, smashing windows, and
burning letter-boxes; focussed attention on their
campaign for Votes for Women. Kipling was mildly
opposed to them. They had the support of the
Liberal intelligentsia which, by now, he positively
abhorred. He was a man ruled in all areas except his
public life by a strong wife and, like many such men,
he thought he ought to keep that last area to himself.
He wrote a wry little poem which satisfactorily
expressed his somewhat quirky anti-feminism. And
he worried a little over the expostulations he
anticipated when Elsie read it:

So it comes that Man, the coward, when
          he gathers to confer
With his fellow-braves in council, dare
          not leave a place for her
Where, at war with Life and Conscience,
          he uplifts his erring hands
To some God of Abstract Justice –
          which no Woman understands.

And Man knows it! Knows, moreover,
          that the Woman that God gave him
Must command but may not govern –
          shall enthral but not enslave him.
And *She* knows, because She warns him,
          and Her instincts never fail,
That the Female of Her Species is more
          deadly than the Male.

It was clearly not an issue that he confronted with
bile or indignation.

Imperialism, on the other hand, was an intensely
serious matter. Kipling was capable of describing
Imperial Preferential Tariffs as though honour,
valour and the whole of public morality were at
stake should any Tory threaten to abandon them.
He reprehended the new status of Commonwealth
Dominions. An old-fashioned Empire was what he
wanted, and he appeared on platforms with Max
Aitken to say so to newly founded Imperialist
Associations. Even Aitken and Bonar Law did not
seem adequate replacements for the recently dead
Joseph Chamberlain: a political leader was wanted
to rally the imperialists and maintain the mood of
hysteria which, for Kipling, was the minimum
amount of support he found acceptable to any of the
great out-dated causes he favoured.

His own hysteria could be bitterly abusive. The
Irish Question called up all his reserves of rage. The
promise of Home Rule was an affront to the memory
of Chamberlain, whose breach with Gladstone had
been made over the issue of Ireland. But in those glad
days, the hiving off of Unionists had reduced the
Liberals to a minority, and empowered the Conservatives. Before his death, Chamberlain's obsessive imperialism had divided his new party, and his
survivors were condemned to live under a powerful
Liberal government that clearly intended to allow
Catholic Ireland to govern itself if it chose.

Kipling was enraged by the affront to England –
the world's natural governing power. Ireland *belonged* to England: it was obvious. Any section of the
Empire that sloped off into self-government was
likely to encourage the dangerous savages of the
overseas territories to try to follow suit. And then
white men might be ruled by black. Which was
unthinkable.

Irrationality of this sort, ironically, brought
Kipling, the staunch loyalist descendant of effective
Punjabi administration, near to a posture of anarchic
treason. He favoured the army's refusal to impose
Home Rule on Ulster. He favoured any opposition
to the Liberal government, no matter how uncon-
stitutional and disruptive. He was one of the die-
hards who would have liked to see the House of
Lords go on and on throwing out Lloyd George's
budgets, even if the King were to be compelled to
create so many Liberal peers that they could not be
voted down.

Boiling belligerency on petty issues characterised
Kipling in 1914. So that the events of August
suddenly provided a refreshing outlet; an area of
release from the mounting tension that could
accomplish nothing in England. The Kiplings were
on holiday near Lowestoft in a house borrowed from
Rider Haggard when the Great Powers of the pre-
1914 treaties began to call in their diplomatic debts.
Rudyard responded by watching passing shipping
with the interested eye of a naval amateur, and
greeted the ultimatum to Germany with unalloyed
delight. There was no sense of lights going out over
Europe for him; all he wanted was a war, as fast as
possible, and he wrote what, with hindsight, must be
regarded as frighteningly misguided words to a

Fleet Street friend who was keeping him posted on events:

'Many thanks for your wire *re* ultimatum. I somehow fancy that these sons of Belial will wriggle out of the mess after all – or it may be worth Germany's while to avoid Belgium if we stay neutral. *How* the Teutons must despise us – and how justly! Meanwhile we look as if we were losing time.'

In justice to Kipling, it must be pointed out that it was not only jingoist imperialists who felt that a war would prove cleansing. Public life had started to look dull and squalid, even to supporters of the Liberal government. The Marconi affair, a matter of the misuse of information about government contracts, brought British politics closer to genuine corruption in the highest places than it had been for over a hundred years. Kipling's furious verses, *Gehazi*, rightly reproved Rufus Isaacs, the Attorney-General who had investigated and whitewashed an abuse with which he had been personally connected. Lloyd George, the most open threat to personal honesty in British public life that the twentieth century has seen, was of course involved.

Other matters, that won Kipling's approval, were equally depressing. Asquith's treatment of suffragettes by repeated imprisonment and force-feeding was rather distant from the impression of educated Liberal humanism he sought to create. The mutinous

officers of the Curragh threatened, for the first time since Cromwell, to remove the army from constitutional civilian control. Their convoluted case for this was an assertion that loyalty to the King did not involve carrying out the commands of his ministers: treason was not treason if loyal officers said it wasn't.

All these dismal trivia – the bread and butter stuff of democratic politics in reasonably secure times – led a generation of young men to respond with enthusiasm to what appeared to be a simple, moral, decisive, political opportunity. German militarism threatened brave little Belgium. Diplomatic agreements were being held in contempt by the Prussian government. Life could be made clean and simple again by a little blood-letting and a little sacrifice in 1914. The poets whose disillusioned, bitter descriptions of incompetently fought trench warfare three years later would persuade succeeding generations that King and Country were not worth fighting for, went off to battle in a mood of crusading optimism. Siegfried Sassoon, Norman Nicolson, Robert Graves, all joined the army in a mood of modest, heroic confidence. As Sassoon wrote later, 'To me, the War was inevitable and justifiable. Courage remained a virtue.' Rupert Brooke, a Liberal intellectual, spoke for them all, when he greeted the War like a lover.

John Kipling was not yet seventeen. But it was unthinkable that the son of the nation's foremost patriotic publicist should fail to join up instantly. And in the need for an army, the disability of his eyesight should be easily overcome. In answer to Kitchener's call for volunteers, he hurried up to London seeking a commission as Temporary Second Lieutenant in the New Army.

Kitchener was no particular friend of the Kiplings.

Rudyard had been unimpressed by his government of Egypt, and when he visited him on a holiday in Cairo in 1913, described him as a 'fatted Pharaoh in spurs'. The outcome of the meeting had been Rudyard's forwarding long lists of statistics to the *Morning Post* to be used in a crusade against his Egyptian agricultural policy. Kitchener was not a War Lord to whom the Kiplings could turn for aid when the recruiting officers, reasonably enough, rejected short-sighted, unexceptionally educated, under-aged John.

John now turned his thoughts to enlisting as a private, though even at this level he might have had difficulty in joining the army in 1914, when fit men were rushing to the colours, expecting the fighting to be over by Christmas. There had been no heavy losses to suggest that an endless supply of cannon-fodder would be needed, and Kitchener himself, though less foolishly optimistic than most about the duration of the war, still expected it to end in three years.

But Rudyard was not without other powerful military friends. Lord Roberts was too old a hero to serve his country at this date but he could still serve his friends. Kipling had made 'Bobs' a household word: 'Bobs', in return, now made John a second lieutenant in his own old regiment, the Irish Guards. John Kipling was inducted into the army in September 1914.

Other old friends, who had experience of uniforms and commissions, were also having difficulty in

The First World War was enormously popular with the English, at first; there was a widespread belief – not shared by Kitchener – that the fighting would be over by the end of the year. A parade of patriotic children marching down Whitehall in August 1914.

joining the active forces. Dunsterville, a colonel in a Sikh regiment, had not carved out the dashing career for himself that might have been expected of 'Stalky'. A welcome guest at Bateman's when on Home Leave, he could not find a similar welcome at the War Office. His active service had all been scrappy fighting with unimportant tribes on the Indian frontier; he had not been drafted to the possible advancement of the South African War. In England on half-pay in 1914, he was clearly given to understand that a retired 'Indian' soldier was an unwanted antique, and it was only by dint of determined persistence that he managed to draw a wretched staff job, escorting prisoners, fresh troops, and supplies on trains in France. His charm remained. He 'got on famously with the French troopers who accompanied him, and they roared with laughter at what they took to be his little joke when he told them he was '*un colonel*'.

Eventually, Kipling managed to persuade the War Office to give his old friend a more distinguished posting, back to the North West Frontier, and at last, after some indecisive scrapping with more unimportant tribesmen, Dunsterville was sent to Persia with a very small command named Dunsterforce, ('I can see Dunster, but where's the force?' asked a jovial Russian ally) and managed to fight a rather 'Stalky' anti-Bolshevik war, which included the use of a car, armoured with papiermâché, to impress the surrounding peasantry.

Baden-Powell was in less difficult straits. His army career had been a spectacular success from the moment of Mafeking. He had become the youngest general in the British army, and, after the Boer War had been appointed Inspector-General of Cavalry, a post for which his stickling smartness might have suited him. But the Boy Scout movement, starting on a small and amateur basis, had taken up more and more of his time. Royalty had declared itself interested in this work with and for the nation's youth, and Baden-Powell had taken the difficult decision to resign his commission and devote himself full-time to Boy Scouting.

In 1914 he offered his services to the War Office but Kitchener was not impressed, and he was politely asked to carry on with his valuable national youth work as the best contribution he could make to the war effort. In a way this seems unfortunate: given B-P's proven capacity to sit tight on supplies, a sector of trenches under his strategic command might have been spared some of the appalling loss of life achieved by the 'Big Pushes' of more adventurous generals.

John Kipling enjoyed the life of a young officer in barracks. He worked hard, got on well with his men, and quickly gained something of a reputation for his capacity to handle batches of drunken recruits fresh from Dublin – a reputation that did credit to the son of Mulvaney's creator. He was stationed at Warley, and motored over to see his family whenever

John Kipling, Rudyard's only son, as an officer in the Irish Guards.

they were staying at Brown's Hotel in London. This became their temporary residence for increasing periods. Rudyard and Carrie hoped Bateman's might be used as a temporary military hospital, but their offer was not taken up.

John sometimes brought with him young brother-officers and Rudyard was enchanted by the company of simple, direct, patriotic young men, engaged in the businesslike pursuit of his ideals and the profession of arms. John's conversation was principally about motor-bikes. Elsie remained his dearly-loved sister: she bought him things from Fortnum & Mason, and knitted socks for him, and he laughed fraternally at her fashionable clothes. Rudyard suppressed any worries that the possession of a soldier-son might have given him, and actually managed to see the front line before young Lieutenant Kipling.

Perceval Landon and Rudyard Kipling, as experienced war correspondents, were invited to visit the armies in France during the summer of 1915, while John was still awaiting orders to leave for the front. Rudyard met France's politicians before he met her soldiers, and he was impressed. Clemenceau might be a man of the left, but in someone else's country – particularly one he loved as deeply as France – Kipling could admire the man without letting his political adherence distract him. He had liked the 'Tiger' when he met him on a previous visit to Paris; the old man's determined patriotism and his furious insistence that Frenchmen must be as disciplined as Germans to fight the Boche effectively, harmonised with the beliefs of the author of *Soldiers of the Queen*.

Briand, too much the intellectual leftist for old Clemenceau, was not so obnoxious to Kipling, even though he reminded him of Lloyd George. An unscrupulous windbag might still be a useful foreign ally in wartime.

The stories that stuck in his mind from this visit were all tales of harsh French military discipline: a sentry shot for sleeping on duty, '*pour encourager les autres*', and dying with his general's arm around him because this 'more difficult' death did not really mean that he was personally in disgrace. And a young lover of Amiens, permitted twice to desert to his sweetheart, but finally shot in a chalk-pit. These things seem to have won Kipling's austere approval.

The trenches at the front had a clean, almost unused look. At Troyes, Kipling came within 'the length of a cricket pitch' of the German front line. It all seemed rather like a game:

> 'They were Bavarians and had been carefully attended to the night before with the result that they were *quite* tame, and I had peeps at 'em through loopholes blocked with plugs. The Colonel pulled the plugs and bade me look. I saw two green sandbags in a wilderness of tree trunks and stones and no Bavarians saw me.'

To John, he suggested useful rules for the game, as Beetle might have directed a fag on the best mode of japing:

> 'I found boric acid in my socks a great comfort. I walked 2 hours in the dam' trenches.
>
> Don't forget the beauty of rabbit netting overhead against hand-grenades. Even tennis netting is better than nothing.'

It was still essentially a civilian's war for Rudyard. He had no real idea of the nature of a trench life: no recognition of the cruel exploitation of courage which, Sassoon was to suggest, was the most tragic feature of the war. How could he? He was one of the exploiters. He never did join those whom Sassoon took to be 'everyone' after the war: the people who recognised the war itself as a 'crime against humanity'. Rudyard had made his mind up too early and too decisively that all crime against humanity was committed by 'the Hun'.

He wrote three war stories in 1915. The worst of them, *Swept and Garnished*, was a crude, sentimental piece of propaganda. Lady Edward Cecil had reported some atrocity stories, which the Kiplings eagerly lapped up. Rudyard now wrote a vindictive little piece about a hypochondriac German lady, driven to pietistic frenzy by a vision of child victims of the German army. The conception is marred by Kipling's own cruelty. The author is evidently enjoying his creation's distress, slowly though he allows it to penetrate her complacent Teutonic mind, and the restrained and externalised hint that Germans somewhere are behaving with remarkable brutality, is lost in the spectacle of an Englishman enjoying a peculiarly refined sadistic fantasy.

It is astonishing that the author of *Mary Postgate* should have written it. The two pieces present an extraordinary juxtaposition in the volume *A Diversity of Creatures*. *Mary Postgate* is a brilliant study of frustrated middle age strained by war and bereavement. The writing is unsentimental and detached. Mary Postgate's unloved existence as a lady's companion; the total lack of affection she receives from her employer's terribly commonplace nephew; her unstinting devotion to him, and shock at his death, followed by her observation of a child victim of a bombing raid; all these things culminate in the most positive act of her life: a sadistic refusal to bring help for a dying German airman. Mary Postgate's mental state very precisely *is* that of the author of *Swept and Garnished*. She attributes all atrocity to the enemy, with blinkered unimaginativeness. Her dead protégé was an airman, but, 'Wynn was a gentleman who for no consideration on earth would have torn little Edna into those vividly coloured strips and strings.' She is more deadly than the male as she reflects that a man would have helped the

Kitchener in 1914. Less optimistic about the duration of the war than his contemporaries, he did not live to see its conclusion. Kipling disapproved of Kitchener's administration in Egypt, and described him as a 'fatted Pharaoh in spurs'.

dying German, and she feels the first real satisfaction of her life after hearing him expire.

It may be that Kipling privately thought he had created an ideal picture of a humble patriot. But his artistry is unfaltering. He is quite detached from his character. Mary Postgate's behaviour is psychologically convincing, and as there is no pressure on the reader to fall into her error of imagining Wynn to be a young hero, there is no need to imagine a pressure to see her as any the less deluded in her final image of herself as a necessary heroine. She is a momentarily unbalanced woman, as the author of *Swept and Garnished* was a momentarily unbalanced man, and the continent of Europe in 1915 was an unbalanced continent.

Sea Constables, Kipling's third active war story, was marked by the increasing tendency in his later work for technique to outweigh content. A rather simple tale of an American ship failing to run a cargo of oil past the British blockade is narrated over dinner by a group of captains who have each played a part in harrassing the neutral. Their dialogue is not easy to follow, but the story is neither so difficult nor so vindictive as has sometimes been suggested. Although the neutral captain finally dies of pneumonia, and the serving British officers refuse to abandon their duty to take him to hospital, Kipling's point was sound enough: war is not a game in which greedy, enterprising buccaneers can lightly cut themselves in to make a few bucks, and then expect sporting assistance from the combatants. It would have been more tactful, however, to have minimised the amateurish, sporting tone of the British captains.

The reality of war was finally brought home to Rudyard in October 1915. In a straggling attack on some houses beyond a small wood, at the farthest point of advance made by any British troops in the Battle of Loos, John Kipling was shot in the head, and laid in a shell-hole by a sergeant. At the end of the battle, 20,000 British soldiers were lost, and the Kiplings received the War Office telegram to say that their boy was wounded and missing.

Rudyard had little doubt about the meaning of this but Carrie continued to hope desperately. Enquiries were made through the American embassies at Geneva and the Vatican, but John was not a prisoner of the Germans. Gradually, patiently, Rudyard sought out survivors from the Irish Guards' advance, and pieced together the story. Stanley Baldwin's son Oliver heard final confirmation of the truth from a surviving eye-witness, two years later. John's body was never found.

There was little consolation for Rudyard. He was not a convinced Christian. A large and mainly sympathetic post-bag on John's death was horribly marred by spiteful letters from a handful of people who presumed to tell him that his loss was the well-deserved consequence of his pre-war belligerence and militarism. The name of Kipling was now doomed: there were neither male sons nor cousins to carry on

Rudyard Kipling in Paris as a war correspondent.

the line. Years later, when a Yorkshire antiquarian wrote to Kipling in the course of his research into the writer's ancestry in and around Whitby, Rudyard refused to help him, because the melancholy loss of John made him unwilling to contemplate work on a surname without a future.

What the stiff upper lip could do it did. Kipling tried to take a simple pride in the achievement of his boy's short life:

> 'He was the senior ensign tho' only 18 yrs and 6 weeks, and he worked like the devil for a year at Warley,' he told Dunsterville. 'He was reported on as one of the best subalterns and was gym instructor and signaller. I'm sorry that all the years' work ended in that one afternoon but – lots of people are in our position – and it's something to have bred a man.'

The father's reactions were in harmony with those of 'lots of people'. Although obviously an exceptional man Kipling was rarely able to command unusual resources of generosity. He joined his fellow-citizens in a rancid hatred of Germany and longed for vengeance in the prosecution of the war.

When Asquith's government fell, to be replaced by a Coalition determined to fight more furiously, Kipling was delighted, even though his *bête noire*, Lloyd George, became Prime Minister. In compensation there were friends in office: Bonar Law, Aitken (now Lord Beaverbrook), Milner, and in a junior position, Stanley Baldwin. Beaverbrook, at the Ministry of Information, wanted Kipling to work with him. But Kipling preferred to go on independently chronicling the doings of the navy, whose invisible operations seemed to him to be underrated by the public.

From Bateman's the gloomy rumble of the guns in France could sometimes be heard. Elsie now became a vital emotional prop for her parents: she was closer to Rudyard, and Carrie's life must have been lonely and difficult. She still had to shield her husband from undue strain. He had been ill with gastritis when the news of John's disappearance arrived, and for the second time in her life she had borne her own grief silently, until he was strong enough to be told of the loss of a child. She was bearing up wonderfully, Rudyard told Stalky. But he was himself still suffering from stress ailments: a partial facial paralysis attacked him more than once.

As the end of the war approached, he began to fear that Germany would be let off too lightly. He disliked President Wilson: he had stayed neutral for so long, and now prated of 'Fourteen Points', and a 'League of Nations', when Rudyard wanted bloody revenge. Theodore Roosevelt, still a correspondent, agreed by and large with Rudyard's dislike for Wilson, but as a practical politician he realised that his old friend was no longer in touch with the realities of political possibility.

Church bells ringing in Burwash told Rudyard and Carrie that the Armistice had been signed. And Rudyard faced a future that would be made sombre by the tragedy of the Great War, into which he had plunged with such high spirits.

Stanley Baldwin was faced with some embarrassment for a rising young politician: his ironworks had come out of the war much richer than it went in. But Rudyard was not concerned with the rebuilding of Britain. His face was, for the moment, turned firmly to the immediate past. The two large tasks that lay ahead of him were the composition of a History of the Irish Guards, and administrative duties on the Imperial War Graves Commission, to which he had been appointed.

'A National Possession'

PEACE WAS FLAT, AND KIPLING WAS DESPONDENT. His health kept him in a permanent state of depression. The gastritis that preceded John's death seemed recurrent. Doctors were unable to produce any effective relief, and Kipling began to fear that he was suffering from cancer. At every examination and operation he was assured that this was not the case, yet he did not improve. Finally, two years before he died, a French doctor diagnosed duodenal ulcers; regretted that it was now too late for effective treatment, but eased the private fear.

The war itself had eased another anxiety. 'Shell-shock' eased the national attitude to mental collapse overnight. Obviously the heroes had not gone mad. Equally obviously, their minds and emotions were not under normal rational control. Stress, then, could cause temporary unbalance, which might be rectified. And it was nothing to be ashamed of. The relief for Rudyard Kipling was immense.

Both these concerns found their way into post-war stories. Cancer became associated with the pain of jealous, sacrificial love, and forms, as such, a part of the masterpiece *The Wish House*. This examines crude love and raw superstition in an old working class woman. By conventional standards she is a deplorable creature, sexually and culturally. Kipling allows her vital humanity to emerge without blurring or admiring her faults, and uses the effective technical device of dialogue in dialect – quite convincing dialect by now – to keep his distance.

Shell-shock recurred as a topic. Simple cures through affection and mild deceptions seem to have been Kipling's preferred therapy. A whole sequence of stories, mostly of very limited interest to non-Masons, relate to an imaginary Masonic Lodge which specially concerns itself with returned front-line men and their difficulty in remembering the rituals. Masonry itself, Kipling clearly believed, was an important aid to mental health.

It was also one of the few remaining unchanged institutions in the new world that had emerged from the war. An unashamed reactionary, Kipling detested most of the changes he saw around him, and, after the manner of the politically simple-minded, he slipped into the Conspiracy Theory. He looked for a group who could be accused of conspiring to overthrow all that is decent, and as is usual in such unsophisticated political thinking, he came up with a mighty unoriginal candidate.

The Jews were his first target. They have the unusual distinction of suiting conspiracy theorists of right and left alike, for notable Jewish Bolsheviks can be matched by notable Jewish Bankers. Thus they may be behind The International Red Conspiracy, or The International Money Conspiracy, or, quite madly, both at once. Happily for his reputation, Kipling never publicly declared, and soon abandoned formal anti-Semitic thinking, which received its quietus a few years later in consequence of the results of its adoption as state policy in Germany.

Silence in public also protected Kipling's reputation in India. He wrote no striking public verses on General Dyer's massacre of unarmed civilians in the enclosed Jalianwala Bagh at Amritsar. The Liberals, represented by Winston Churchill, whom Kipling disliked, had Dyer dismissed from the army, although he escaped cashiering. The diehard conservatives thereupon started a fund for the 'hero' who, they maintained, had 'saved the Punjab' by his decisive action. Kipling would have been a natural leader for the pro-Dyer forces, and had he written as pungently on the Amritsar atrocities as he wrote on other political topics, it would not yet have been possible to resuscitate his reputation in India. For this crass act of imperialist brutality brought Mahatma Gandhi into active politics, and may be seen as the formative experience of modern, independent India. But Kipling was discreet, and even hinted disapproval of undue force in imperial government when he referred back to his own time in India as a period when 'killing in Civil Administration was . . . reckoned confession of failure'.

He was confidently incautious in his denunciations of socialism and Bolshevism. He saw them as fearful and meaningless evils which threatened to spread over the world, leaving a trail of dead and dispossessed men of wealth behind them. Theodore Roosevelt died unexpectedly, of natural causes, in 1919. But Kipling thought he knew what had *really* killed him: the bullet of a socialist assassin fired seven years earlier in Milwaukee, which had appeared only to crack a rib at the time – but had now done its devilish work in bringing down the statesman Kipling called 'Greatheart'.

The major political fear in Kipling's mind at this time was the 'handing over of India'. Not that (as the Jalianwala Bagh incident had shown) any English

133

government was yet willing to consider true independence. But the increased use of Indian officials, with a view to training a Civil Service capable of taking over the country in the case of eventual independence *was* government policy. Kipling detested it, and decided that an idea of Rider Haggard's might be pressed into service in opposition.

The two proposed the formation of a 'Liberty League' of all good men and true throughout England and the Empire – all men of any religion – to oppose the policies advocated by godless Bolsheviks. There was some doubt in Kipling's mind about launching so serious a project from the Letters page of *The Times*. Alfred Harmsworth (now Lord Northcliffe) had bought that venerable organ of the establishment, and was suspected of using it for cheap stunts such as already masqueraded as 'crusades' in his *Daily Mail*. The *Morning Post* was at this time more clearly a *gentleman's* ultra-right paper.

But *The Times* had the reputation and the circulation, and from *The Times* the League was launched, supported by a leader describing Kipling as 'poet, seer, . . . patriot, . . . national possession'. The *Daily Herald*, under the lively editorship of George Lansbury, took a more realistic and humorous view of the practical value of the Liberty League:

> 'Every Bolsh is a blackguard',
> Said Kipling to Haggard
> – 'And given to tippling',
> Said Haggard to Kipling
> 'And a blooming outsider',
> Said Rudyard to Rider.
> – 'Their domain is a blood-yard',
> Said Rider to Rudyard.

Rudyard and Carrie at the inauguration of the War Cemetery at Loos, where their son John lost his life.

In March 1920 the League began soliciting subscriptions, and received a reasonable response from the charitable and well-heeled right wing. By the middle of April, Haggard and Kipling were engaged in nervous correspondence about the fiasco on their hands. One of the good men and true who had joined them in organising the defence of liberty had embezzled the funds! Responsibility for dealing with the situation fell most heavily on Haggard, the League's president. He would have liked to return all subscriptions to members and say no more about it. But he realised that to do so openly would be to make a laughing stock of themselves, and the propaganda value to the left of a league of gentlemen who picked their own pockets would be immense. Within a month, the Liberty League had been quietly buried.

Haggard was, by now, one of Kipling's closest, as well as oldest literary friends. He alternated his popular romances with books on farming and land management, and these topics interested Kipling more and more. The Kiplings had increased their holdings around Bateman's and were interested in getting the best out of their property. As Rudyard grew older, management and direction of the farming land fell increasingly on Carrie. Informed local opinion was that she was too parsimonious, and would have got more out of her land if she had been willing to put more into it.

Haggard's frequent visits to Bateman's were marked by one peculiarity. Kipling could work in his presence and he in Kipling's. He was the only visitor who was habitually invited to accompany Rudyard to his study. There they would sometimes sit opposite each other at the long desk, and write with concentration; sometimes one would work at the desk while the other read on the settee; and sometimes one would jot down the ideas that both threw out, and they would exchange notes and sketches over the planning stages of a new work of Haggard's.

There were many other visitors to the house. Although Rudyard was gaining the reputation of a recluse, this was largely because he refused most speaking invitations that came his way; because Carrie jealously protected him from enthusiastic admirers when they were out together; and because there was short shrift for the casual, unannounced, uninvited visitor to Bateman's, though Frank Buchman got away with bringing some of his Oxford Groupers to sing hymns on the lawn.

But invited visitors often filled the house. Young men from the Irish Guards, who gave Rudyard colour and information for his history of the regiment; artists, writers, colonial administrators, soldiers; sons of old friends; favourite servants from Brown's Hotel; any of these might be found taking tea in the big, square hall, when Kipling came down from working in his study.

When children came they were expected to wear their oldest, shabbiest clothes, and their parents were warned that they might be expected to fall into

LATEST NEWS

LATEST STRIKE NEWS.

Miners Fed—On inquires late last night it was stated that the Situation is unchanged.

Two Warships landed at Liverpool last night with food supplies.

The Police had some trouble at Poplar and Canning Town yesterday, gangs chiefly composed of youths made rushes near Poplar Hospital, a baton charge by the Police was necessary and several casaulties were taken to Poplar Hospital, youths tried to prevent passengers on cars and one new car was destroyed. The Chief Commissioner states that the general position satisfactory throughout the country.

10,000 strikers out at Crewe.

Five cars overturned between Canal Bridge, Kinsland road and Liverpool street.

A few buses and lorrers have been stopped in parts of London and at Nottingham.

There has been some interferance, the situation is well in Hand and gives no cause for anxiety.

The Prime minister precided over a full Attendance To Day.

The Rumour that two Policemen Killed at Poplar is Denied.

the pond. For the gardens at Bateman's, beautifully laid out with formal lawns and yew hedges and little lead figures – a task Rudyard and Carrie had thoroughly enjoyed – included a small pond on which Rudyard loved to paddle visitors in a little boat. Nor did he mind if older and more distinguished guests Fell in the Pond; an occurrence so common that it was abbreviated to F.i.P. in the Bateman's visitor's book.

A frequent visitor was cousin Stanley Baldwin. He was almost as bookish as Rudyard, and enjoyed the complete rest from practical political and business affairs which Bateman's held out. When George Saintsbury, from his retirement at Bath, published his *History of French Literature* Baldwin, a guest at Bateman's, bagged volume two to see what was said about Balzac, while Kipling accepted volume one and turned up Rabelais.

Although both men had formed their tastes in the 1880s, and Baldwin's had not been carried forward within hailing distance of the present by the practice of letters as had his cousin's, he was by no means the bucolic middlebrow that his incautiously declared preference for Mary Webb made him seem. He liked good music and good literature, and he was even more fond of hearty country walks than Rudyard. They appealed to that part of his personality that had once made him wish to take Holy Orders. But he walked too fast for the Kiplings, and too far. They prepared a note for him, which he found pinned up on his bedroom door when he arrived for one visit:

Rules for Guests

1. No guest to walk more than 5 miles an hour.
2. No guest to walk more than 2 hours at a time.
3. Guests are strictly forbidden to coerce or cajole the natives to accompany them in said walks, as the proprietors cannot be responsible for the consequences.

Signed R K, C K, E K (natives).

When Stanley became Prime Minister his relatives were justifiably proud. Rudyard and Carrie were welcome guests at Chequers, and Rudyard's actual political influence increased. For Stanley used him to draft Conservative Party manifestoes, and contribute ideas and phrases for non-political royal speeches on which the Prime Minister's advice was required. Kipling had begun to break with Beaverbrook; the man's personal ambition was distasteful, and their political views were no longer in harmony. Baldwin's famous attack on the press lords, in which he accused them of seeking 'power without responsibility, the prerogative of the harlot', has been ascribed to Kipling.

Kipling's political position in the 1920s was curious and threefold. His writings made him the foremost spokesman of simple, more or less non-political conservatism. The romantic vision of the eastern empire, and the personal and moral responsibilities it laid on its servants were all that most readers would identify as 'political' in his most widely read works.

Within more informed circles he was recognised as the friend and occasional adviser of leading Conservative politicians. He and Carrie regularly undertook electioneering duties for the party, and on several occasions he refused offers of safe Conservative parliamentary seats.

General Dyer, the man responsible for the Amritsar massacre. Reactionary opinion held that Dyer had 'saved the Punjab', and a fund was opened for his benefit. Kipling may have disapproved: he regarded the use of force in civil administration as a confession of failure.

Stanley Baldwin in 1922.

But in private life he was so deep-dyed a reactionary as to merit the description 'lunatic right-wing'. He continued to love his cousin Stan, and put family affection before all other considerations. But he frequently told friends that Stan was 'a socialist at heart'. And when an old friend impertinently reported his private conversation at the tea-table to the American press, his vehement denunciation of that country's late entry into the war, and emergence with undeserved riches and power intact, was so drastic and dangerous that the governments of both Britain and France felt compelled to issue public repudiations of his views.

Conservative seats in parliament were not the only tribute to his greatness that he refused. Only universities were secure enough in their 'academic freedom' for Rudyard to permit himself to accept their honours. He collected another honorary doctorate at Edinburgh, and, to his great delight, was similarly honoured at Paris and Alsace. In 1923 he was elected Lord Rector of St Andrew's University, and made a good and effective speech on Independence.

It was a paradox that he should be a very rich man, for he never relinquished his determination not to let money get such a hold over him that he could ever be bought. It was a further paradox that he should be the proud spokesman of sturdily independent self-made men, for his social life was deliberately led among those county families whose inherited wealth gave them the not altogether undeserved title of the Idle Rich.

His sturdy independence even managed to embarrass royalty. He refused the O.M. and the C.H. on separate occasions, and since he had refused a decoration that was known to be in the personal gift of the King, Buckingham Palace felt the need to issue a modest statement to the effect that it was through no ill-will on the part of the monarch that Rudyard remained plain Mr Kipling.

Kipling regretted the publicity of the statement. But he also regretted having embarrassed the King for George V was not a remote monarch to Rudyard. He met him first in the course of his duties on the Imperial War Graves Commission. Kipling had devised the universal inscription, 'Their name liveth for evermore'. He was one of the group which proposed the burial of 'an unknown soldier' in Westminster Abbey, and it was appropriate that he should have been associated with this, as the father of a son whose last resting place was unknown. He inspected cemeteries whenever he visited France, and this work inevitably brought him into contact with the conscientious George V.

After 1928, their acquaintance ripened into intimacy, when they met at a private party and the King spent the entire evening talking to Rudyard, to the possible discomfiture of the other guests. Soon after this, Rudyard and Carrie were weekend guests at Balmoral. Later Kipling advised the King on light reading to see him through an attack of pneumonia, and sent a parcel of his own Edgar Wallace thrillers down to Bognor, which the King's sojourn caused to be re-named Bognor Regis.

The Kiplings' home life became lonelier in 1924, when Elsie married Captain George Bambridge, who had served with John's regiment. Bambridge was following a diplomatic career, and the daughter to whom Kipling had, inevitably, grown closest, left England, and saw her parents only when they came to winter on the Riviera.

Rudyard became more and more dependent on Carrie. Hugh Walpole saw them together at a house party in Kent, and described

> 'Ma Kipling . . . a good strong-minded woman who has played watch-dog to him so long that she knows now just how to save him from any kind of disturbance, mental, physical, or spiritual. That's *her* job and she does it superbly. . . .
>
> '"Carrie," he says turning to Mrs K., and at once you see that she is the only real person here to him – so she takes him, wraps him up in her bosom and conveys him back to their uncomfortable hard chaired home. He is quite content.'

Not everyone was so content. Carrie's weakness was a jealous and possessive love, which may once have been necessary to wean Rudyard from his mother's overwhelming and dominating affection, but which, by the end of his life, simply seemed to cut him off from the spontaneous, easy friendships that were probably still within the capacity of his nature, and which gave him deep gratification. At the same house-party where Walpole observed the two of them together, he heard Kipling say that there had been men friends in his life who had been more to him than any woman. But Carrie did not hear that.

The health of neither seemed altogether reliable. In 1927 they took a really long trip, to Brazil, for Rudyard's health. It proved thoroughly enjoyable, and two years later they went to the West Indies. This time it was Carrie whose health was in question, and on the way back she had to stop in hospital at Bermuda with appendicitis for four months.

The last ten years of Kipling's life were not a time

Caroline Kipling in later life.

he really enjoyed living through. Political changes far removed from Bolshevism seemed to him dishonourable. He resigned from his Rhodes trusteeship in 1925, when Milner was succeeded by a young Liberal, and a majority of the Trustees took the view that their function was to use Rhodes' scholarships in the interest of Liberal internationalism and an independent Commonwealth. Rudyard knew that Rhodes had intended his money to be used to reflect his own Conservative nationalism, and a strong, traditional empire. He insisted that his resignation be made public, as it was a protest against a breach of the principle of trust.

Writing fashions also seemed to be passing him by. He disliked the Liberalism of fashionable Bloomsbury, but stuck to his private rule of refraining from adverse comment on another writer's work. But he did not mind letting friends know that he thought Lytton Strachey's *Eminent Victorians* a cheap, hollow, and ultimately immoral book. He himself had never flattered his readers by deliberately denigrating people whose culture differed from his own in time or place. Even his racism had always been concerned with looking at the different *positive* capacities of different races, and stressing that different talents suited different races for different functions.

E. M. Forster's *A Passage to India* was vague about this point. All men were equal, for Forster; at least, all educated men were. The Indians who interested Forster were western-educated and intelligent. Almost all his Anglo-Indians were bone-headed bigots.

It was a book which treated India without love and without feeling. At the heart of the sub-continent's mystery was a desiccating, 'Boom!', which reduced and annihilated all human greatness and glory. The land and climate were vaguely called in as supernumerary villains, preventing Englishmen of good will from enjoying friendship with Indians. The few passages of 'truly oriental splendour' were obvious bravura insertions, linked to a half-mysticism in which Forster himself did not really believe.

A spirited attack on the British Raj, yes. A typical, sly, Forsterian attack on upper-middle-class England's eggshell-china teacup manners, concealing the jaws of cast-iron self-interest. But a tepid book about India, and a novel whose structure was as faulty as *Kim's*, and which lacked Kipling's great and glorious density. Yet, for a generation Forster seemed the truer commentator, the finer artist, the profounder observer of India.

Kipling was a back number in advanced intellectual circles. His two post-war collections, *Debits and Credits* and *Limits and Renewals*, contained some of his most sensitive writing, and, in the spirit of the time, technical experimentation so extreme as to make some stories exceptionally obscure. A generation that accepted the obscurity of Eliot and the vulgarity of Pound roundly damned Kipling for both faults.

At Thomas Hardy's funeral the last great public turn-out of English men of letters took place. Kipling was placed next to Shaw in the procession. He would have preferred the merely Liberal Galsworthy to the actually Socialist Irishman. Shaw was faintly embarrassed by the fact that the gulf between their heights seemed no less than that between their opinions. Kipling was not actually below average height, but his stocky figure and short neck always made him look shorter than he was.

For his faithful audience of middle class non-intellectuals he wrote one more book. He turned to his and their passion for dogs, and wrote, in a baby-talk appropriate, he felt, to a canine mind, an account of life as it might be observed by one of his own Aberdeen terriers. *Thy Servant a Dog* sold 100,000 copies in six months, and almost doomed his serious reputation. Few major writers have written so bad a book: almost none when in their maturity.

Rudyard was embarrassed by the existence of a Kipling Society, headed by Dunsterville and Beresford, and filled with admirers who idolised his works. And he missed the respect and support of his intellectual equals. Literary society took its idea of Kipling from the cartoons and parodies of Max Beerbohm, who had pilloried him without mercy since the turn of the century.

An essentially kindly man, Beerbohm's drawings of men of letters were usually very gentle jokes. He was himself disturbed by the animus with which he hit out at Kipling. But each re-reading of the works made it seem inevitable that he must attack again. The apparent brutality and vulgarity pained the aesthetic dandy, and the very vigour and talent which breathe unmistakeable life and force into Kipling's writing made it the more distasteful.

In 1936, with his reputation at its lowest ebb, Kipling died. His vast following among the elderly and conservative meant that he merited full obituaries and a funeral in Westminster Abbey. But there was a note of uncertainty in the obituarists' writing. Fleet Street dared not lay itself open to the scorn of

THE ILLUSTRATED LONDON NEWS

The World Copyright of all the Editorial Matter, both Illustrations and Letterpress, is Strictly Reserved in Great Britain, the British Dominions and Colonies, Europe, and the United States of America.

SATURDAY, JANUARY 18, 1936.

RUDYARD KIPLING: VETERAN OF ENGLISH LETTERS, POET OF EMPIRE, AND A MASTER OF FICTION.

The world was shocked to hear, on January 13, of the sudden illness of Mr. Rudyard Kipling, which necessitated an urgent operation. He reached seventy a fortnight before, having been born in Bombay on December 30, 1865. It was in India that he first became famous, with "Plain Tales from the Hills" (1887) and subsequent stories, including "Soldiers Three." Later he made a fresh reputation in poetry, especially with "Barrack-Room Ballads," "The Seven Seas," and "Recessional." Yet another phase of his genius appeared in the "Jungle Books" and "Just So Stories."

FROM THE DRAWING BY SIR WILLIAM ROTHENSTEIN: REPRODUCED BY COURTESY OF THE ARTIST.

The title page of The Illustrated London News, *18 January 1936, which went to press with the news of Kipling's illness. By the time the issue appeared Kipling was dead. The drawing is by Sir William Rothenstein.*

139

the intelligentsia.

When George V died two days later, the cheap comment was that 'The King had sent his trumpeter ahead of him'. Kipling's funeral at the Abbey was packed, but the distinguished mourners were military and naval men and politicians: not the gathering of intellectuals who had mourned the passing of Thomas Hardy. Before long, the man who had removed the swastika emblem from the covers of his books when he saw German Nationalism consolidating around Hitler was himself being accused of having been a Fascist.

Yet his readers remained. The middle classes continued to offer their children Kipling's books to read, and the experience of his powerful prose left an inevitable mark. Before ten years had passed, four major critics had urged a reconsideration of Kipling's merits.

Edmund Wilson, always keen to rescue British writers who were undervalued by the 'gentlemanly' traditions of their own country, examined Kipling's life: noted with disapproval his withdrawal from an early democratic stance, but praised his latest short stories highly.

T. S. Eliot cautiously admitted to a liking for Kipling's verse, as he published a selection. He was not willing to say clearly why he did not regard it as poetry (though he did not), but his intellectual prestige was sufficient to cause a tremor in those intellectual Stock Markets which had sold off all shares in Kipling.

George Orwell, always an enemy to parlour pink aestheticism, praised Kipling's earthy appeal to the common reader and common sense, and expressed convincing admiration for his grasp of the realities of power and government. And, authoritatively, Orwell cleared Kipling of the charge of Fascism.

The most diffident of Kipling's new defenders was Lionel Trilling. *Almost* he felt that Kipling was a Fascist; *almost* he wanted to attack him. But critical honesty compelled this leading liberal humanist to admit that he found in Kipling a writer he could enjoy, and that there would be something ungrateful about discarding books that had made him take writing so seriously in his youth. And Kipling did deal with some unfashionable virtues that were again needed in time of war.

These lone voices had no immediate, powerful effect. The Second World War made all too clear the point that Orwell had established: Kipling could never have been a real Fascist, because he had never sufficiently come to terms with the twentieth century to grasp so essentially twentieth-century a doctrine as Fascism. The 1950s, however, saw E. M. Forster at the peak of his fame, and Kipling was obviously not compatible with Forsterian humanism. The typical Kipling defender continued to be a more or less critical conservative, who, slightly shamefacedly hoped to slip in some defence of some unfashionable political views in the course of a robust defence of the unfashionable writer.

Bonamy Dobrée represented the only consistent, reputable supporter Kipling had enjoyed since before his death. And Dobrée could be made to seem slightly suspect: his criticism a little patchy, as when he undervalues Teshoo Lama severely by calling him 'lovable': his upper class social background an easy means of evasion for readers who did not want to listen to what he said, anyway. Not until C. S. Lewis wrote his essay on Kipling did it seem that a critic could confidently take up this piece of political dynamite, and handle it as a purely literary phenomenon.

Nor is it yet entirely possible. The issues Kipling defended with so much vehemence and vitriol may now be dead. His ideals, like his appearance, may be lightly caricatured in Alf Garnett. But nobody old enough to have worked for or against the independence of India can treat Kipling with quite the same detachment as might be brought to, say, Charles Lamb. One of the greatest of today's literary panjandrums – a man who has probably done more than anyone else to ensure that young critics today try to estimate the worth of books from the value of the words on the page alone – once dismissed Kipling in the author's hearing with the words, 'Oh, no! *I* was brought up in a *Lib*eral household.'

Still, time is on Kipling's side. If, as a matter of history, his political manners were often indefensible, and his opinions were, by the end of his life, diametrically opposed to what most of the world would see as the worthwhile developments of the time, nonetheless the critic cannot avoid recognising a great writer. He is, perhaps, most easily compared with Browning, whom he admired and imitated. Browning has his patches of appalling vulgarity. Browning has energy which sweeps the unwary past his lapses of taste. Browning was excessively admired by the wrong people in his lifetime, and excessively deplored for the wrong reasons by some of his successors. Browning's total output is uneven. He defies many of the canons of criticism, which makes his work difficult to evaluate.

But a general consensus has been reached on the best of Browning. We know, in general, how much he matters for our time, and what we can safely ignore. His essential ideas and habits have been analysed and described. That he *has* greatness and importance is not in dispute.

And it is to be hoped that Kipling, too, will soon have his greatness recognised. The universal acceptance of almost all he wrote, and the high moral validity given his ideas by the Kipling Society cannot be accepted as an ultimate verdict. But ivory tower dismissal of him cannot be accepted, either. Kipling is one of our great writers. We cannot afford to dismiss great writing because we do not like its setting: that way lies the acceptance of any charlatan who is willing to appeal to momentary fashion.

News ⚜ Chronicle

No. 27900   SATURDAY, JANUARY 18, 1936   ONE PENNY

WHITE HORSE WHISKY
EQUAL TO A FINE LIQUEUR
Various sizes of sealed flasks on sale

THE KING: A DISQUIETING BULLETIN
Prince of Wales Takes Special Train to Sandringham

A JUBILEE PORTRAIT OF THE KING

HEART TROUBLE REPORT BY THREE DOCTORS

Bronchial Catarrh Declared Not To Be Severe

OXYGEN DISPATCHED FROM LONDON LAST NIGHT

5 a.m. EDITION

SIX minutes after 11 o'clock last night the following alarming bulletin was issued from Sandringham House, the Norfolk country home of the Royal Family:

"THE BRONCHIAL CATARRH FROM WHICH HIS MAJESTY THE KING IS SUFFERING IS NOT SEVERE, BUT THERE HAVE APPEARED SIGNS OF CARDIAC WEAKNESS WHICH MUST BE REGARDED WITH SOME DISQUIET.

(Signed) FREDERIC WILLANS.
STANLEY HEWETT.
DAWSON OF PENN.

At midnight the "News Chronicle" Special Correspondent telephoning from Sandringham, stated : " I am officially informed that the King's condition is less comfortable ":

At two o'clock this morning he again came to the telephone to say :

"There has been no change during the last two hours in the state of His Majesty's health."

It was not until 4 a.m. that good news came. Then it was semi-officially stated that the patient was "sleeping peacefully."

The Prince of Wales travelled from London to join the Royal Family at Sandringham yesterday.

Lord Dawson and Sir Stanley Hewett are remaining with the King. Oxygen has been dispatched from London.

SNOWSTORM SWEEPS ROYAL HOME

From Our Special Correspondent

SANDRINGHAM, Friday Night.

THE "disquieting" bulletin on his Majesty's health which was issued shortly after eleven o'clock tonight will be followed tomorrow by another pronouncement from the royal medical advisers. It had been learned early yesterday that the King was confined to his own room with a cold.

First reports declared that his condition was not regarded as being in any way serious.

Wireless broadcasting was interrupted during the night for the first announcement to the nation of the physicians' views regarding his Majesty's health.

The Duke of York had been in residence at Sandringham House for some time, leading the shooting parties which his father, when in normal health, usually enjoys.

During the day the Prince of Wales arrived. He took a special train from London to Wolferton Station. Thence he motored to his parents' home.

Sir Frederic Willans had been called in when the royal patient showed signs of a chill two days ago.

Now he has been reinforced by Lord Dawson of Penn and Sir Stanley Hewett.

Two Nurses Called In

There are two nurses in the house. Oxygen has been brought from London.

The weather here is severe. Early today snow fell heavily, giving the countryside a white mantle. The storm eventually became a blizzard. Tonight the thermometer dropped 10 degrees below freezing oint.

At a late hour villagers were still standing in groups outside their homes discussing the reports from their "Squire's" bedside. Sandringham House was aglow, lights appearing at almost every window.

The King was last seen out on Wednesday. He was then mounted on his favourite white pony.

Villagers tell me that he then looked in the best of health, his cheeks being bronzed.

He has spent much time here since Christmas in the company of his grandchildren, Princess Elizabeth and Princess Margaret Rose.

His Majesty celebrated his seventieth birthday on June 3 last. In that month he had his last indisposition, it being announced that bronchial catarrh was affecting him. His doctors ordered two months' rest.

The King's last grave illness was announced to his subjects in November of 1928, but by April of the following year he seemed to have made a splendid recovery, despite operations.

His Majesty, in the view of those who are daily about him, came through the Jubilee celebrations very well, but last month he suffered a great grief in the death of his sister, Princess Victoria.

BLIZZARD, GALE AND FROST

Widespread Peril of Icy Roads

This promise to be one of the worst weekends of the winter. Here are the conditions as forecast by the weather experts :

A heavy snow with a lot of ice and Northern England.

A ninety gale extending southward to the South-East Coast.

Rain and sleet over wide inland areas.

Snow floats everywhere at night. Snow which began to thaw yesterday, and then froze hard again at night. Makes roads all over the country icy and dangerous.

The A.A. advises all motorists not to take their cars out unless they have to. "It is the worst night for motorists of the whole winter," an A.A. official said last night.

In no part of England or Scotland is the temperature likely to rise much above freezing point until well into next week, and last night a gale warning for all coasts was broadcast.

THREE DEATHS FROM COLD

While sweeping snow from the back of her house, Elsie Gertrude Benton (80), of Sarehole Road, Birmingham, collapsed and died in hospital.

Today at work in the snow, Charles Hammersley (61), of Corfton Leek, clocked on at the Paper Mills and then collapsed and died.

Walking in St. Paul's Road, Tufnell Park, yesterday, Daniel Jones, of Foxham Road, Tufnell Park, collapsed from the cold. When taken to hospital he was dead.

Heavy snowstorms over the greater

TURN TO PAGE THIRTEEN, COL. 1

Is Lindbergh Baby Still Alive?

DETECTIVES HOLD MYSTERY CHILD

Late last night a Reuter message from Akron, Ohio, stated that the police there are inquiring into an astonishing story by an Ohio woman that a fair-haired boy, living at the home of a lorry driver named Andrew Dolsen, "may be the kidnapped Lindbergh baby."

The boy has been taken in charge by detectives, one of whom went to Akron from Trenton, New Jersey, after, it is stated, receiving a report from a woman who claims to know "all about the Lindbergh plot."

The woman's name is withheld.

She is declared to have said that Mrs. Dolsen, the lorry driver's wife who died two years ago, was a friend of the late Violet Sharp (the servant of the Lindberghs who committed suicide after the kidnapping).

"WIFE HAD PLENTY OF MONEY"

"When my child was a baby," Dolsen is reported to have said, "I was summoned home from a long trip by word that he was ill. When I got home I found this boy; he was not ill, and he did not resemble my baby.

"I said to my wife : 'This isn't our child. Ours didn't have curly hair.'

"Later, I noticed that my wife had plenty of money. I saw her with 600 dollars in 20-dollar notes. She couldn't explain where she got it from."

It will be recalled that the body of the Lindbergh baby was identified by scraps of clothing.

GOVERNOR'S REASONS

With New Jersey in an uproar over Governor Hoffman's reprieve of Hauptmann, and scathing denunciation of him by newspapers all over the country, Mr. Hoffman yesterday afternoon, says the "News Chronicle" New York Correspondent, was goaded into hitting back at his critics.

In a statement the Governor gives his reasons for the reprieve. He attacks the prosecution and declares :

I doubt that the crime could have been committed by any one man

I question the truthfulness and mental competency of several witnesses for the prosecution.

I doubt the evidence at the trial purporting to show that Hauptmann was the man who entered the Lindbergh nursery and kidnapped the baby.

The statement concludes with the assertion that he "does not fear impeachment because of his action," and that he would "welcome an investigation of the entire case."

COLD

(See Page Thirteen)

Special Week-end Section
Pages 9, 10, 11, 12

	Page
Thirty Miles an Hour	
By Robert Lynd	8
Loughran-Farr Fight Protest	13
Paul Robeson's Ambition	3
Stuart Emeny Dispatch	5
Hypnotist Censured	13
WIRELESS PROGRAMMES	12

Mr. F. W. Norwood, who is to leave the pastorate of the City Temple and take up evangelistic work (See Page Three)

LORD DAWSON   SIR STANLEY HEWETT

TWO OF THE KING'S DOCTORS

FOREIGN SITUATION DEVELOPS

GERMANY : Dr. Goebbels, foreshadowing a German demand for the return of colonies, declared last night that some day " the bomb will explode." See Page Two.

ITALY protested to the League yesterday against alleged Abyssinian atrocities, declaring that captured soldiers have been mutilated. Page Two.

BRITAIN : Mr. Eden, who leaves for Geneva tomorrow, last night reaffirmed faith in collective security, but was silent on sanctions. Page Seven.

LONDON SHIP IN CRASH

New York, Friday.

The American steamer Cherokee (5,896 tons) has sunk in St. John's River, near Jacksonville, Florida, after being in collision with the London steamer Welcombe (5,122 tons). The Welcombe is reported to be badly damaged and aground, but no one was hurt.—Reuter.

LATE NEWS

Death of Mr. Rudyard Kipling

THE "News Chronicle" regrets to announce that Mr. Rudyard Kipling died in the Middlesex Hospital at 12.10 this morning.

An operation had been performed on Monday for gastric trouble, a perforated ulcer in the stomach. Mr. Kipling had not spoken for several hours before he died.

Major-General Dunsterville, the original of Stalky, in "Stalky and Co," paid the following tribute to the friend of schooldays, in a special interview with the "News Chronicle" :

"In three score years and ten no man's outlook on life could have changed less than that of Rudyard Kipling, a lover of men of action, the under-dog, children and animals, never in all his writings probing the morbid psychology of his characters."

"His loyalty to his personal friends, as well as to his many numerous, was never shaken or lessened by the lapse of time—in my own case a friendship of nearly 60 years."

Stalky's appreciation of "the boy genius he knew" appears on Page Five.

LOUIS WINS BY K.O.

Chicago, Friday Night.

Joe ("Sepia Slugger") Louis knocked out Charlie Retzlaff, in the first round of a 10-round bout, here, tonight.

Pre-fight betting was 20 to 1 on Louis.—Reuter.

The News Chronicle, 18 January 1936. King George V died two days later – but his illness almost edged the news of Kipling's death off the front page.

Sources and Acknowledgments

The first debt of any writer seeking biographical data on Kipling is to C. E. Carrington's standard *Life*, and I am grateful to the Macmillan Company of London and Basingstoke, the Macmillan Company of Canada and Doubleday & Company, Inc for permission to use quotations drawn from this source. Kipling's own writings, particularly the evasive autobiography *Something of Myself*, the *Letters of Travel*, and the *Souvenirs of France* are useful primary sources, and I am grateful to Mrs George Bambridge, the Macmillan Company of London and Basingstoke, the Macmillan Company of Canada and Doubleday & Company, Inc for permission to reproduce short extracts. A. W. Baldwin's *The Macdonald Sisters* provides copious information about Kipling's antecedents and relatives, and I am grateful to Peter Davies Ltd, for permission to extract occasional quotations from this.

Kipling in India by John Cornell is perhaps the most detailed and documented published account of a substantial period of Kipling's life, and I corrected and rejected one or two familiar myths after studying some of Mr Cornell's footnotes. Morton Cohen's *Kipling and Rider Haggard* is useful and informative on Kipling's literary life in England. Michael Edwardes' various books on the British in India were my main source for the political and social history of the Raj.

Kipling's schooldays are thoroughly remembered in G. C. Beresford's *Schooldays with Kipling*, and glanced at in L. C. Dunsterville's *Stalky Reminiscences*. I am grateful to Victor Gollancz Ltd for permission to reproduce Beresford's account of an English lesson at Westward Ho!

The 'Rules for Guests' addressed to Stanley Baldwin are taken from K. Middlemass and J. Barnes' *Baldwin*, by kind permission of Weidenfeld (Publishers) Ltd and Collier-Macmillan International.

I have also read and taken into account better known critical studies of Kipling: those by Le Gallienne, Hilton Browne, J. I. M. Stewart and Joyce Tompkins, as well as those collected by Roger Lancelyn Green and Andrew Rutherford, and those I mention in the text.

Friends and colleagues with whom I have discussed Kipling over several years, and whose critical views have stimulated or modified my own, include Professors Jack Gallagher, Arnold Kettle, Douglas Jefferson and Wallace Robson, and Messrs. Maqboul Aziz, John Spencer and Stephen Wicks. In almost all the above cases, I am grateful for support for an enthusiasm for Kipling's writing, which opposed intellectual fashion.

I am most grateful to my mother for having introduced me to the *Just So Stories* and *Jungle Books* almost as soon as I could read; to *Puck of Pook's Hill* a few years later, and to *Kim* a few years after that. She gave me a knowledge of Kipling's verse which enabled me to make my first use of the English Faculty Library in Oxford (when it was housed in an attic in the Examination Schools) to win a bet on the authorship of *A Smugglers' Song*. But she never carried me over towards the opinion she once heard expressed in the 1930s to the effect that Kipling was *undeniably* a greater poet than Shakespeare.

My publishers and their editors, my family and my wife's family, were all wonderfully considerate when, at rather short notice, I found that I had a post abroad to take up on the same day as my typescript was due to be delivered. My warmest thanks must go to Elaine for enabling me to concentrate on writing and revising, while she so coped with things that my typescript was deposited in London exactly as she and I were deposited in Barbados, without any hitch.

Index

Figures in italics refer to illustrations

EMBRACING EARTH

NEW VIEWS OF OUR CHANGING PLANET

EMBRACING EARTH

New Views of Our Changing Planet

Payson R. Stevens and Kevin W. Kelley

Foreword by James Burke

Essay by W. Stanley Wilson, NASA

Chronicle Books · San Francisco

May our one Earth become one world.

Printed in Hong Kong.

Library of Congress Cataloging-in-Publication Data
Stevens, Payson R.
    Embracing earth : new views of our changing planet / by Payson R.
Stevens and Kevin W. Kelley : with a foreword by James Burke.
        p.   cm.
    Includes index.
    ISBN 0-8118-0135-7
    1. Earth. 2. Earth—Photographs from space.   I. Kelley, Kevin W.
II. Title.
QB631.S66 1992
508—dc20   91-41022
                                     CIP

Distributed in Canada by Raincoast Books,
112 East Third Avenue, Vancouver,
B.C. V5T 1C8

10 9 8 7 6 5 4 3 2 1

Chronicle Books
275 Fifth Street
San Francisco, CA 94103

CONTENTS

FOREWORD
by James Burke

More than a hundred thousand years ago, a small group of the first modern humans came north out of Africa to colonize the Earth. Somewhere, perhaps in the Sinai, they split, bade goodbye to each other, and went their separate ways to separate destinies. Their descendents would not meet again for twelve hundred centuries.

For the next eighty thousand years the inquisitive wanderers hunted their way across the world. From time to time individual groups would break off the great journey to settle permanently: in the forest glades, on the savannah, along lakes and seas.

Over the course of centuries these tiny communities would take on the characteristics of their new homes. Body shape and coloring would adapt to fit local climatic conditions. Tools and lifestyles would emerge to suit the physical constraints of the immediate environment. Language would develop to reflect surrounding reality.

Personal identity would become one with place.

Thus it is that humans are the children of the planet, selected for survival by the ecosystems with which they have coexisted for millennia.

Unlike all other life-forms, however, we descendents of those first ax-maker Africans have gone forth and multiplied because of the tools bequeathed us by our ancient predecessors.

In an extraordinarily brief span of time we have used those tools to change the world. With the help of plough and sword, printing press and electron, we have freed ourselves from total dependence on nature.

As part of that process we have also succeeded in enhancing the Earth's carrying capacity beyond anything our distant ancestors could have dreamt of. But we have succeeded too well. Today we are within sight of what appears to be the final planetary limit on population growth. In all probability we will reach that limit by 2050.

And as our global presence has grown, so too has our effect on the environment. Particularly since the Industrial Revolution, we have made ourselves felt, chemically, throughout the biosphere.

We are exterminating plant and animal species at an unknown rate. Desertification and deforestation radically perturb the balance of natural ecocycles.

However, the technology that has brought us to the brink of disaster could also save us. The convergence of data processing and telecommunications, which makes possible the enthralling images in this book, offers the hope of a new understanding of the planet.

As we move closer to the completion of a global information network, we have become aware that these advances have not made it a shrinking world, but one which, fortunately for our survival, still retains much of its original physical and cultural richness and variety.

In spite of our best efforts, we have not entirely succeeded in destroying the heterogeneity of the human species. Most important, many of the thousands of different cultures still alive around the planet have retained much of their archaic intimacy with their environment. If we can find ways to make use of that ancient knowledge in the next century, it may help us to retrieve some of our diminished sense of belonging.

Earth is our home, vividly and majestically displayed in this magnificent volume. Each picture shows a different face of our common mother. The evocative power of these wonderful images should stir genetic memories of our origins, reminding us of how far we have come and warning us of what our end might be.

Above all, this book serves as a timely reminder that, if we are to survive as a global community in the next century, it will be here, where we began, on Earth.

There is nowhere else to go.

PREFACE
by Payson R. Stevens and Kevin W. Kelley

Payson R. Stevens. In writing and designing this book, two images have stood out for me as quintessential visions of the twentieth century. One looms with horrifying darkness, disgorging waves of incinerating heat and clouds of mushrooming radiation. It was the time when one small Japanese watch was charred still and silent forever at the beginning of the nuclear countdown. It was a snapshot ushering in the age of the bomb—whose destructive power first burst on Hiroshima and Nagasaki, and continues to be a sword of Damocles.

The other image is of the Earth from space as first seen by the NASA Apollo missions over twenty years ago. In it, our exquisitely beautiful planet floats amid the darkness of space, a jewel of blue awash with water, surrounded by a pale reddish blue atmosphere as thin as a hair glowing against the blackness of eternity, with fleecy white clouds and continents as familiar as those on a childhood school map. Our home seen as a whole is a powerful symbol of the only life in our solar system— a place to cherish, protect, and value.

Two images: powerful, awesome, and encompassing alternative realities—one destructive and pessimistic, the other constructive and expansive. Both rely on the power of the human intellect and the disciplines of science and technology to be realized. They also offer widely divergent options for our species.

Viewed from space, our planet, our home, has a sense of oneness that must become an emblem for a higher order of existence. Everything around us, however, seems to indicate that the human species has reached a very precarious time in its evolution. Life is out of balance. Aggressive behavior has become the simplest, most direct form of diplomacy. War between nations and with the environment emerges as the backdrop for the daily news. The consequences that are unleashed cut into the fabric of our existence and into the ecosphere.

Warnings of great danger are everywhere: a global population that will double in fifty years, causing severe stresses on resources and resulting in increased human misery; a thinning of the ozone layer in the atmosphere over Antarctica and the rest of the planet; the hottest year on record in 1990; the largest oil spill in human history as the consequence of the 1991 war in the Persian Gulf. These and many other indicators, including the destruction of species and bioregions, are all linked to the same metaphor: we are fragmenting because we are afraid to trust wholeness. In spite of these dangers, holistic views are entering mass consciousness. Our need to understand the Earth as a system, with its interdependent, interconnected components, is why the different views from space are so exciting for contemporary science: they provide us with a potentially liberating perspective. *Embracing Earth: New Views of Our Changing Planet* contains striking images of our planet seen from space, offered as reflections on both its beauty and its vulnerability to human impact.

The science of remote sensing—observing and analyzing the Earth from a distance—has given us eyes in space that observe with superhuman powers once only the privilege of mythic gods. Sophisticated sensors can "see" day or night, through fog and clouds. They are sensitive to temperatures, water vapor, the amount of chlorophyll (and therefore plant life) in water and on land, seasonal changes in the concentration of ice, yearly changes in ozone levels, winds blowing over the water and roughening its surface, even ancient aquifers under the desert. Remote sensing images take many visual forms: they can be photographs as well as computer renditions from different sensors, which are enhanced with digital colors that emphasize patterns. These images are forming an enormous portrait, a massive mosaic that shows the state of our planet's health and the interaction of all its components. With this perspective has come a new discipline: earth system science. It is an all-encompassing view that requires an understanding that is more than geology or oceanography alone, more than climatology or meteorology. It is a meta-science that draws on all the natural sciences to help create a new approach for understanding how our planet works and how we affect it.

From the incredible diversity revealed by the imagery of our planet, we must seek inspiration that will help us find balance within a larger whole. The sophisticated technologies we have developed are only the tools of our inventive intellect; the way they are used ultimately reflects our view of ourselves. Technologies may help us understand and deal with some of our environmental problems but they are not the answer to these dilemmas. Solutions will come by developing human values that are global and interconnected, and which recognize that unlimited growth and expansion come at the expense of an ecologically and economically sustainable future.

We must search within ourselves to clear away the negativity and personal pain that is projected out into the larger world and desensitizes us to our destructive behavior toward each other and the Earth. All small acts of conservation, of questioning conformity and authority, of speaking out and demanding responsible behavior from politicians, schools, the media, and ourselves, must be viewed as normal behavior that will be additive, synergistic, and transformational.

All of science and all of art are the tools that allow patterns to be recognized. And within each cultural moment of history, they can be at the service of the status quo—the socioeconomic paradigms that drive us—or they can be elevated through a collective consciousness which rejects fear and requires love, clarity, and balance. Nothing less will do. Nothing else is more needed to welcome the Third Millennium.

Kevin W. Kelley. It is the fundamental beauty of the Earth that draws me to the creation of a book such as *Embracing Earth: New Views of Our Changing Planet.* As seen from space, the awesome majesty of the Earth is particularly exciting and illuminating, and it induces an even more profound reverie. No matter how many times I see these images, no matter how well I understand the important scientific and ecological messages that the images convey, ultimately I am most moved and most satisfied by the exquisite beauty and abundant truths of our planet.

I would encourage the reader to spend time with the images in this book, to really look at them. Allow your intuition and curiosity to lead you to your own discoveries. Your initial response may be an emotional reaction to the abstract beauty of what you see, or it may be the thrill of recognition of a familiar continent or contour from a radically new perspective. Continue to explore the images. You will find your own patterns and connections and significances, often taking you in directions other than the one we, the authors, address in the text.

You might see that the large macro patterns of the Earth resemble, sometimes with remarkable precision, the designs at ground level, or the micro systems of your own body. Rivers and their tributaries ranging over thousands of miles resemble patterns in a leaf or the veins in your hand; the folds of mountain ranges also appear to be ripples in sand dunes. You will notice rhythms in the clouds, in the texture of the land, in the color of the sea.

These rewarding discoveries will lead to new questions that will take you in many directions. Do not let yourself be satisfied with the literal explanations of what you see. You may find, as I sometimes do, that these images of the physical Earth can serve as metaphors for a wide range of mental, cultural, and spiritual processes.

I deeply enjoy the cycle of discovery, reflection, and mystery. Often I go back to my favorite photographs and spend more time with them, roaming the details of terrain and the subtleties of texture to find, once again, another layer of understanding and challenge. Ultimately, for me and perhaps for you, there is more mystery than discovery, more wonder and beauty than cognitive understanding.

This intuitive approach complements and enhances, rather than replaces, a more scientific approach to what the images in the book reveal. One thing that you are certain to discover, no matter how you consider the Earth, is the sobering fact that the planet is in jeopardy. Our resources are being depleted, and the very fabric, balance, and stability of the Earth are being threatened.

How will we create a sustainable future? The information conveyed in the images in this book and the powerful technology that delivered them can be a first step, but they are only the first step. The fabulous images and technology can help us see and understand what is going on in an unprecedented way—the hole in the ozone is now actually visible. We can now see what is beyond our own senses, beyond the limitations of an earthbound perspective.

The best perspective is always from a distance. From the distance and silence of space, from manned and unmanned spacecraft, this book brings us images and messages for survival. But information alone will not save the Earth. Decisions and actions will.

Many people have already been moved to action by the data on our destruction of the planet, and many others will undoubtedly heed the call of the startling information and conclusions in this volume. For some people, including myself, the call to action will come from a different inspiration. When we look closely and fully at the images in this book, we apprehend a wholeness that is more than the sum of its parts, a totality that is more than the sum of numbers. Patterns and textures become rhythms of interdependent systems and metaphors for a chaotic harmony: this vibrant, living Earth, sacred, divine, and immensely beautiful, evokes a love within us, an Epiphany.

For me, that is the power of the beauty of Earth as seen in these images. I hope that this beauty will inspire enough love to move you and me to act.

Note on the images: The images that follow were taken from space by cameras and a variety of remote sensing devices, as explained in the essay that begins on page 164. Satellites equipped with detectors sensitive to visible wavelengths, microwave, and thermal radiation, as well as other bands of the electromagnetic spectrum, send data to computers on Earth that process and display the data, as you will see in this book. In some cases, these images are photographs that capture what was visible to an astronaut's eye; in many other cases, the images reveal what the eye or photographic camera cannot see. These highly informative, visually dramatic, and usually false-colored images highlight vegetation, heat, water and air currents, and other aspects of the Earth and its atmosphere. The captions to the images explain the significance of the color scheme produced by the remote sensors. What may appear to be an imperfection in an image is often a consequence of data transmission. On many pages, there are composite images that show an entire hemisphere or the whole globe at one time, or that superimpose geographic boundaries or data-graphic information over the images. To provide an additional perspective to the view from space, there are occasional Earth-based photographs of places or events. From ground level to the Space Shuttle to a satellite over 1 million miles from Earth, these images present an intimate portrait of our planet as it has never been seen before.

NATURAL RHYTHMS

Patterns and structure. Everywhere we look we see them. What appears random and chaotic also has order. And on Earth much of the order is linked to interrelationships that drive constant change. Cycles and rhythms. Pulses and flows. Changes in magnetic fields. Continental plates moving. Water cycles. Seasons changing. Life and death. Process and connection. Nature flows through webs of structure and shifting time: from ocean to cloud to rain to river to ocean. Natural rhythms.

NATURAL RHYTHMS

The rhythms of the natural world are all around us. They are constantly changing, with countless clocks ticking at different beats, different times. We immediately perceive the moment-to-moment flux of our daily world: the drifting of clouds, the surging of waves, the rustling of wind in trees, the bubbling of water in brooks, the melting of icicles. We know the seasons, from the mantle of summer's green to that of winter's snow. We have faith that the Earth will renew itself each spring. The cycles of human or animal life—from birth to death—are a constant part of our deepest psyche, for they remind us of our own mortality and return to the earth.

Then there is the scale of deep time, spanning millions, even billions of years, with a clock that ticks almost beyond our comprehension. It is the rhythm of continents moving, of mountains uplifting and eroding, of deep canyons slowly being carved by water through countless millennia. It is also the clock of life's evolution: species evolving, and disappearing into the oblivious maw of extinction. Somewhere in between the brief moment and the millions of millennia are time scales that embrace sunspot cycles, poles wandering, and glaciers retreating and expanding.

The natural rhythms of our planet give us a sense of order even when we are faced with catastrophic earthquakes, tornadoes, hurricanes, and avalanches. Everything has its time and place: its origins and evolution, its life and death. We understand that there are processes which drive these events and that we are somehow part of them and part of nature, from volcanoes to ocean currents. These processes are as uplifting as the new spring buds, as comforting as the waves endlessly breaking, and as harrowing as the tornado or tidal wave sweeping the landscape with death and destruction. They are the matrix that helps give order and sets the rhythms of the physical world.

For plants and animals, the cycles of change operate on many scales. As the Earth rotates around the sun, day shifts to night, sunlight to darkness. Flowers close up at night; animals go to sleep or awaken depending on their feeding habits. The seasonal alternation of shorter and longer days, and colder and warmer temperatures, triggers the internal clocks deeply etched into the genetic material of all life-forms. Hormones flow, behaviors manifest, and mating seasons start, all based on cues from the rhythms of the external world.

For five hundred thousand years, humans have learned to survive and adapt to these rhythms and to carefully observe the cycles that would help ensure our survival and the survival of our offspring, our species.

Our perspective for watching change has always been from the vantage point of level ground, a high hill, or a mountain. Storms brew in the distance, fields of flowers blossom, and forests change color. From our beginnings, we have only been able to perceive our immediate landscape. Only recently has our view expanded beyond the evolutionary limits of our vision. In the twentieth century, airplanes gave us a larger regional perspective that expanded our awareness to hundreds of miles. The last three decades have taken us out into space and given us views of thousands of miles and even the entire planet.

Satellites have become technological sentinels orbiting the Earth, taking countless snapshots with numerous sensors. Images of whole continents and ocean basins allow us to track change at daily, weekly, monthly, and annual rhythms. Satellites allow us to watch fires burning in Yellowstone National Park and storms forming around the world, shown on the daily television weather report. We can see the oceans bloom, the land lose vegetation and turn to desert, and the seasons change. A new global vision is emerging. Seen from space, our planet is not only a beautiful blue marble, but a complex interaction of many components: land, air, water, snow and ice, life. We are in the process of gathering a portrait of our planet that will enable us to understand how these elements interact and interrelate. Without this satellite perspective, we would never advance beyond struggling to tell the forest from the trees.

The cycles of change, part of the dynamics of the Earth system, affect all of its components. Our planet has natural archives that can reveal past episodes of some of these changes. Tree rings can record events over thousands of years. Ice cores sample time going back hundreds of thousands of years. Ocean cores and sedimentary rocks reveal events that occurred millions of years ago. These records tell us about past temperatures, rainfall, vegetation patterns, air composition, sea levels, and solar activity. Our understanding of future global change relies on our ability to read and interpret these past records. They are part of the planetary library that will help us to predict the effect of our activities on the Earth.

What follows is a panorama of these rhythms as seen from the perspective of space. Their inherent beauty and order are apparent. Yet our appreciation of natural rhythms is essential not only to delight in an understanding of the way the world works but to realize our place within these rhythms and our impact on them.

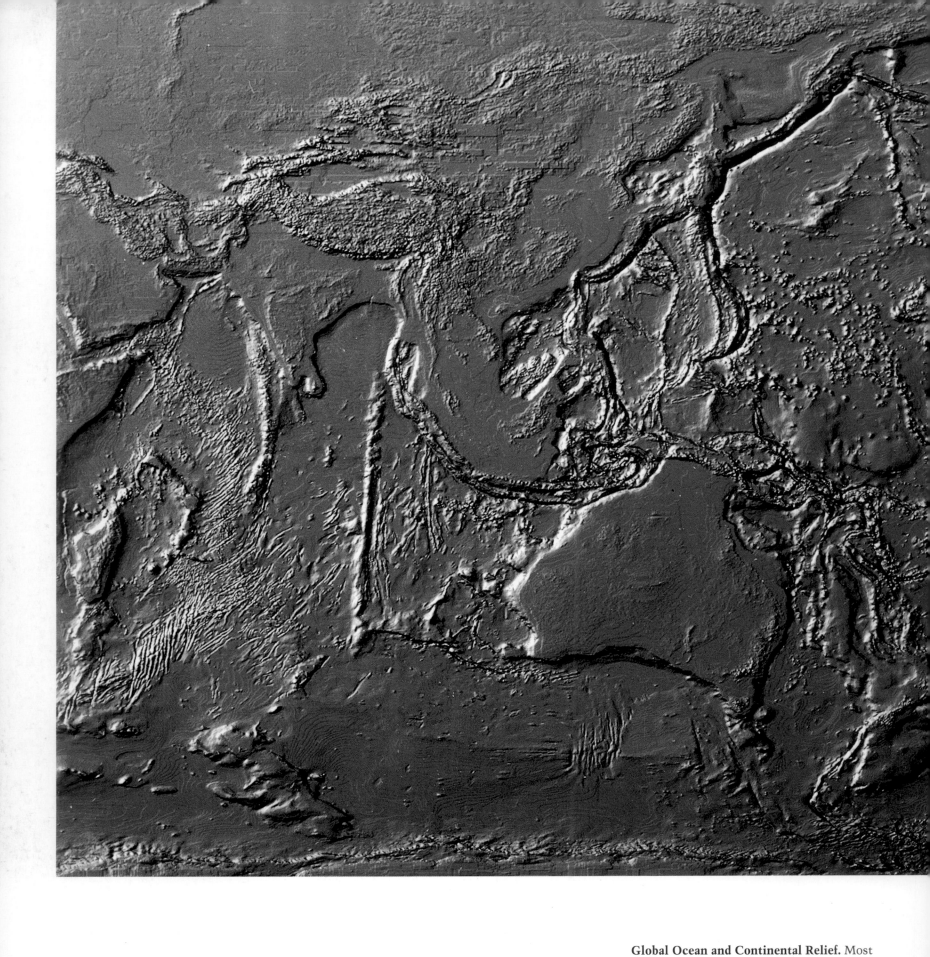

LAND

Global Ocean and Continental Relief. Most of us think of the earth beneath us as solid and immovable. But those who have experienced the force of an earthquake know that even the seemingly solid earth moves and changes. Only in the last few decades has science revealed that the Earth's surface is made up of a series of huge plates that have been moving for hundreds of millions of years. This theory of plate tectonics and seafloor spreading is one of the great discoveries of recent times. Volcanoes, earthquakes, underwater seafloor relief, the movement of continents, and even the evolution of certain organisms can be explained by this elegant theory.

These huge plates move as if on a gigantic conveyor belt. They are driven by a heat engine from deep within the Earth, which generates magma that comes to the surface at ridges beneath the ocean. As the plates move,

they collide into each other, one plate riding on the top, the other subsiding below it. Mountains are formed, the earth trembles and quakes, and where the magma comes close to the surface, volcanoes spew their fiery, molten rock.

There is a flow to all this movement that can accurately be measured by satellites using lasers. Scientists have found that the Atlantic Ocean is widening at the rate of one inch a year, so that the continents on either side are drifting farther apart from each other. The fit of South America and Africa confirms that the continents were once part of a super landmass, called Pangaea.

Many of the Earth's most spectacular geological features are hidden from view deep beneath the ocean's surface. There are trenches six times deeper than the Grand Canyon and mountains several times taller

than Mount Everest. The image shown above is a representation of that waterless view of Earth. It has been made by a combination of ship depth-sounding technology and an altimeter sensor aboard NASA's Seasat satellite. The altimeter sends down a radar beam that can measure differences in the height of the sea surface with a precision of two inches. These measurements can map the relief of the ocean's surface, which actually reflects how gravity affects the ocean water surface. Over a midocean ridge, water piles up, while over a trench, the sea surface may be depressed as much as 190 feet.

This global ocean and continental relief shows that continental borders are extended farther by their shelves and slopes, which are normally hidden from view. Deep trenches can be seen at the margins of South America and North America and along the rim of the

eastern Pacific. Midocean ridges are visible at the center of the Atlantic and at varying points in the Pacific and Indian oceans. These and many other features all fit together like a giant puzzle, the pieces being the plates of North and South America, Eurasia, Africa, and the Pacific.

The creation of uplifted mountains from plate motion and volcanic islands is the beginning of an endless cycle for the solid Earth. Then, wind and water begin the process of erosion, which further defines the appearance and evolution of geologic features. At each scale, from the mighty Himalayas to the trickle of water eroding the desert floor, the solid surface of our planet is constantly being altered.

◄ **Grand Canyon, United States.** The Grand Canyon in Arizona is a dramatic example of the power of water to erode the land. The Colorado River took 4 million years to cut a 278-mile-long canyon, whose width varies from less than 1 mile to over 18 miles, and whose depth extends as much as 1 mile. The great variation in the altitude of the canyon, from 1,200 to 9,100 feet, has created desert to subarctic ecosystems.

The appearance of the canyon walls was shaped by geologic events that go back almost 2 billion years. It was a drama with many forces: volcanoes erupting, mountains thrusting upward and twisting, land subsiding, water and wind constantly eroding the land. All of these are phases of the geologic cycle that determine the look and lay of the land.

▲ A view of the Grand Canyon from the South Rim looking toward the North Rim.

Tibet and Nepal. These two countries are part of the great 1,500-mile-long Himalaya mountain range, created when the Indian Plate collided with the Asian subcontinent 40 to 60 million years ago. Nepal rises to great mountainous heights, while Tibet, to the north, occupies a high plateau averaging 16,000 feet. Tibet dominates this Space Shuttle image of approximately 150 square miles. A glacier in the upper right flows off the north slope of the Gangdise Shan mountains in southern Tibet. A small lake, Konggyu-tso, is in the center, and a portion of another lake, Manasarowar, is in the top left. Nepal is in the lower left.

When we talk about preservation of the environment, it is related to many other things. Ultimately the decision must come from the human heart. The key point is to have a genuine sense of universal responsibility, based on love and compassion, and clear awareness.

The Dalai Lama

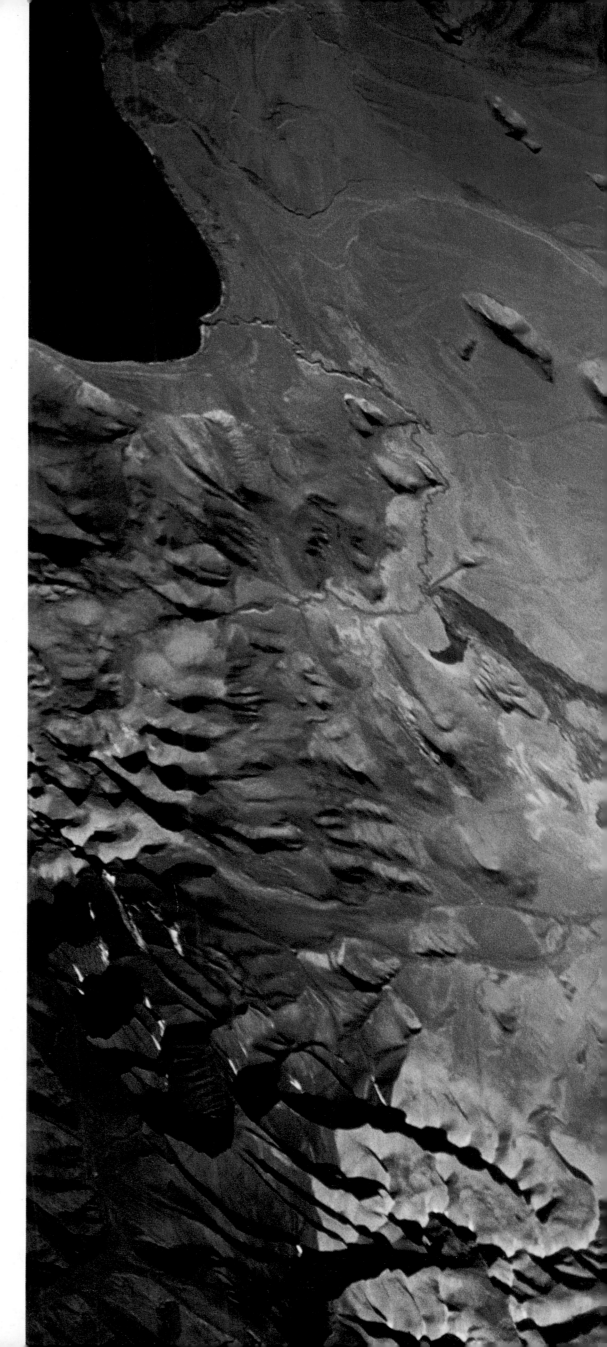

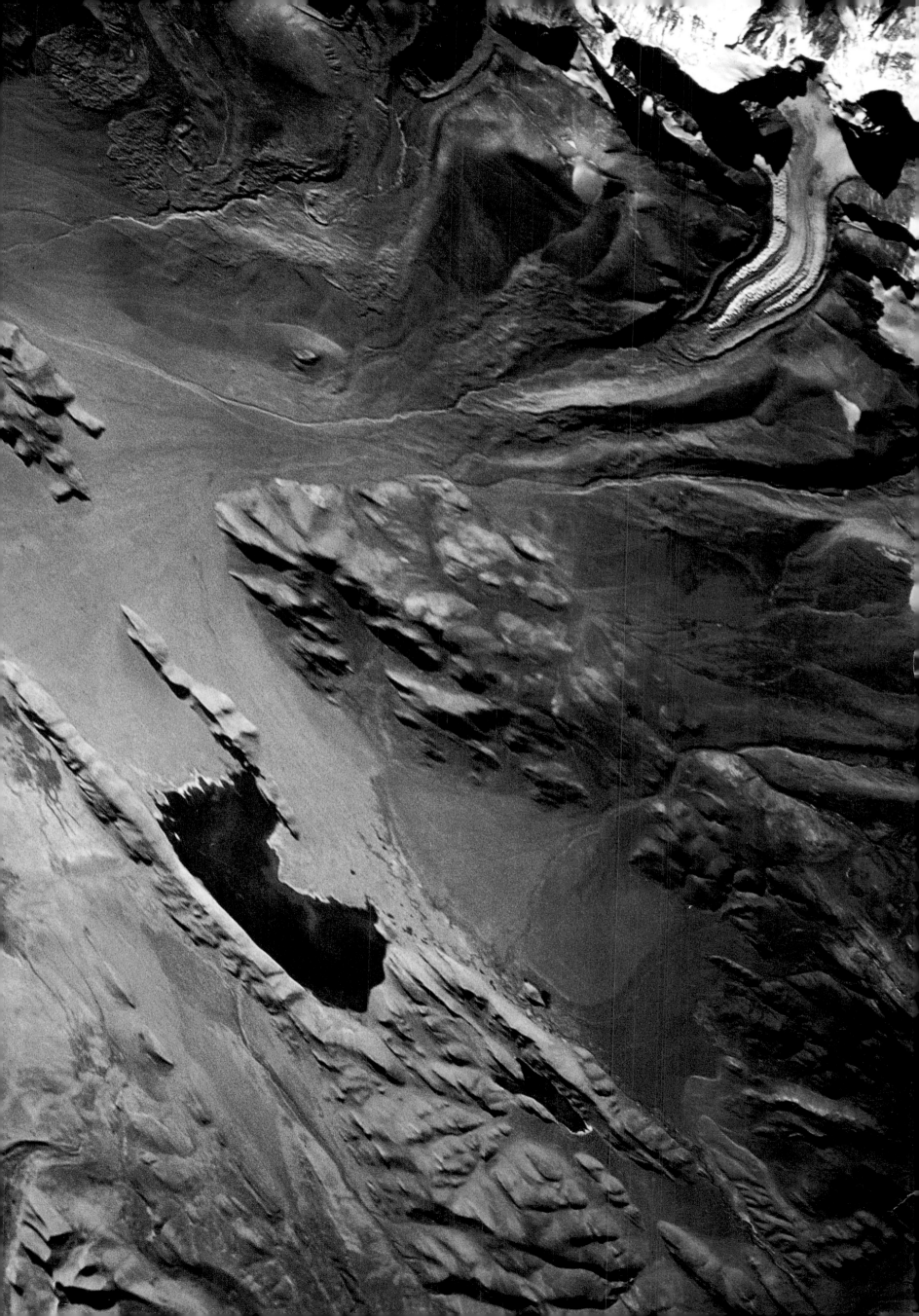

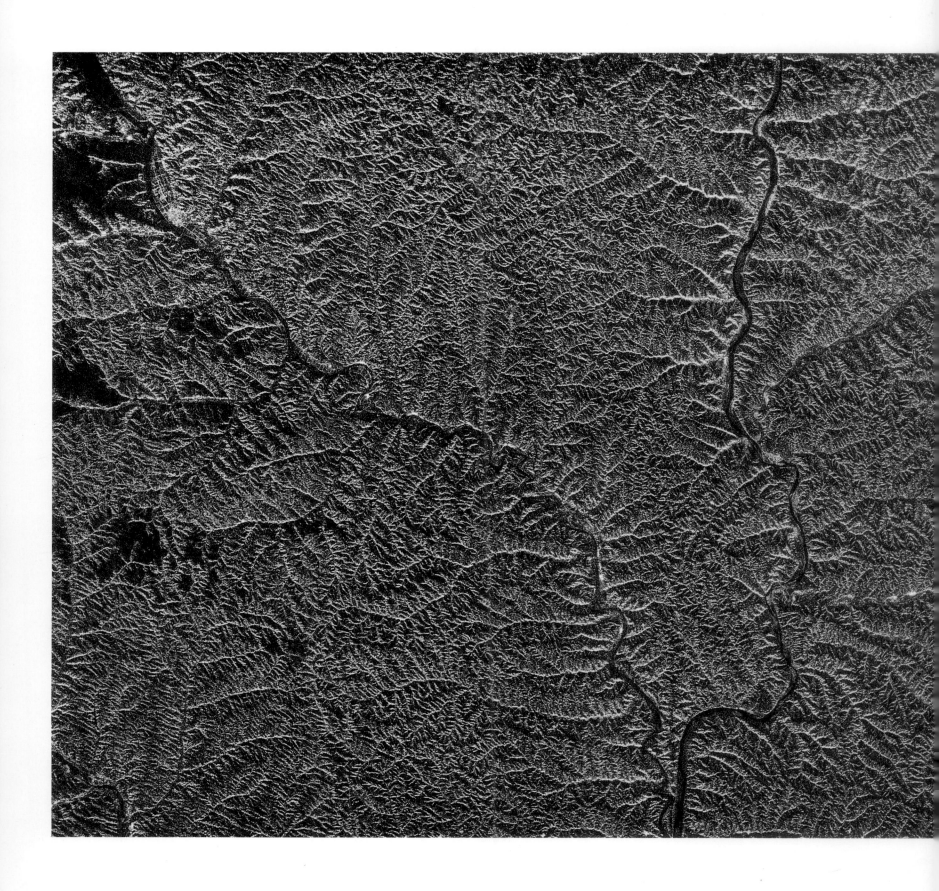

The wind blows pebbles across the fields. Sheep cannot find even dry grass. In every ten years, nine yield no food. If it rains, there's a harvest. If not, all is lost.

Gansu, China, folk saying

Windblown Silt, Loess Plateau, China.
Dust storms, a part of nature's rhythms, arise when the turbulent movement of the wind sweeps up the surface soil. Loess is a form of windblown silt or dust that can bury landforms over the course of time. The Loess Plateau of central China is probably the largest accumulation of windblown silt on the planet, having been carried over many centuries from the Gobi Desert of Mongolia nearly 1,000 miles away. The plateau,

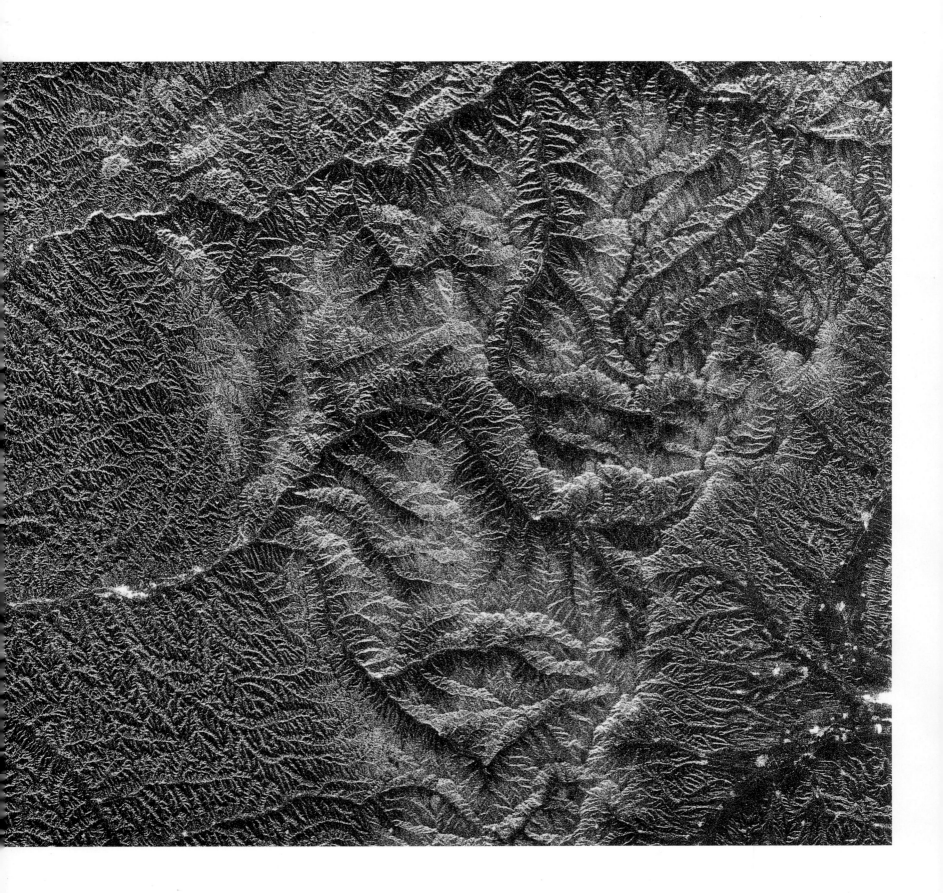

covering an area of almost 200,000 square miles, is a powerful example of the wind's capacity to transport the earth.

This radar image is centered on the Huang He, or Yellow River, in the Shanxi Province of China, as it flows south. The Kuye He joins it at the bottom. The entire scene reveals the effects of intense water erosion. Because the windblown silts are not very compacted and easily wash away, rainstorms and runoff have created an extensive terrain of elongated ridges and gullies. The tremendous erosion contributes to the sediment load of the river. Hence its name: Huang He, or Yellow River. The city of Xing Xian is the bright spot at the center of the image to the east of the river. The villagers living on the Loess Plateau often struggle in this desolate and harsh environment, where a constant and reliable source of water for irrigation is difficult to obtain.

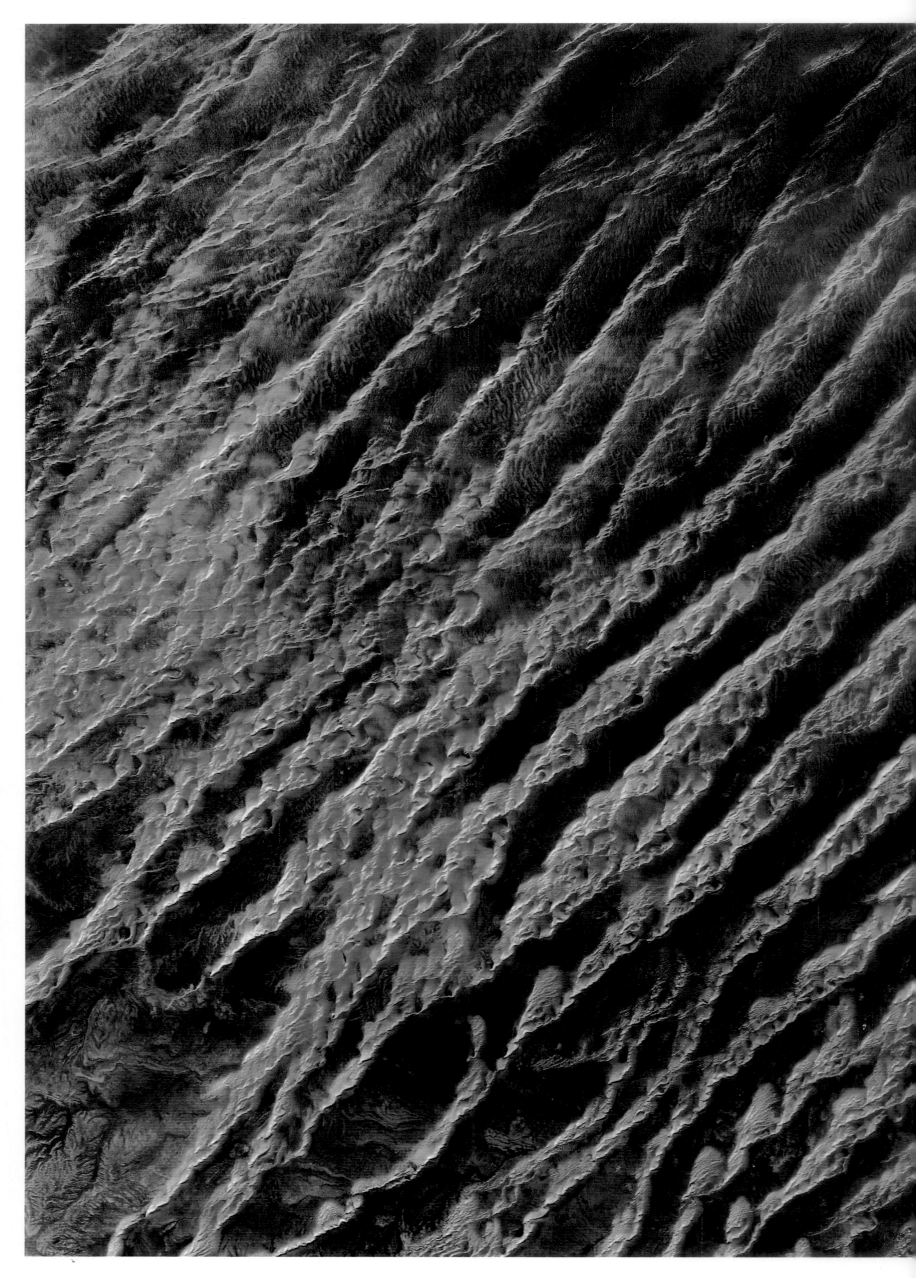

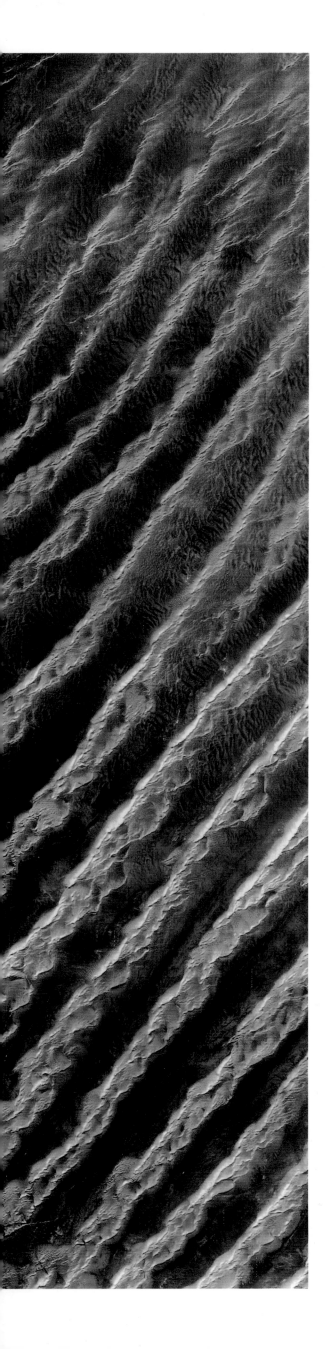

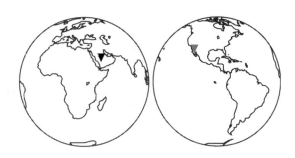

◄ **Empty Quarter, Saudi Arabia.** Winds blowing across the Arabian Peninsula have created vast regions of undulating dunes resembling the ocean surface. The Grand Rub' al Khali Erg is an extensive sand basin in the southwestern quadrant of Saudi Arabia. Known as the Empty Quarter, it is a desolate expanse of crested dunes shaped into long parallel ridges by continuously blowing southwesterly winds. The light blue regions in the image are oases, where water collects. Formations caused by water erosion are in the lower left.

▲ **Baja California, Mexico.** This image of the surface of a dune in Baja was taken from a distance of only a few feet. The pattern in the sand was caused by the same forces that formed the dunes covering 250,000 square miles in the Empty Quarter of Saudi Arabia.

Western Andes Mountains, Peru. The Andes Mountains, like the Himalayas, were formed by the collision of huge tectonic plates moving over the Earth's surface. As the Nazca Plate in the Pacific Ocean moved east, it struck the South American Plate. The Nazca Plate slipped under the South American continent, uplifting the terrain into a 4,500-mile-long mountain range whose highest peak is nearly 23,000 feet.

This false-color image shows the region in the Andean foothills surrounding Nazca, Peru, after which the plate is named. The elevation of the area ranges from 2,000 to 6,000 feet. The mountains, in the upper right, are veined with numerous rivers draining westward toward the lower-lying land (gray-green). Villages and cities surround the major rivers, along which farm plots are clearly visible. Vegetation appears in reddish brown. The image indicates that much of this region is semiarid, with little vegetation, hence the proximity of the farms and villages to the main sources of water for irrigation. The white fan shapes are older river deposits that streamed from the longer valleys of the mountains.

It is lovely indeed, it is lovely
indeed ...
I, I am the spirit within the Earth;
The bodily strength of the Earth is my strength;
The thoughts of the Earth are my thoughts;
All that belongs to the Earth belongs to me;
I, I am the sacred words of the Earth;
It is lovely indeed, it is lovely
indeed.

Navaho Creation Chant of Changing Woman

If the doors of perception were cleansed every thing would appear to man as it is, infinite.

William Blake, poet

◄ **The Himalayas**. This sweeping view takes in the plateaus of Tibet (bottom), the Himalayas and Nepal, and the great plains of the Ganges River in India (top). The scene is late summer, when minimal snow covers the mountains. The Himalayas, the highest land range on our planet, include Mount Everest, at 29,030 feet. The mountains were created when the area now known as India collided into the landmass of Asia over 40 million years ago. The mountain-building processes caused by plate tectonics and continental drift, which formed the Himalayas and other ranges, such as the Andes, continue to change the Earth today.

▲ The Himalayas, near Dudh Kund, Nepal, at an elevation of 12,000 feet.

Gibson Desert, Australia. Almost two-thirds of Australia is arid or semiarid, with extensive deserts of sand. Wind-driven processes have created this patchwork of color and texture. The predominant features are the linear sand dunes caused by winds. The colors, which are computer enhanced, signify a variety of natural processes. The faint red areas are sparse grasses and shrubs, the main desert vegetation, which stabilizes the dunes. The dark areas are scars from many years of fires that have burnt back the plants. The cycle of fire and plant regrowth is evidenced by the red regions amid the black scars. Areas of bright yellow are exposed shifting sands with little vegetation. The brilliant blue highlights show water collected in shallow depressions.

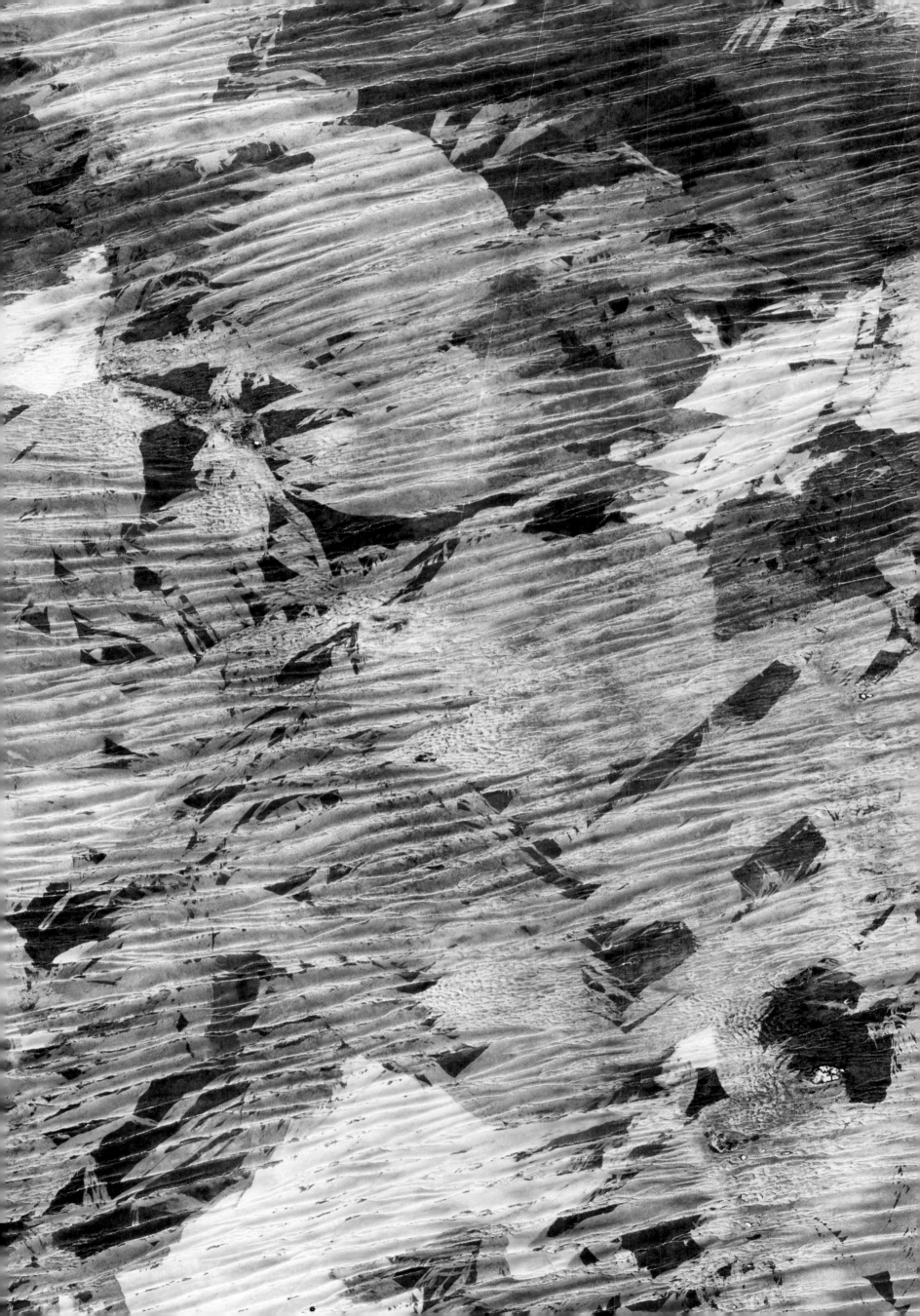

Mount Ararat, Turkey. Most of the active volcanoes in the world today lie along the circumference of the Pacific Ocean. Another area of sporadic activity extends from Armenia through Iran. It is a zone where the Arabian Plate collides with the Eurasian Plate in the ongoing process of continental drift and the continual action of plate tectonics. Earthquakes are common here, often with devastating impact on small villages and poorly built homes, which are not prepared to withstand earth tremors. There is also a history of older volcanic activity going back millions of years.

Mount Ararat is a large, extinct volcanic cone, measuring over 22 miles at its base, located in eastern Turkey near the border with Iran and Soviet Armenia. Shown here are the two major peaks, the larger, cloud-topped Great Ararat (16,945 feet) at the center towering above Little Ararat (12,077 feet) to its right. The sensor used to make these images can distinguish between the white clouds above Great Ararat and the ice cap (in blue) to the left of the peak, even though both are normally seen as white. The lava and ash deposits are warm brown. The bright red regions are fire scars from burnt brush and vegetation. Lava channels and gutters are apparent along the slopes of both volcanoes. The Razdan River and its fertile plain with numerous agricultural plots can be seen at the top of the image.

Mountain ranges, volcanoes appeared in salt-and-flour relief. It was easy to imagine the dynamic upheavals that created jutting mountain ranges and smoking craters.... I became an instant believer in plate tectonics.... The view from overhead makes theory come alive.

Sally Ride, astronaut

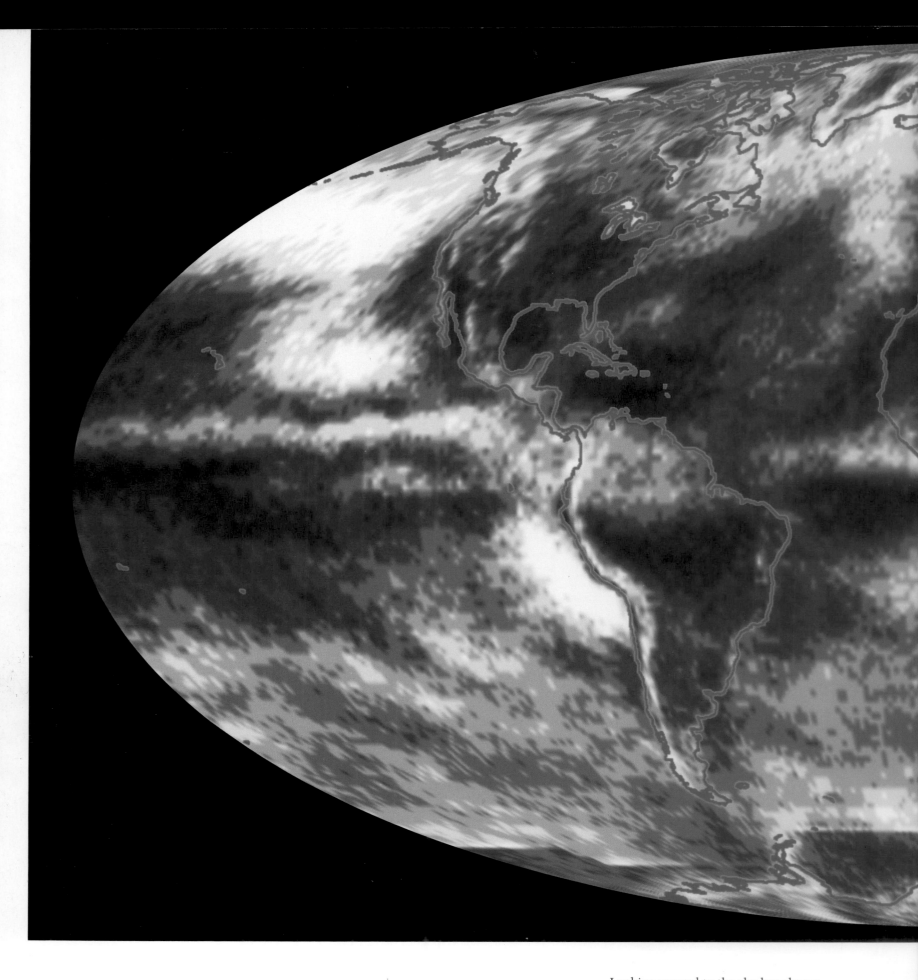

AIR

Looking upward to the sky has always presented us with an ever-changing spectacle of beauty and often of immense power. Clouds move endlessly, storms roll in with ominous darkness, and sunsets fill the horizon with vibrant hues. It is a thin veil through which we look, for our planet is surrounded by an invisible ocean of air that forms the boundary between Earth and outer space. This shell of gases and particles rises some 300 miles, becoming thinner and lighter as it ascends. It is more than a boundary, for it protects and shelters life from damaging solar rays, heat, and cold. Countless meteors are rendered harmless each day as they burn up before they reach the Earth's surface. The great weather machine—of heat, water, and wind, of energies transformed—plays out its daily drama in this constantly moving veil.

The atmosphere, which science has probed for four hundred years, has been shown to be divided into a number of regions. The first 10

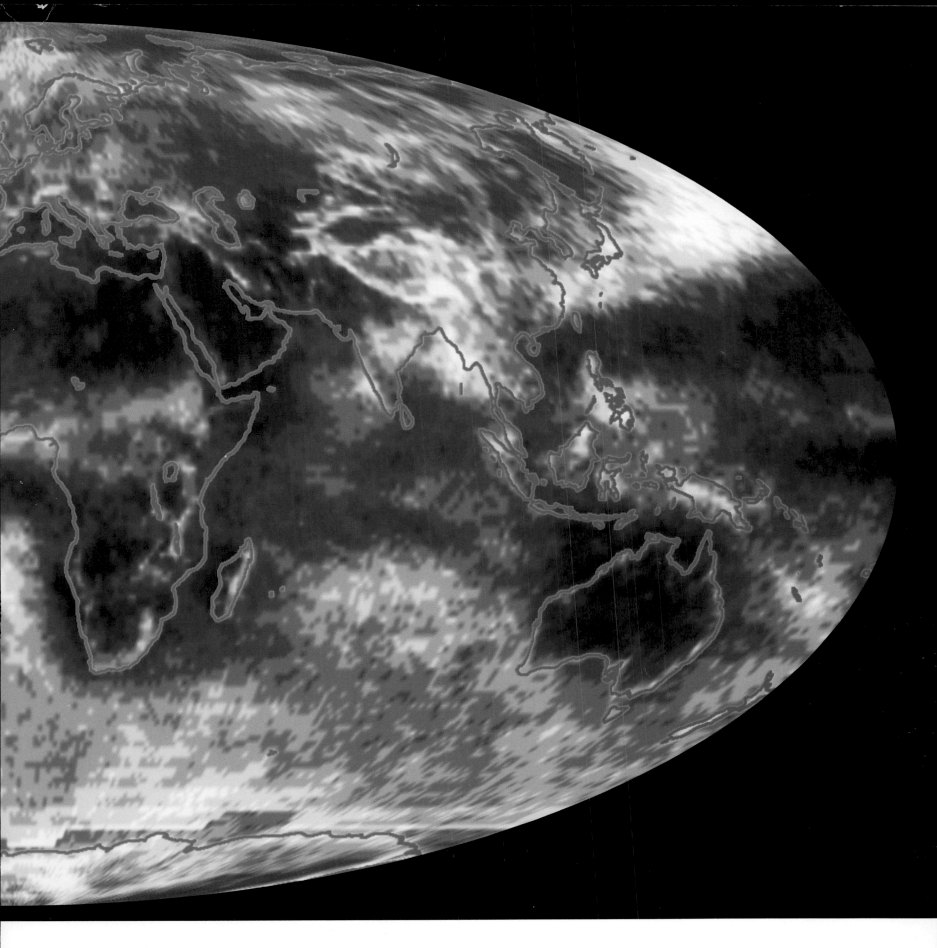

miles is the troposphere, where weather and clouds form. This region is followed by the stratosphere (10–30 miles); the mesophere (30–50 miles); the ionosphere (50–180 miles), where auroras glow and meteors leave burning trails; the thermosphere (up to 300 miles); and the exosphere (over 300 miles).

The atmosphere is a vast chemical soup of molecules interacting with each other and also is affected by photochemical reactions driven by solar radiation. The gases trapped in the atmosphere make our planet habitable. Oxygen sustains life. Carbon dioxide, a by-product of that same life, regulates the planet's temperature through the greenhouse effect. Ozone helps protect life from damaging ultraviolet radiation.

Satellites continuously supply data and images that expand our knowledge of the atmosphere. Clouds and winds, the harbingers of changing weather, are monitored daily and appear nightly on television. Hurricanes are

tracked with concern and interest. Winds are shown to etch vast regions with dunes or to blow dust off Africa that ends up in South America. The ozone hole over Antarctica is monitored annually, and these images have motivated international treaties governing the production of chemicals that destroy ozone. In the fall of 1991, NASA launched the Upper Atmosphere Research Satellite (UARS), the first spacecraft dedicated to conducting a systematic, comprehensive study of the stratosphere. UARS will also provide data on the mesosphere and thermosphere— regions of the upper atmosphere that are especially susceptible to changes caused by human activities.

The satellite image above depicts mean (or average) global cloud cover for June 1988. A combination of different sensors was used to determine the opacity and height of clouds. Cloud cover ranges from the lowest levels, in dark blue, to the higher levels, in pale blue

to white. The image also shows the essential features of global cloud dynamics. A white band extends across the tropics from Africa to South America to the Pacific Ocean. Known as the Intertropical Convergence Zone, it is a region of high concentrations of large clouds that is nearly continuous around the equator. The zone of high cloud levels that covers India and the Bay of Bengal is associated with Indian monsoons.

Exploration of space has revealed the atmosphere to appear as a blue-violet glow surrounding the Earth. Only recently have we been conscious of the fragility of this delicate, life-giving membrane. Now that we see its aura from space, and understand the impacts of potential global climate change, air pollution, and ozone depletion, we realize that our atmosphere can no longer be taken for granted.

There is inward beauty only when you feel real love for people and for all the things of the earth; and with that love there comes a tremendous sense of consideration, watchfulness, patience.

Krishnamurti, philosopher

Atmospheric Veil. The atmosphere is a veil of gases and particles that forms the boundary between the Earth and outer space. It shelters us from the intense heat and cold of space, damaging forms of solar radiation, and billions of small meteors that bombard the Earth daily. Comprising a series of layers, the atmosphere is about 300 miles thick, and the life-protecting stratosphere extends to only 30 miles above the surface of the Earth.

In this Space Shuttle image, the sun illuminates the Earth's atmosphere as a red-, violet-, and blue-tinted band. This band is actually made up of many layers. The red-to-orange region is the troposphere; the blue region is the upper atmosphere, which consists of three regions: stratosphere, mesosphere, and thermosphere. Clouds are seen in silhouette.

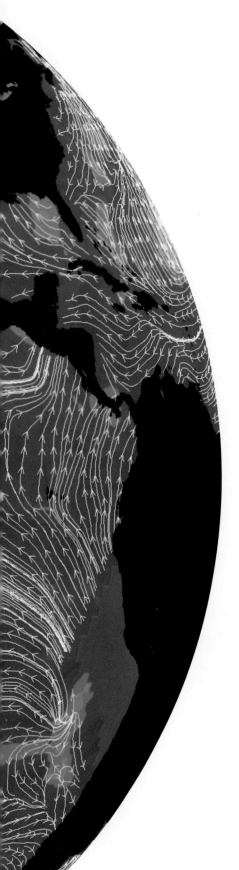

◄ **Winds over the Pacific.** The wind is a principal engine driving ocean waves and currents. It is one of the main forces that move water over our planet's surface and influence the exchange of heat between the atmosphere and the oceans. Wind also helps redistribute solar heat from the tropics into the cooler polar regions. The dynamics of wind is crucial to the Earth's weather and climate.

Satellites can observe global wind patterns on the ocean surface that are impossible to measure at sea by ships and buoys. This image is based on more than 150,000 satellite measurements made during a single day. A radar beam measures the roughness of the sea surface, which is caused by wind action. Computer programs turn this information into wind speed and direction, shown here. The silhouettes of North and South America are added for reference. Wind speed increases from blue-purple to yellow-orange, with the strongest winds being at 20 miles per hour. White lines with arrows show the direction of wind flow.

Winds swirl in a counterclockwise direction in the Northern Hemisphere and clockwise in the Southern Hemisphere. Small storms appear in the Gulf of Alaska, and two giant storms are shown in the bottom center of the image, between New Zealand and Chile.

▼ This black-and-white image shows the same scene in a satellite photo. It is similar to the daily weather pictures we see on the television news. The main storms and cloud patterns are visible but without any indication of their strength or direction.

ONE-FIFTH OF THE EARTH'S LAND, WITH 80 MILLION PEOPLE,
IS THREATENED BY DESERTIFICATION.

Desertification, Western Africa. In many semiarid regions of the tropics, the loss of vegetation through either natural or human forces has caused a loss of topsoil. Overgrazing, particularly by livestock, results in the degradation of plants that otherwise would help hold water and soil during rainstorms. In the absence of plant life, floods wash away valuable topsoil, and what is left is often picked up by the wind, leaving only sand behind. This insidious process that destroys

the fertility of the soil is known as desertification. It is an environmental disaster that has occurred chiefly in the dry areas of the tropics and most recently has contributed to the famine in the Sahel, the southern area of the Sahara Desert that extends from Senegal on the Atlantic Ocean inland to Chad.

In this large satellite image of the west coast of Africa, Senegal is in the center, with the capital of Dakar located on the long pointed promontory jutting into the Atlantic

Ocean. To the south of the promontory is Gambia, which is surrounded by Senegal. To the north of Senegal is Mauritania. Part of Guinea-Bissau is visible to the south. Vegetation is red; desert regions, beige. The most striking feature is the dust storm blowing off the coast of Mauritania and passing over the capital, Nouakchott. Dust from such storms can be carried by winds across the entire Atlantic to as far away as Brazil.

Tropical Storms. These powerful engines of energy are born at sea and can cause great destruction when they reach land. Their winds can blow with a fury of up to 250 miles per hour, enough to drive straw through steel. Tropical storms form in the latitudes between 20° north and 20° south of the equator and are known by many names around the world: hurricanes in the Atlantic Ocean and eastern Pacific Ocean, typhoons in the western Pacific Ocean, and cyclones in the Indian Ocean. These storms are generated by the interaction of the sun with the ocean and the atmosphere. As the sun warms the ocean, evaporation transfers heat from the water to the atmosphere. The warm ocean serves not only as a source of heat but also as an unlimited source of water that fuels these tempests. The rotation of the Earth sets the winds spiraling around a calm center with a counterclockwise direction in the Northern Hemisphere and a clockwise direction in the Southern Hemisphere.

▶ **Hurricane Elena, Gulf of Mexico.** This large photograph shows Hurricane Elena on September 1, 1985. The storm is many hundreds of miles across, with a calm eye in the center.

▼ **Hurricane Gilbert, Gulf of Mexico.** These two weather satellite images were made on September 14 and 15, 1988. Over the two days, Hurricane Gilbert moved rapidly west through the Gulf of Mexico. The hurricane, which is over 1,000 miles across, occupies the entire gulf.

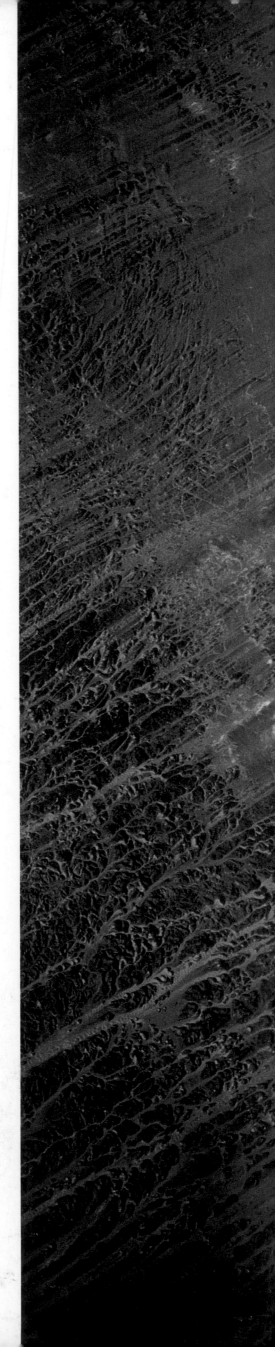

*It is the wind that comes out of
our mouths now that gives us life.
When this ceases to blow, we die.
In the skin of our fingers we can
see the trail of the wind; it shows
us where the wind blew when our
ancestors were created.*

Navaho legend

► **Sahara Desert Winds, Tibesti Mountains.**
The power of the wind not only picks up
and disperses soil into the air, but also slowly
gouges the land, leaving distinct erosional
features. This Space Shuttle image of the
Sahara Desert along the borders of Chad and
Libya in north-central Africa shows the two
aspects of air: how it marks the land and how
it absorbs other gases and particulate matter.
The long, linear features result from the
force of winds sweeping down the Tibesti
Mountains. Parallel bands of long trails of
sand and darker volcanic material are also
seen. The circular feature in the center is
the remnant of an ancient volcano that has
been totally eroded. Smoke from fires appears
in the lower left. The remaining trees and
shrubs of the Sahara continue to be cleared
for fuelwood and charcoal production,
further leaving the soil bare and vulnerable
to erosion by the desert winds.

►► **Thunderheads, Africa** (following pages).
Thunderstorms are part of the cycle of the
global heat transport system. Without them,
the solar energy absorbed by the Earth would
be trapped at the surface, causing a significant
global rise in temperature. Thunderstorms
efficiently and effectively transfer this heat
back to the upper troposphere (the lowest
region of the atmosphere) where most weather
occurs. The condensation of water vapor into
the towering thunderheads releases the heat
up to 5 miles into the atmosphere.
  Thunderheads, a popular term for the
anvil of cumulonimbus clouds, punch up into
the stratosphere (above the troposphere) over
tropical Africa. The low angle of the sun
highlights the shapes of the clouds. At the
Earth's surface, the thunderstorm releases
heavy winds and rain.

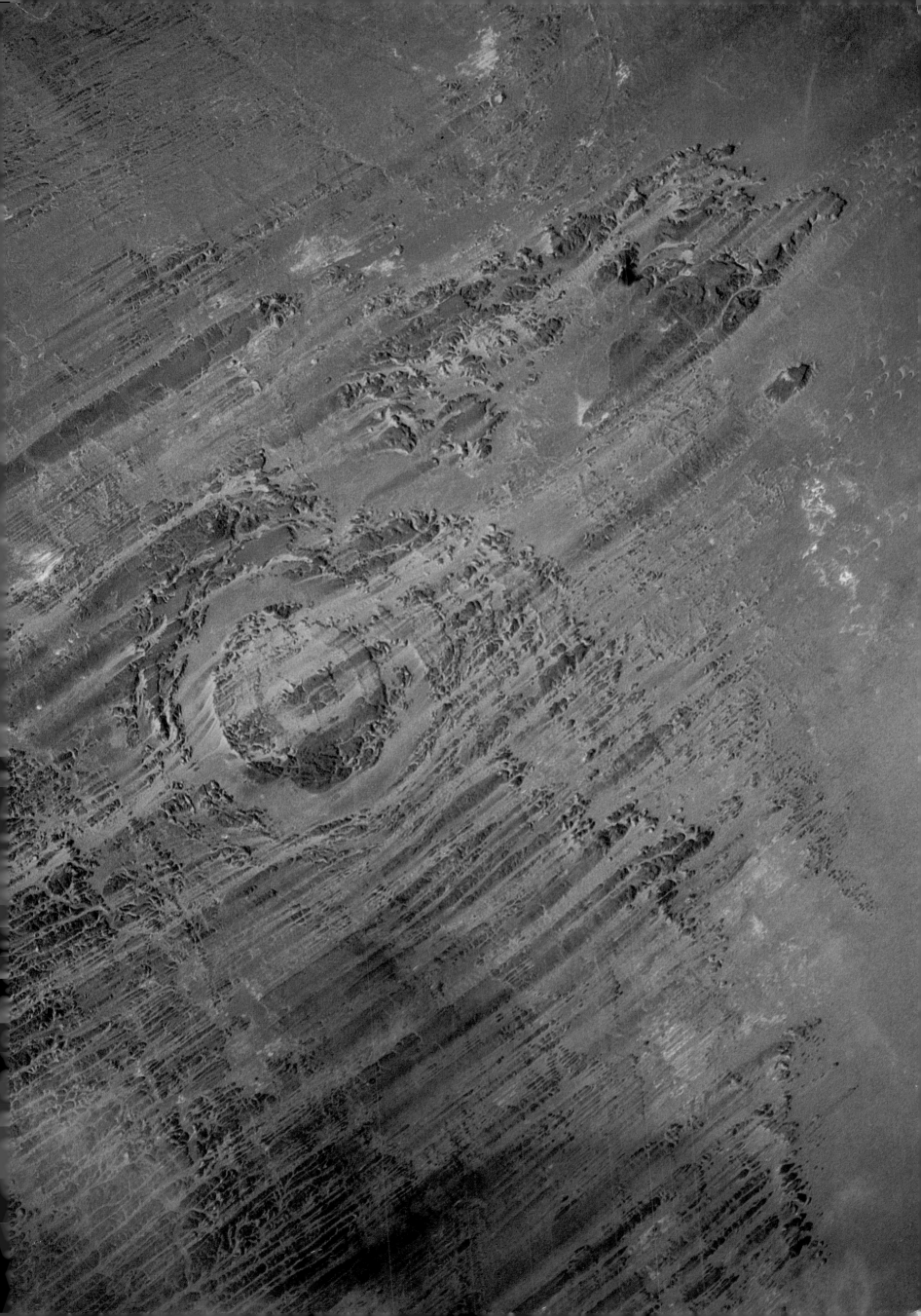

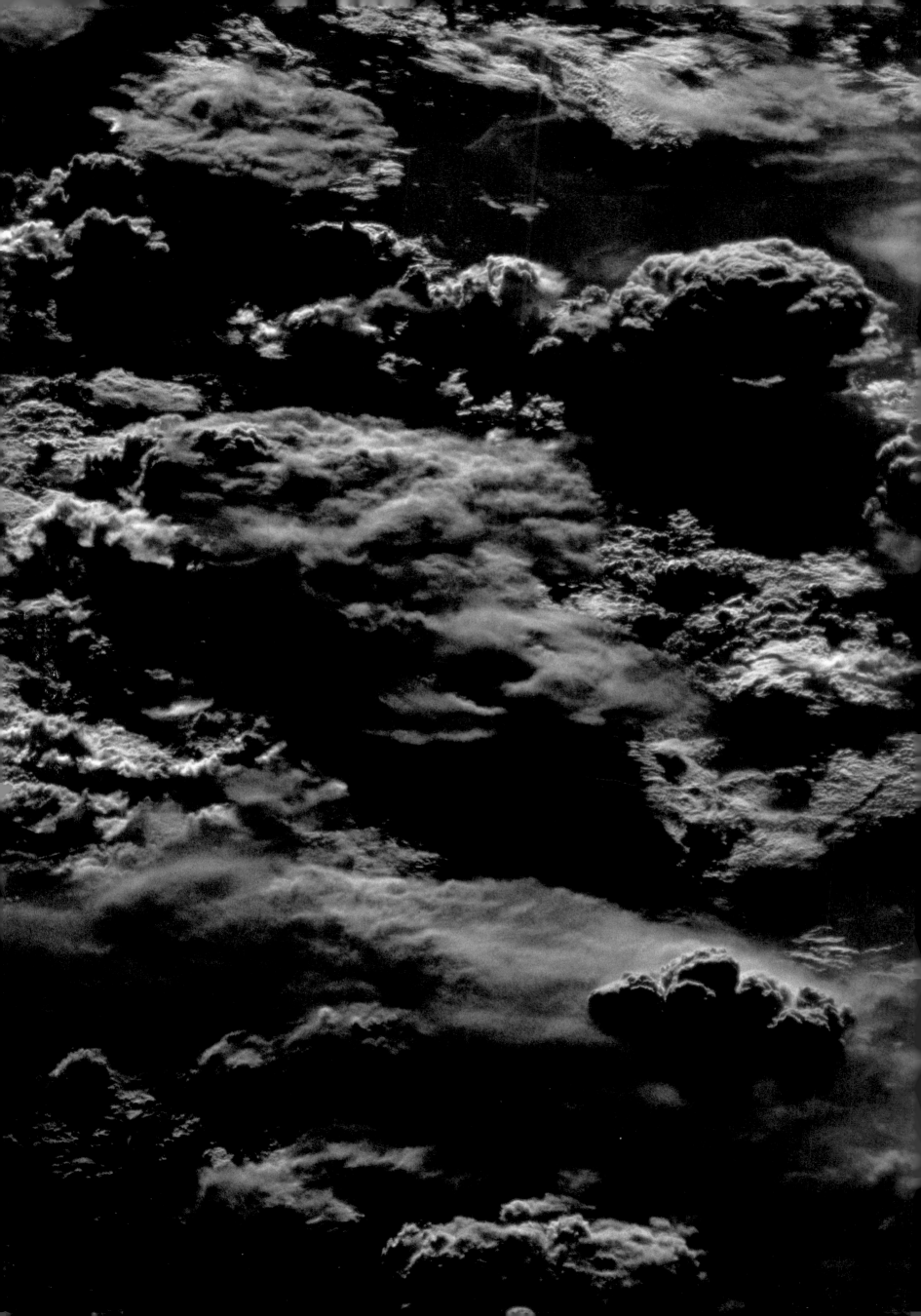

Guadalupe Island Wakes, Mexico. The trade winds propel clouds from east to west across the Pacific Ocean. The warm air, combined with the hundreds of square miles of warm ocean, results in the formation of cumulus and stratocumulus clouds. Cloud patterns generally show the direction of the winds. When the air currents are intercepted by a high landmass, such as an island, complex airflow patterns are created, and the clouds divide in order to bypass the obstacle. An island wake or ship wave pattern is formed, similar to the deflection of water around a boat or of air around an airplane wing.

▲ This wake effect occurs around Guadalupe Island, in the Pacific Ocean, 180 miles to the west of Baja California, as the even rows of cumulus clouds circumnavigate the island.

► Another view of the Guadalupe Island wake, center right of the image, includes downstream turbulence developing into cloud vortices. Punta Eugenia on the west coast of Baja California appears at the top of the image. Isla Cedros, located offshore, also manifests the island wake effect.

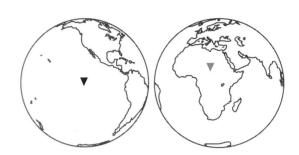

Weather and Clouds. Satellite weather pictures are part of our daily television diet. The movements of storms and clouds are tracked hour by hour and can be used to forecast general weather conditions at least a few days in advance. Weather satellites orbit the Earth at over 22,000 miles. Synchronized with the planet's daily orbit, they are always above the same point on the surface. The cloud patterns that are revealed, combined with balloon and meteorological ground measurements, help us to interpret the weather. Even though 160 nations share data, predicting the weather for more than a fortnight can be difficult. The complexity of the Earth's atmosphere, with many forces interacting and creating chaotic events, is still beyond the predictive calculations of the best supercomputers.

▶ The full image of the Earth shows the partially cloud-covered North American continent at the top. South America is clearly seen in the lower right. The Pacific Ocean dominates most of the image, with major storms in the North and South Pacific. The storm to the west of Baja California contains a hurricane moving in a counterclockwise direction. A large storm is in the center of the South Pacific to the west of South America.

▼ This image, taken during one of the Apollo moon missions, shows the Earth from an altitude of 23,000 miles. The African continent and part of the Arabian Peninsula are clearly visible. Storms and associated clouds swirl above the Earth's surface.

Mount Pinatubo, Philippines. Mount Pinatubo was dormant for over six hundred years, but when it began spewing smoke, gases, and rocks in mid-June of 1991, it produced the most powerful volcanic eruption of the century. For hundreds of years, titanic pressures of magma had built up inside the 4,795-foot-high mountain. When the volcano finally erupted, it blew a deadly mixture of volcanic fragments and gases that roared down the mountain at speeds of up to 100 miles per hour. Hundreds of thousands of inhabitants fled the area. Although approximately three hundred individuals died, the toll could have been much worse. Fortunately, geologists had been monitoring the volcano and were able to warn most residents prior to the main eruption. The various satellites that observed the eruption provided scientists with the opportunity to study its impact on climate.

▼ This image shows the main island of Luzon on July 5, 1991, a few weeks after the main eruption, with Mount Pinatubo still smoking. The smoke clouds, measured by radar, reached 15 miles high. The South China Sea is on the left; the Philippine Sea is on the right.

► This series of images shows the eruption over a twelve-week period. The massive amounts of sulfur dioxide released into the atmosphere combined with water droplets to form sulfuric acid, which may linger in the stratosphere for up to three years. Note the dramatic progression of the sulfuric acid aerosol as it completely encircled the Earth north and south of the equator. These droplets act as a shield that reflects the rays of the sun back into space, causing a slight global cooling, predicted to last for several years. This cooling may temporarily counteract the greenhouse warming of the past decades but could complicate research into global climate change. Another impact of the stratospheric volcanic cloud may be a dramatic, though temporary, depletion of ozone resulting from additional chemical reactions.

BLASTING 15 TO 20 MILLION TONS OF SULFUR DIOXIDE INTO THE STRATOSPHERE,
MOUNT PINATUBO WAS THE LARGEST VOLCANIC ERUPTION OF THE CENTURY.

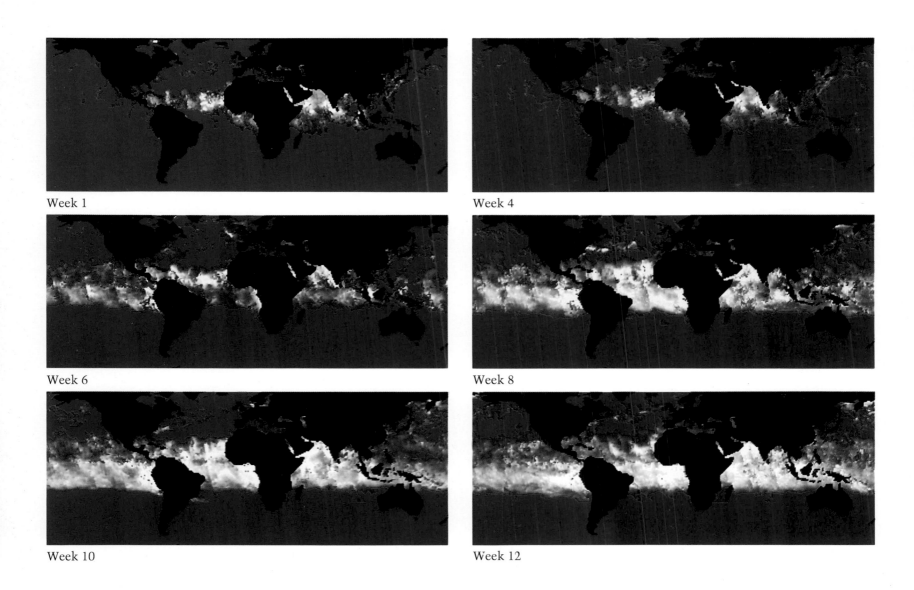

Week 1

Week 4

Week 6

Week 8

Week 10

Week 12

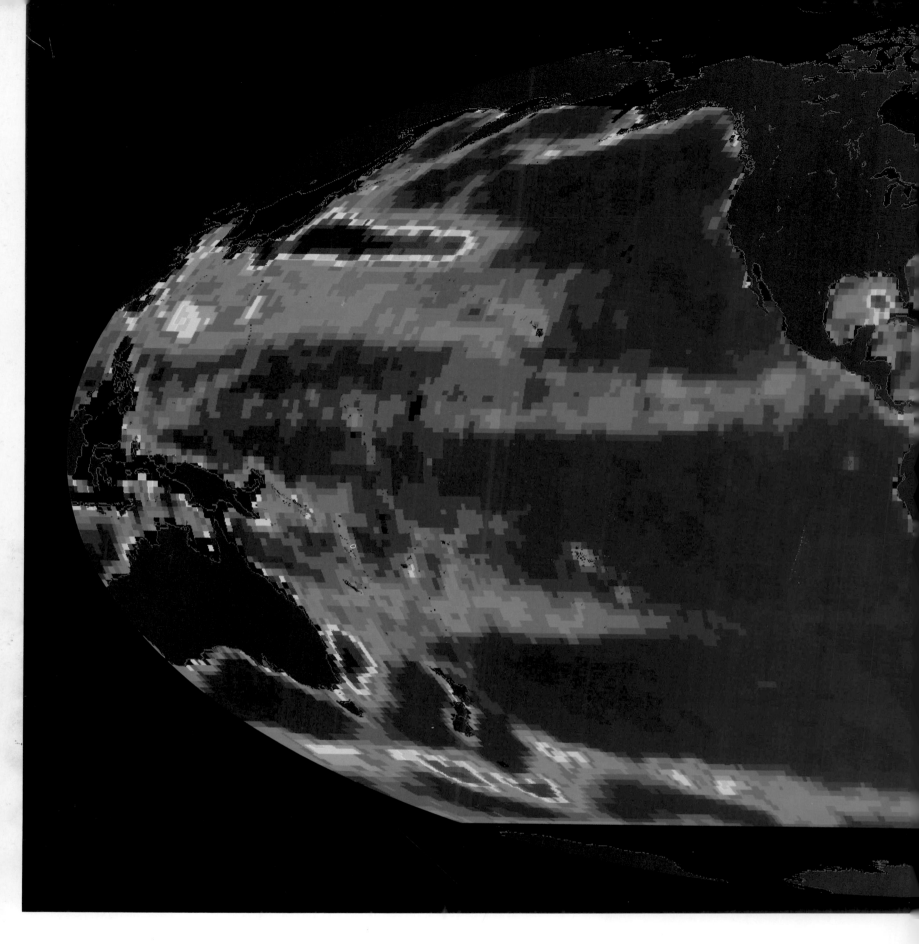

Our planet really should be called "Water" rather than "Earth," since water covers over 70 percent of its surface. As a liquid in the ocean, a solid in snow and ice, and a gas in water vapor, water plays the essential role in the global climate machine.

Water is the matrix of life on our planet. It is the only substance that naturally exists as a liquid, a solid, and a gas. Water evaporates from the oceans into the air, falls from the clouds as rain or snow, and flows from streams and rivers to return again to the sea, constantly replenishing and recycling itself. Where there is water there is usually life.

The largest water component is the ocean. Without oceans our planet would be unbearably hot or cold. Ocean currents help to modulate global temperatures by redistributing heat from the tropics to the poles. Oceans are also like a great thermostat that holds more

WATER

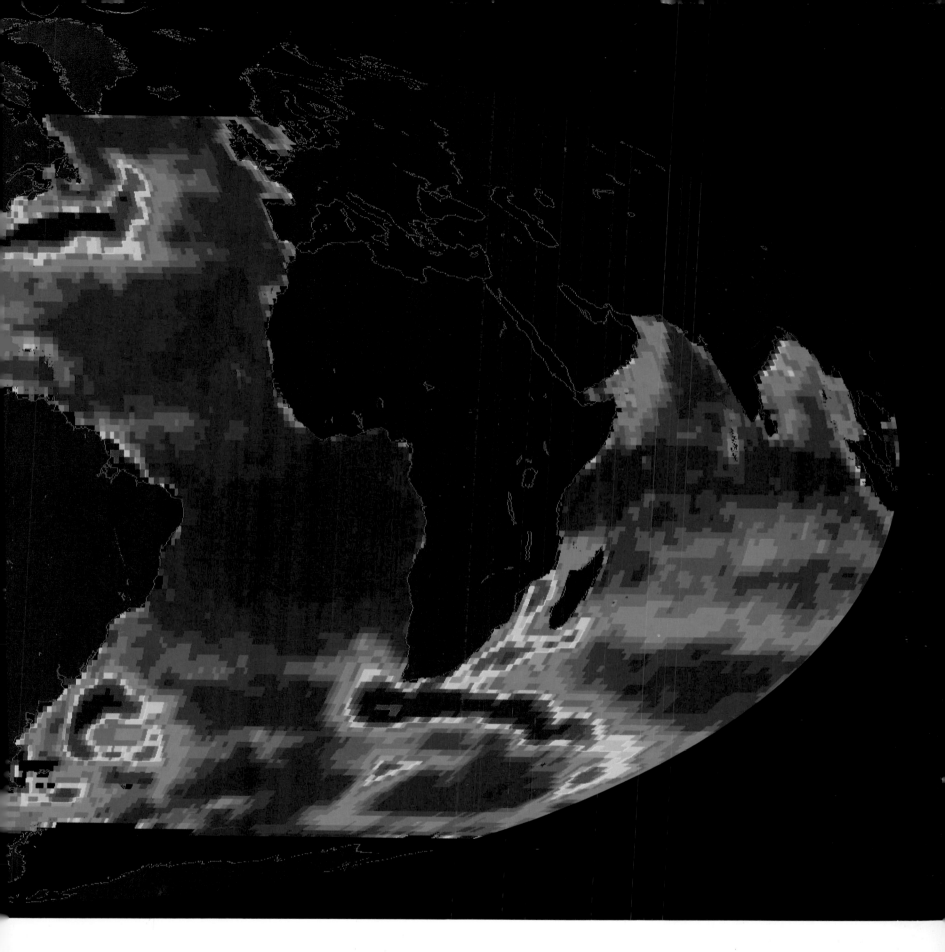

heat than the atmosphere and gives it up slowly, thus moderating temperatures.

Water vapor is the most changing constituent of the atmosphere and is a main contributor to the greenhouse effect that warms our planet. As a solid in the form of snow and ice, water further influences the heat distribution on Earth.

Traditionally the oceans have been studied by ship surveys. But this is a very costly and time-consuming effort and can never give a complete picture of the entire ocean at one time. Satellite imagery and a wide variety of ocean sensors offer the unique opportunity to study the water of our planet both globally and locally. Some sensors have gathered more data in three months than oceanographic sampling did in one hundred years. When combined with data collected by ships, buoys, and current

meters, satellite imagery gives us a more accurate view of the global oceans.

The global ocean currents shown above were recorded by an altimeter using a radar beam that measures the distance between the spacecraft and the sea surface with a precision of two inches. This image of the differences in the height of the sea surface is a composite of millions of repeated measurements taken over a three-month period. The topography of the ocean surface is directly related to the fluctuation of its currents. The most active, rapid-moving currents show the most variability; slower currents show less change. The major strong currents, known as Western Boundary Currents, are seen in red and orange. These currents include the Gulf Stream in the North Atlantic, the Kuroshio of Japan, the Agulhas Current of South Africa, and the Brazil Falkland off South America.

The red patches around Antarctica are part of the West Wind Drift. The satellite sensors revealed the relatively calm nature of the ocean currents (seen as blue) over most of the ocean surface.

Water is everywhere, in crashing waves, drenching storms, and rivers eroding the land. Moist soil allows plants to grow, and large reservoirs and small wells quench our thirst. By understanding water and its flow, we expand our penetration of the mystery of this almost magical substance on which many people desperately depend, and which others often take for granted.

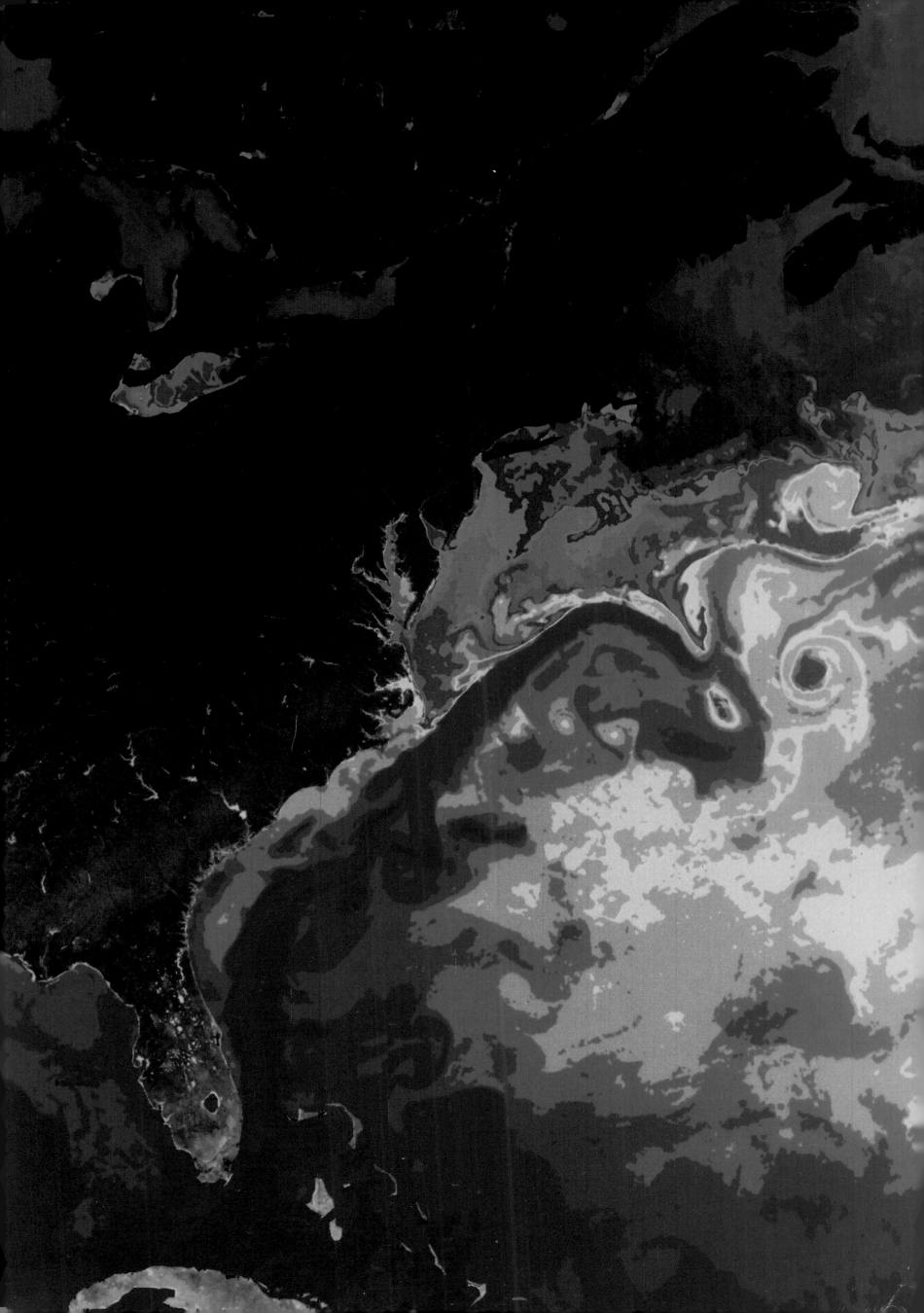

63

Dead Sea, Israel, and Jordan. The process of continental drift not only forms mountain ranges when the Earth's plates collide, but also creates other important geologic features. In certain regions, the spreading of the Earth can result in the formation of new oceans or seas, such as the Gulf of California. The splitting of the Arabian Peninsula from Africa 35 million years ago created the Red Sea. The same forces caused a rift valley, or trench, in the Earth's crust separating what is now Israel and Jordan. The images here are a pictorial sequence zooming in on the Dead Sea.

▲ The image on the top left is an overview of Israel, Jordan, Lebanon, and Syria. Israel bounds the Mediterranean Sea and appears dark green-brown due to the extensive agricultural development in the arid tan desert, clearly defined at the border between Israel and Egypt in the lower left. The Dead Sea is at the bottom, and the Sea of Galilee is at the top. The rift valley between them is seen as a lighter line to the right of the Jordan River, which connects them. The river separates Israel from Jordan and Syria.

The image on the top right shows the Dead Sea with the Jordan River flowing into it from the north. The river descends in elevation as it flows through the rift valley at the top of the image, dropping from 700 feet above sea level to 1,300 feet below sea level when it enters the Dead Sea. The numerous hot springs that surround the Dead Sea reflect the geologic activity in the region. Tel Aviv, Israel, is the dark gray area on the Mediterranean coast partially obscured by clouds. The Dead Sea is shrinking due to evaporation and has the highest salinity of any body of water in the world.

► The detailed image of the southern portion of the Dead Sea shows the evaporation flats (in light blue) that are being used for commercial salt and mineral production.

NINETY-SEVEN PERCENT OF EGYPT'S POPULATION LIVE AND WORK ALONG THE
NILE RIVER, WHICH REPRESENTS ONLY 2-1/2 PERCENT OF THE LAND.

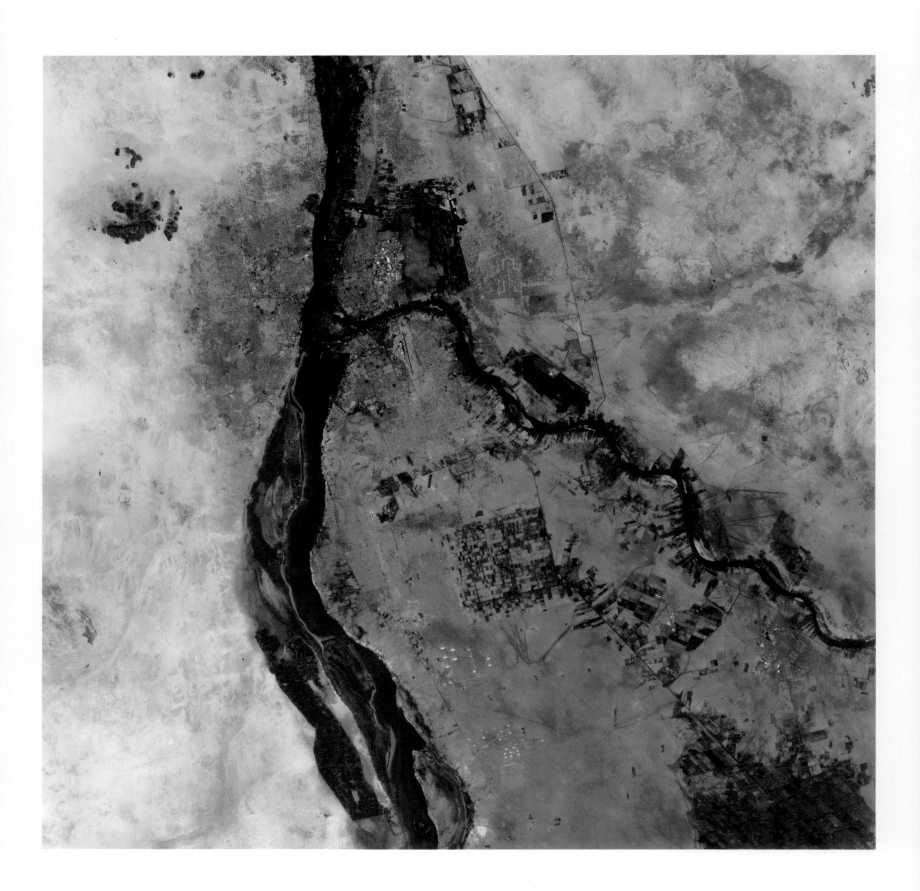

Nile River Flood Cycle. The flooding of the Nile River into its valleys was a symbol of resurrection for the ancient desert civilizations of Africa. The yearly flood enriched the land with water and nutrients. Since most of this region is desert, with little rainfall, the overflowing of the river beyond its banks was seen as miraculous. For thousands of years, the Nile sustained the agriculture that allowed the Egyptian civilization to evolve and prosper.

The annual flood cycle of the Nile River continues to bring to the surrounding land rich mud and soft silt—the natural fertilizers that allow crops to flourish. We now know its waters come from the mountains of Ethiopia and the highlands of east Africa. These two images compare the Nile before and after flooding in Khartoum, the capital of Sudan.

◄ Taken before the flood, this image shows the narrow Blue Nile flowing into the broader White Nile. The urban areas of the capital city are gray-blue, the vegetation is red, and the surrounding desert is tan. Here the Nile merges into one river from its two branches: the White Nile, to the west, and the Blue Nile, to the east.

▼ When the White Nile overflows its banks, the width of the river triples in some regions, leaving a few small islands, which are higher in elevation. The Blue Nile doubles in width. Numerous ponds and lakes are scattered throughout Khartoum. Increased cultivation is seen in the rectangular grid in the center of the image.

► **Kuskokwim River, United States.** Water plays a critical role in the erosion of the land. Rivers are one of the main forces that cut through the landscape and carry sediments on their journey to the sea. The sediments often contain nutrients important for the growth of marine life. As the rivers enter the ocean, they deposit sediments in fan-shaped deltas.

The radar sensor that took this image of the Kuskokwim River in Alaska and its sediment deposits in Kuskokwim Bay, an inlet of the Bering Sea, operates independent of weather and sunlight. Because radar sensors can penetrate clouds and transmit images day or night, they are very useful in providing high-resolution images of polar regions such as those in Alaska, where clouds and darkness are frequent.

The 600-mile-long Kuskokwim drains the large Kuskokwim Mountains in central Alaska. The sediment deposits are the dark areas in the bay and along the coastline. They are separated by bright, curving water channels, which are deeper than the darker deposits. The appearance of the channel changes daily due to the combination of strong tidal forces, the variable flow of the river into the bay, and local wind conditions.

▼ **Denali National Park, United States.** A stream fed by melting ice flows down from the lower mountain ranges of central Alaska.

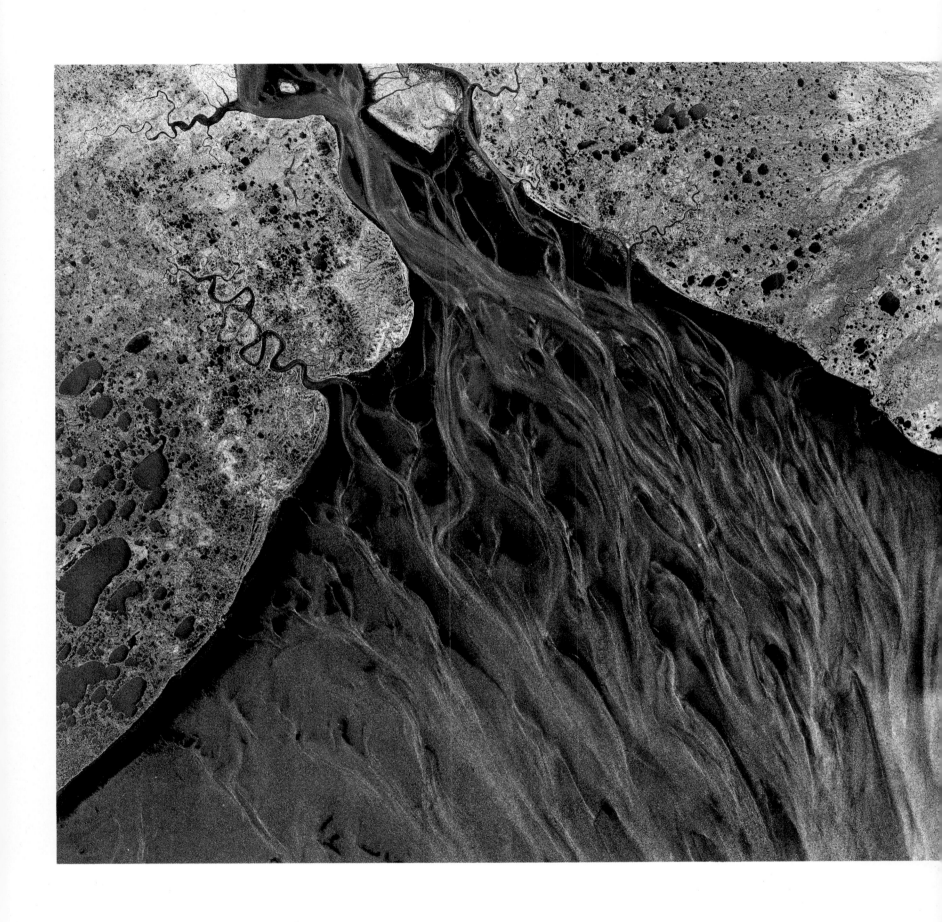

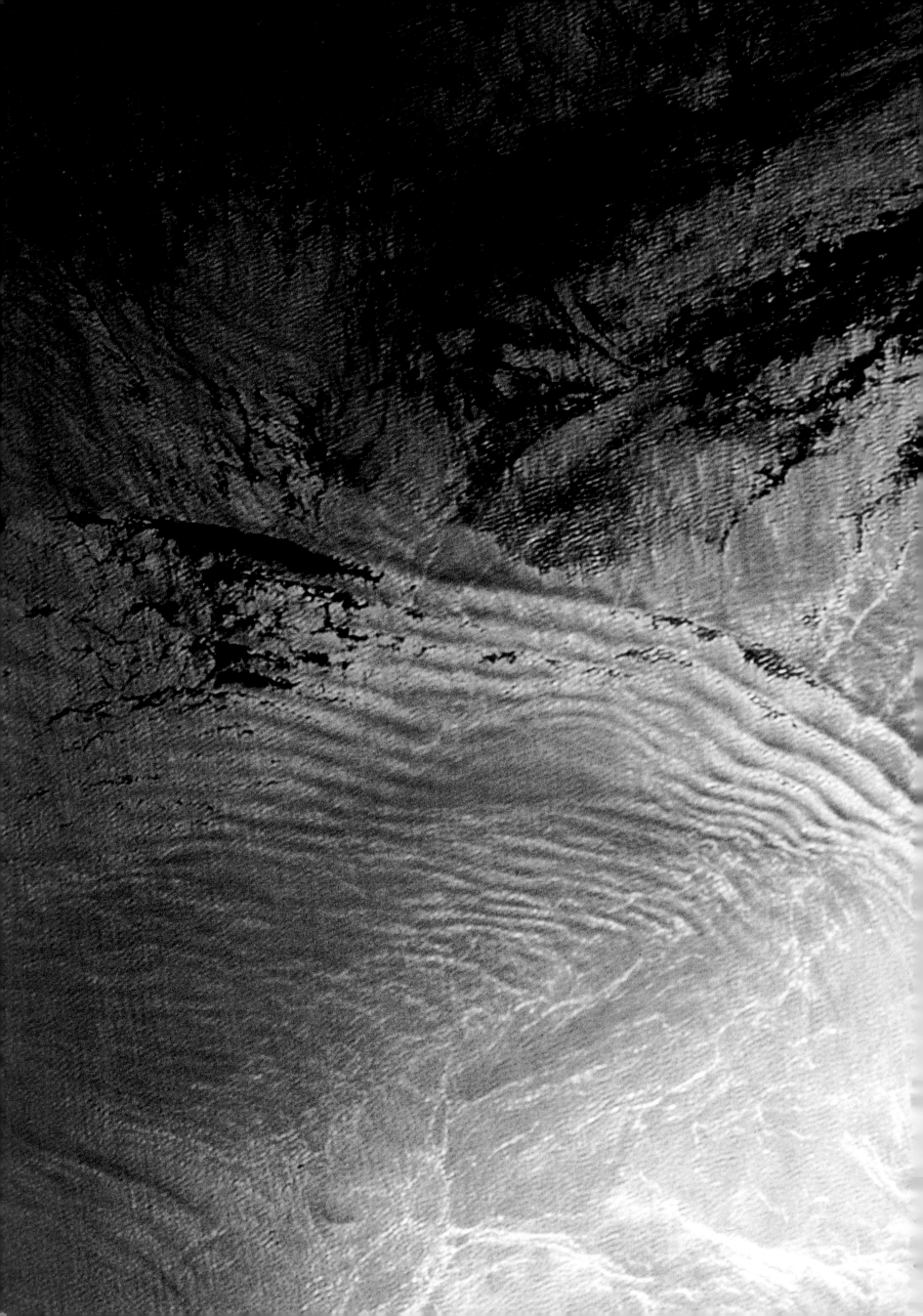

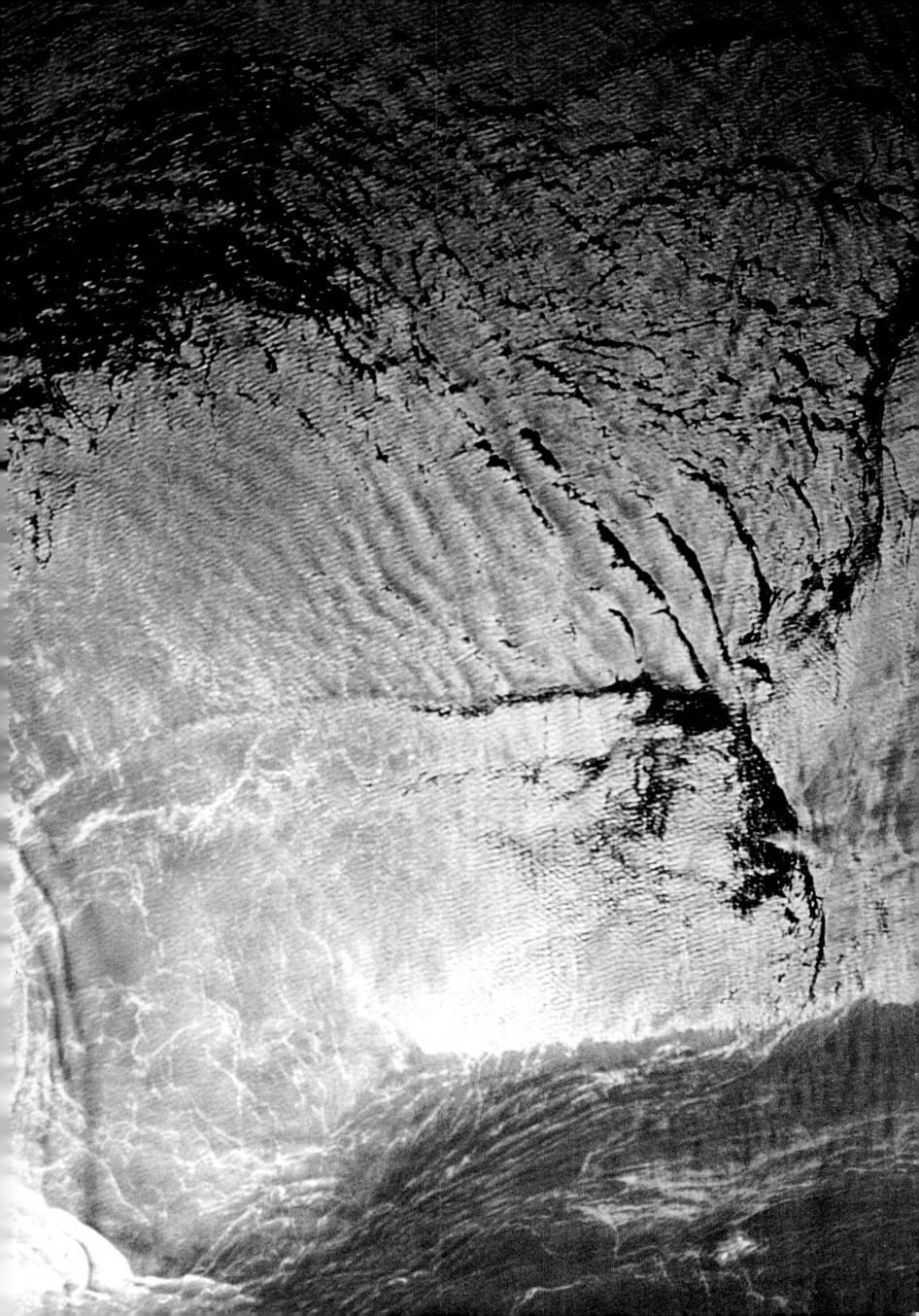

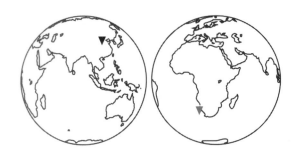

► **Yangtze River, China.** The flow of rivers plays a very important role in the water cycle by carrying fresh water and sediments to the ocean. The long journey often starts with snow melting in distant mountains and rain filling streams that eventually merge with rivers. As the streams and rivers head to the sea, they bring dissolved salts and minerals from the land. Throughout the great clock of geologic time, this process contributed to the salinity of the ocean.

Rivers are also important conduits of transportation for human activity. Many great cities grew along large rivers. Here, the Yangtze River, or Chang Jiang, flows past the city of Shanghai, on the east coast of China, on its way to the East China Sea. Shanghai is the dark black-gray region at the center bottom of the image. A tributary, the Huangpu Jiang, joins the Yangtze. Variations in the aqua-green of the river reflect the presence of sediment and probable pollution. The river is approximately 25 miles wide at this point. Islands at the mouth of the Yangtze include part of the long Chongming Dao, shown at the top of the image, and the smaller Ruifengsha, below it to the right.

◄◄ **Internal Waves, Atlantic Ocean** (previous pages). Alternating bands of smooth and rough water at the sea surface commonly occur in coastal waters. These patterns reflect surface currents caused by deeper ocean movements known as internal waves, which have best been observed by satellite sensors and Space Shuttle cameras. The formation of internal waves is still not completely understood but is known to be related to the topography of the ocean bottom as well as to the action of the tides. These waves play an important role in helping to mix coastal waters and increase their fertility.

Shown here are internal waves in the coastal Atlantic, off Africa, covering an area of 30 square miles. Two arc-shaped wave trains can be seen converging in the center of the image. The sunglint on the water reveals the complex details of the ocean surface formed by winds, currents, and internal waves. In the darker areas at the top of the image, the sunglint pattern is obscured by winds that ruffle the sea surface.

Impact Crater Lake, Elgygytgyn, Siberia.
Nearly 4 million years ago, an asteroid struck
the Earth in northeastern Siberia and formed
an immense crater called the Elgygytgyn
impact crater. The remoteness of the region
prevented the crater from being discovered
until the early 1960s. Its extraterrestrial origin
was not determined until the 1970s. The
diameter of the crater's rim is approximately
12 miles, and the surrounding area contains
material dispersed from the asteroid's impact.

Satellites have provided unique tools to
study inaccessible regions such as this one
in Siberia and to understand the evolution
of landforms. We can imagine that the
immediate impact of the asteroid would have
resulted in extensive destruction to the land
and forest. After millions of years, water
flowing from many small rivers and streams
filled the crater. In this image, rivers and
streams are thin blue lines, vegetation is red,
and exposed landforms are gray-green.

Its substance reaches everywhere;
it touches the past and prepares
the future; it moves under the
poles and wanders thinly in the
heights of the air....
If there is magic on the planet,
it is contained in water.

Loren Eiseley, naturalist

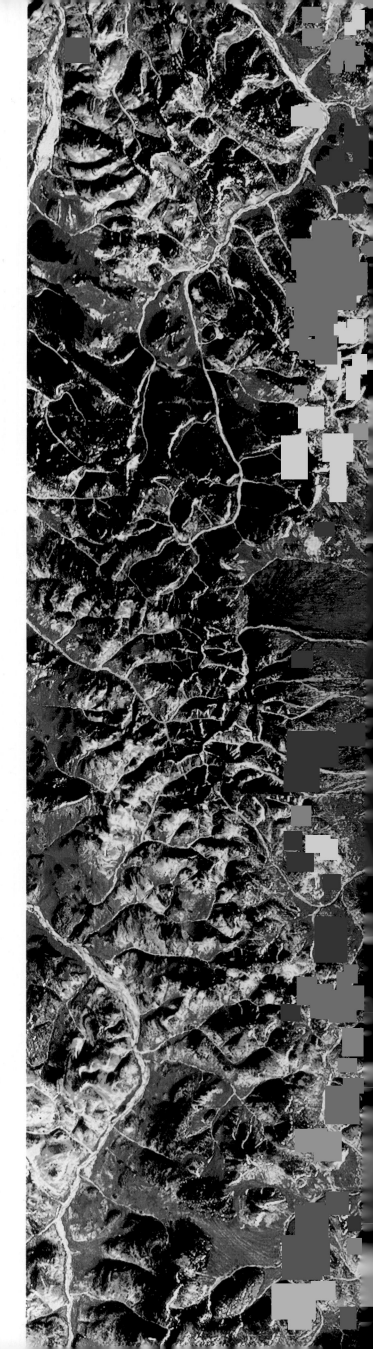

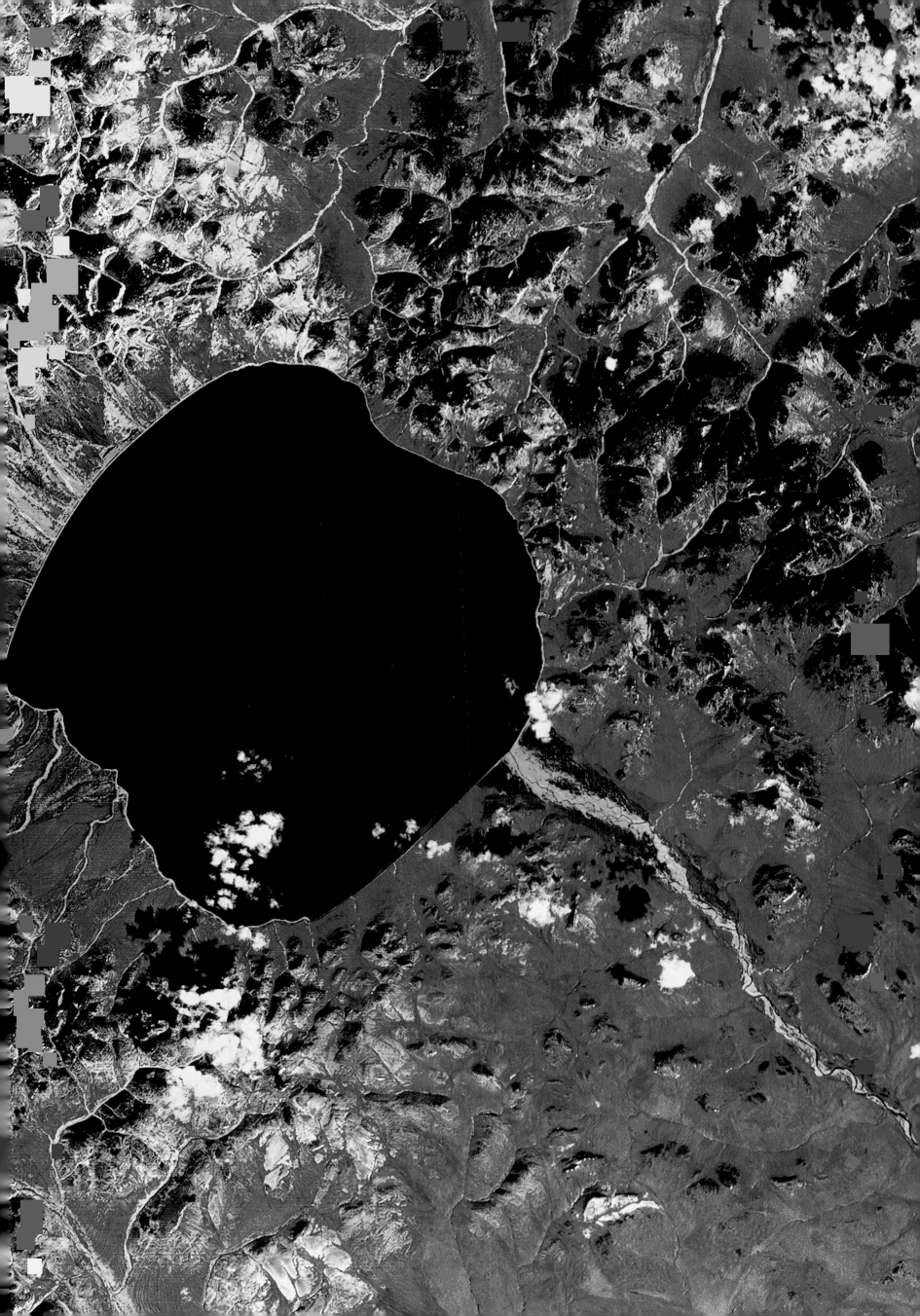

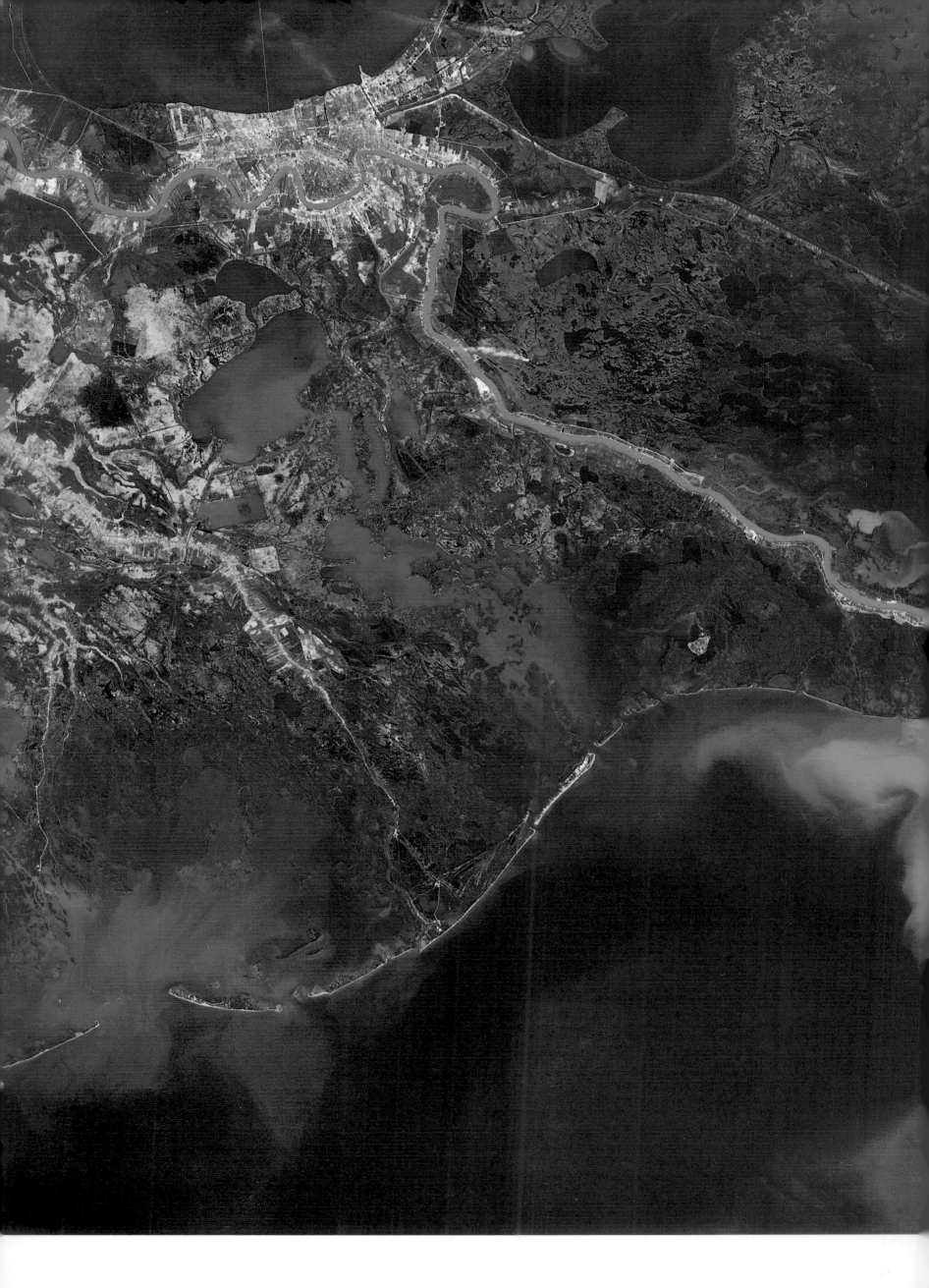

Mississippi River Delta, United States.
River deltas have played an important role in the development of civilizations since ancient times. The word *delta* is derived from the fourth letter of the Greek alphabet, which is triangular in shape. This same shape is formed by sediments that are deposited by rivers flowing into larger bodies of water.

The Mississippi River, the largest river system in North America, drains over 2 million square miles between the Appalachian Mountains to the east, the Rocky Mountains to the west, and Canada to the north. As the river winds south to the Gulf of Mexico, it carries the eroded land suspended in its flow. The sediment load discharged by this great river has been estimated to be over 5 billion pounds annually. The sediments are deposited onto the continental shelf in a pattern known as a birdsfoot delta.

Seen here is the birdsfoot delta of the Mississippi River reaching into the Gulf of Mexico and covering an area of approximately 625 square miles. The sediments carried by the Mississippi force the flow to split into several channels. Vegetation is red. A network of marshes is at the very tip of the river channels. Light blue plumes of muddy water spread into the gulf. The white regions are areas of developed land on the natural levees along the course of the Mississippi.

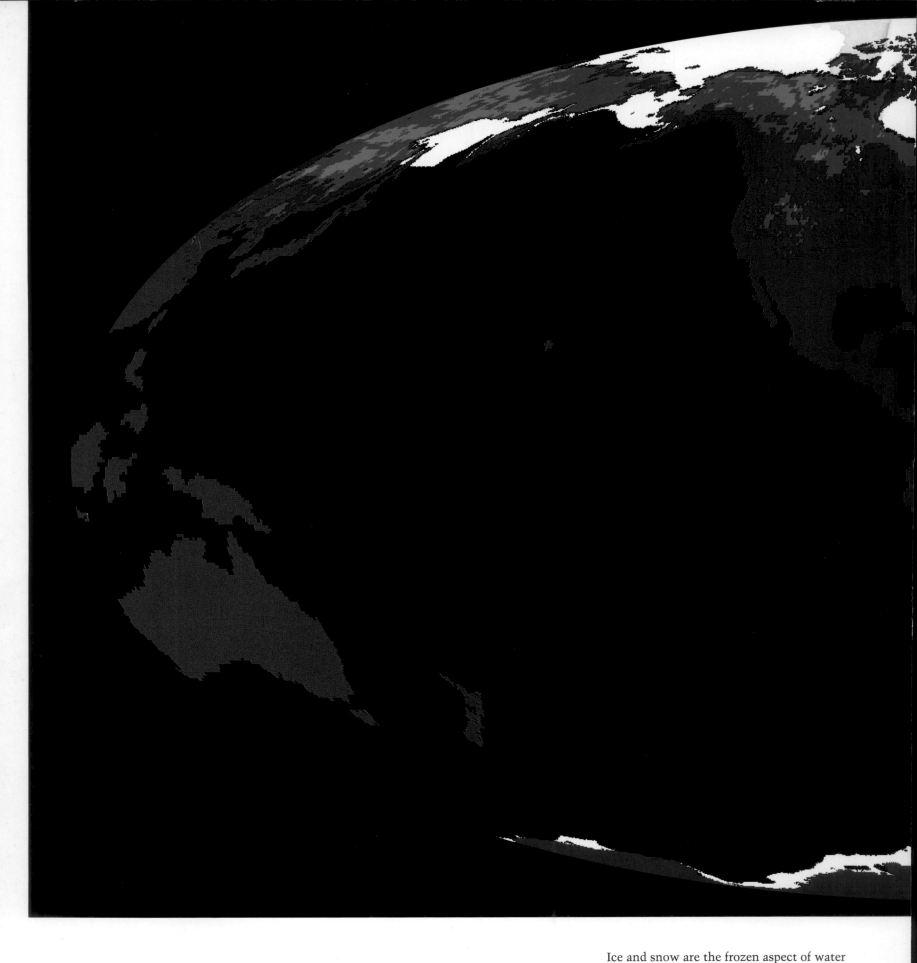

ICE

Ice and snow are the frozen aspect of water and in this unique form play a crucial role in the Earth's climate and heat transport system. The orbit and inclination of the Earth cause the predominant locations of ice and snow to exist in the polar regions, though even at the equator snow can be found at high altitudes. The history of our planet includes many cycles of warming and cooling. There is evidence that massive glacial activity occurred over 2 billion years ago, and there have been at least six ice ages in the last 1 million years. The process of planetary cooling, encompassing periods of glacial advance and retreat, can last millions of years.

The movement of ice sheets during different glacial periods may have influenced the social evolution of the human species, as resources were more limited during times of cooling than during warmer periods. Early humans had to learn to hunt, make clothing

and tools, and communicate more effectively to survive in the colder climate. These challenges created by climate change required adaptations that may have stimulated the development of the human mind and of human society.

Today we know that snow and ice play major roles in shaping our planet. Glaciers are major agents of erosion. They often follow valleys cut by streams and rivers. As glaciers grow and move downslope, they carry huge boulders that gouge the land underneath. When glaciers melt, they leave behind jumbled deposits of rocks and gravel. Ice sheets can cover whole continents, as in Antarctica, an area larger than the United States and Mexico combined. Antarctica holds 90 percent of the Earth's ice, and in places the ice sheet is over 2 miles thick.

The temperature difference between the poles and the equator is one of the main climate engines driving the large-scale circulation of the atmosphere and the oceans. Warm air and water move toward the poles, redistributing heat, water, gases, and nutrients on a global scale. These processes help determine the climate and habitability of our planet.

Among the unique aspects of the polar regions are major annual cycles of snow on land and ice at sea which influence regional and global temperatures. Land and sea experience rigorous cold during the continuous darkness of the winter months. If the ice sheets of Antarctica and Greenland were to melt entirely, the global sea level would rise by over 200 feet. Sea ice also influences the circulation of ocean waters: as temperatures drop, the colder, denser water at the poles sinks and moves to lower latitudes.

The remoteness and inhospitable conditions of the polar regions and of certain mountainous areas on the planet make research difficult, if not impossible. Satellites have helped to overcome these limitations by providing long-term measurements of both land and sea. Passive sensors that measure light and microwave radiation can indicate the extent and type of sea ice, and radar sensors can measure the volume of ice and snow.

The image here shows global snow and ice cover. Sea ice is white; shallow snow, dark blue; moderate snow, medium blue; and deep snow (greater than a foot), light blue. The permanent ice caps of Antarctica and Greenland are purple.

The annual cycles of ice and snow have deep roots in our prehistory, during the ice ages. Today the potential of global warming caused by human activity makes early detection of any changes in snow and ice levels critical for the economic and social well-being of the world.

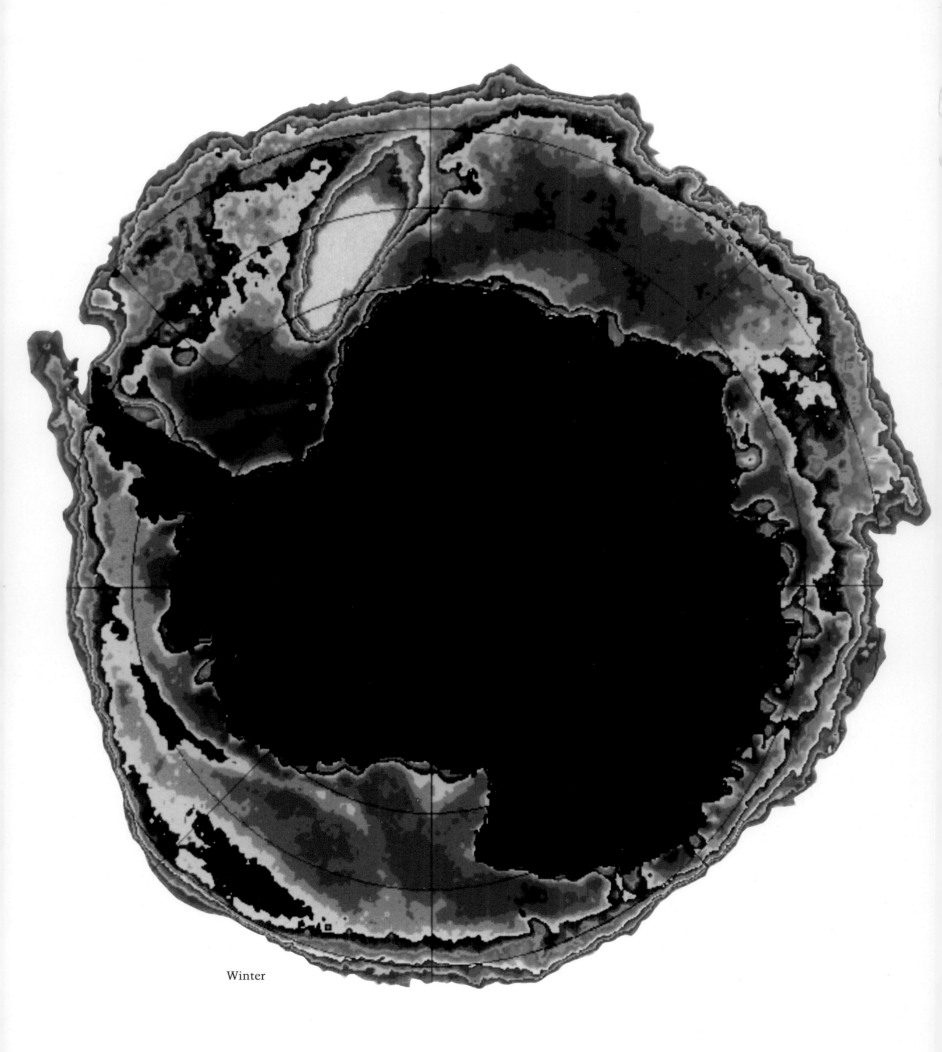

Winter

Antarctic Sea Ice. Antarctica is a foreboding continent. Shrouded in darkness for half the year, it is a desert of ice with the coldest temperatures and fiercest winds ever recorded anywhere on Earth. Its ice and snow influence the Earth's climate, acting as an insulating barrier that regulates the rate at which heat is transferred between the atmosphere and the oceans.

Until the advent of satellite observations, annual and year-to-year changes of polar sea-ice cover were very difficult to obtain and measure accurately. Satellites with microwave sensors allow continuous monitoring of sea ice day or night, even through cloud cover. Microwave radiation is naturally emitted from the Earth's surface, just as heat radiation is emitted from our bodies or from hot rocks on a summer day. Scientists are able to convert these microwave measurements into ice concentrations through a series of mathematical formulas.

This series of images shows seasonal patterns in the freezing and melting of sea ice around Antarctica. The Antarctic landmass is in black. Ice concentration decreases from high levels near the coast (red) to low levels near the outer ice margins (blue and green). Four main Antarctic seasons, from winter through the following fall, are depicted. In winter, Antarctic sea ice covers an area greater than the United States. Ice extends more than 600 miles out from the continent in areas such as the Ross and Weddell seas. During the summer, continuous daylight and heat melt more than 80 percent of the winter ice. These massive seasonal expansions and contractions strongly interact with the atmosphere to affect climate. Any long-term increase or decrease in sea-ice cover may provide an early warning of climate change, a critical monitoring capability available only from satellites.

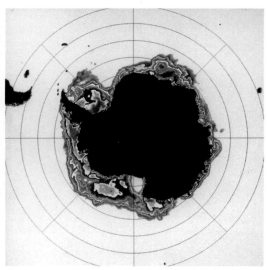

Spring

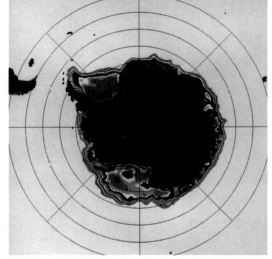

Summer

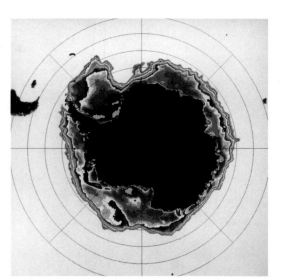

Fall

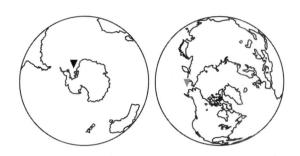

► **Weddell Sea, Antarctica.** A year in Antarctica consists of months of continuous darkness in winter, followed by months of continuous daylight in summer. The annual breakup of the vast sea ice around Antarctica begins with the growing daylight hours and the effect of the sun's warmth. By the end of summer, the sea ice surrounding the continent has diminished by over 80 percent.

In this image, thousands of icebergs have broken off, or calved, from the Filchner Ice Shelf in the Weddell Sea. The ice shelf, in the lower left, with a thickness of hundreds of feet, is a smooth white. The large, trapezoidal iceberg in the center is approximately 3-1/2 by 5-1/2 miles. A smaller iceberg has been heaved, or rafted, on top of it by the currents and moving masses of ice. Sea ice, in between the icebergs, is light blue, and open water is black.

▼ **Bering Sea, the Arctic.** Annual cycles of melting and freezing affect the Arctic as they do Antarctica. In this photograph of first-year ice floes in the Bering Sea, a small-scale version of ice rafting can be seen in the upper right.

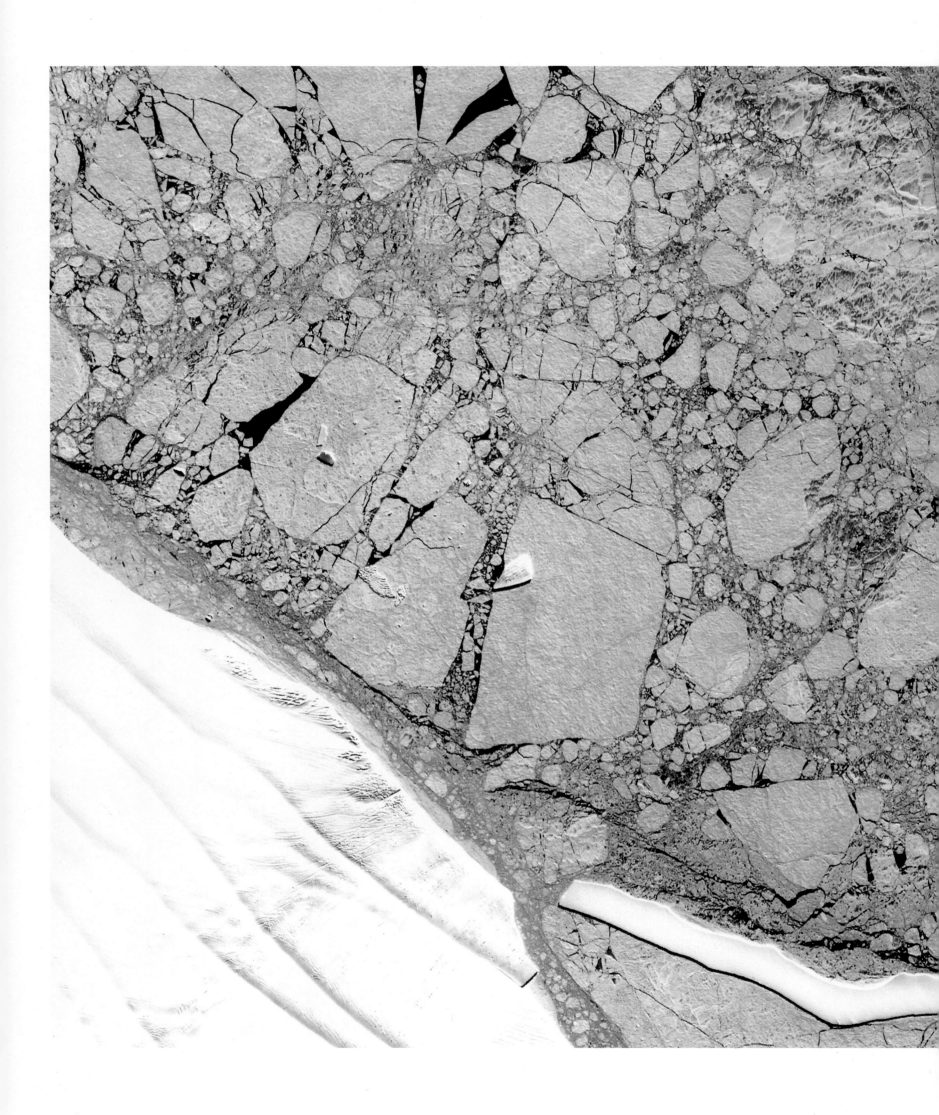

**▶ Byrd Glacier and Ross Ice Shelf,
Antarctica.** Antarctica contains 90 percent
of all the Earth's ice. Its glaciers move ice
from the continent's interior to the sea.
Yet little is known about these glaciers
compared with those in populated regions
such as Switzerland or Alaska. Satellites
provide essential data about their features,
properties, and movement.

Polar ice responds to warming by melting
and flowing from the land and eventually
toward the ocean, thus decreasing in size.
With cooler temperatures, more snow falls
and compacts to ice, thereby increasing a
glacier's size. Long-term warming can cause
a rise in global sea levels. Cooling will result
in the opposite effect: a decrease in sea levels.
Understanding these dynamic changes—the
surge and retreat of glaciers—gives us insight
into past and future climatic environments.

Here we see a false-color image of the
Byrd Glacier and Ross Ice Shelf. Scientists
use satellite and aerial photography to track
changes and movement in glaciers. They
have determined that each year the Byrd
Glacier flows seaward at a rate of 1,300 feet
and discharges some 11 cubic miles of ice
into the Ross Ice Shelf.

▲ Elephant Island, Antarctica. Calving
icebergs and glacier.

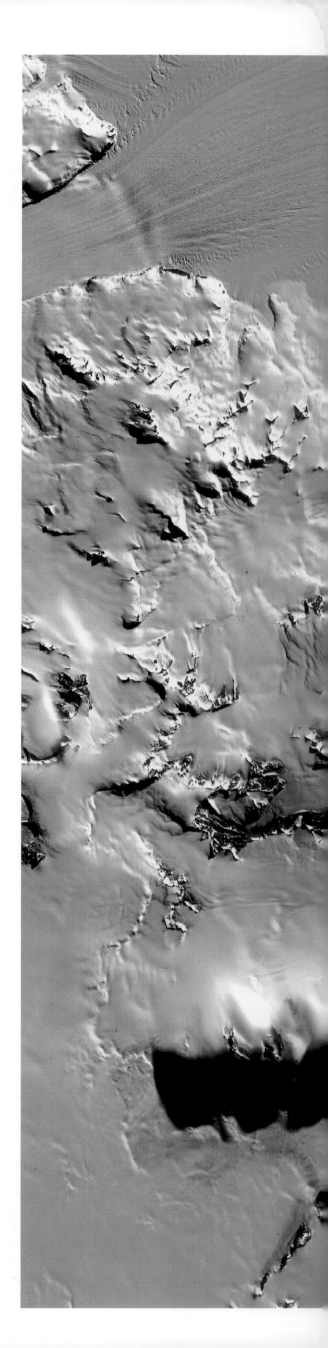

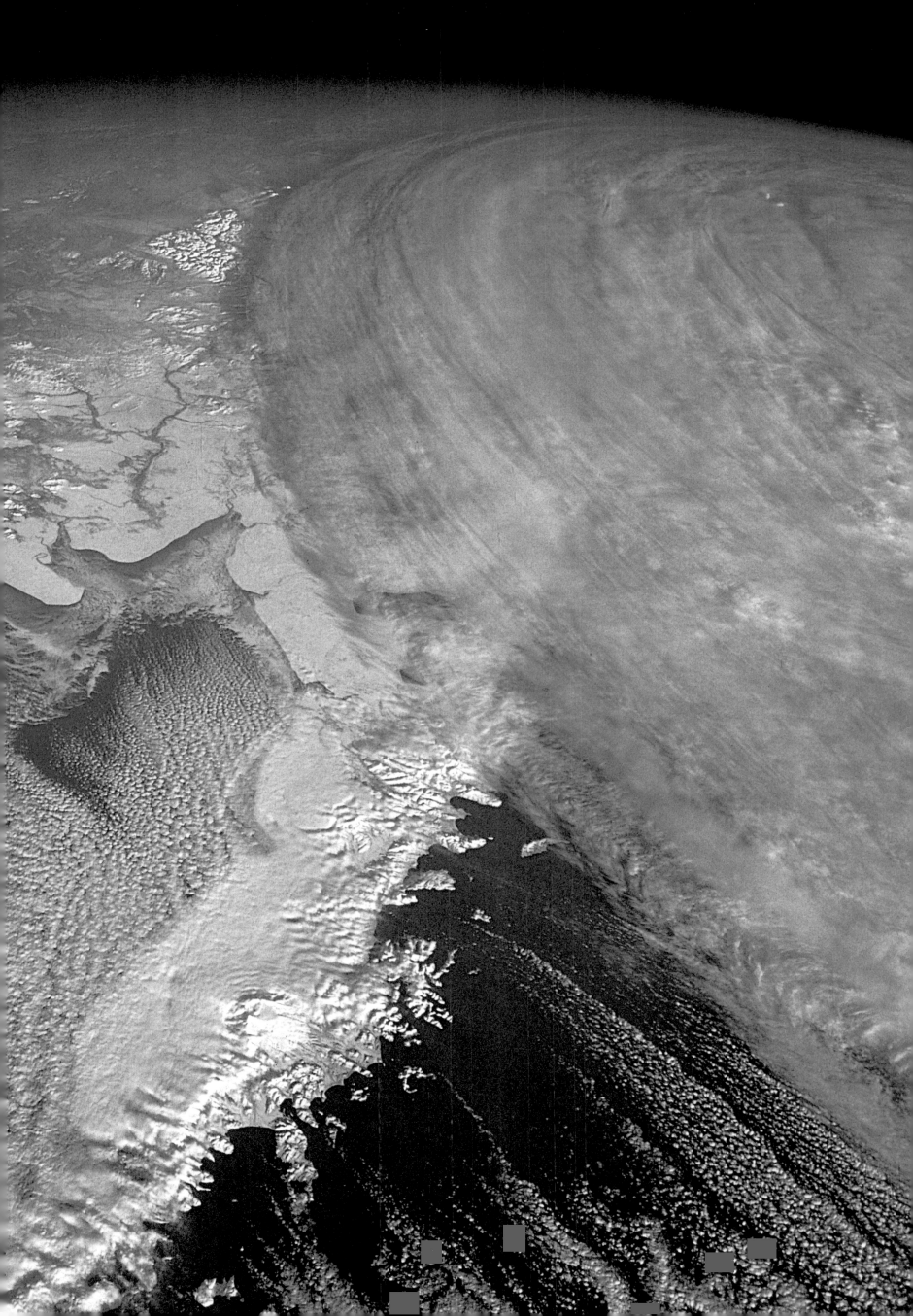

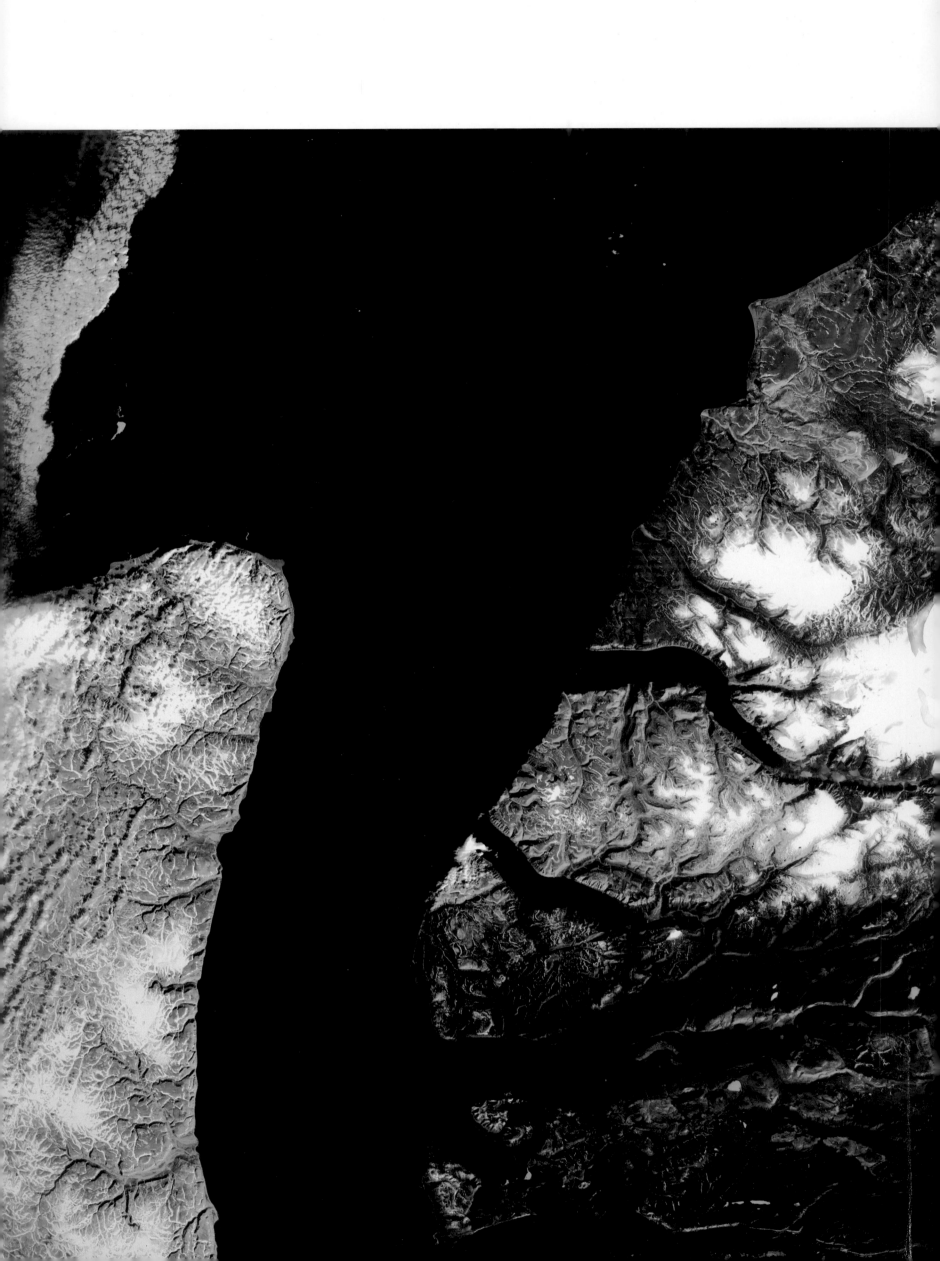

Baffin Island, Canada. Part of the Northwest Territories of Canada, Baffin is the largest island of the Canadian Arctic Archipelago. Admiralty Inlet, a 180-mile-long fjord at the northern tip of the island, empties into Lancaster Sound. The inlet, in the center of this image, is bounded by two peninsulas: Brodeur, to the lower left, and Borden, to the right. Ice is white and shades of blue; glaciers are dark gray-blue. The deep glaciated valleys along the inlet fill with water to form smaller fjords.

*From dark and icy caverns
    called you forth,
Down those precipitous, black,
    jagged rocks,
Forever shattered, and the
    same forever?
Who gave you invulnerable life,
Your strength, your speed,
    your fury and your joy,
Unceasing thunder and
    eternal foam?*

Samuel Taylor Coleridge, poet

◄ **Hubbard Glacier, United States.** The end of the last ice age, about ten thousand years ago, signaled a climatic warming and the retreat of massive glaciers that had covered most of North America. The advance and retreat of glaciers are part of the cycle of temperature and climate shifts on the Earth. Glacial advances can change the local ecology, alter the course of rivers, and destroy human habitation. Glacial retreats can open new bays and expose the underlying land.

High-altitude aerial photography provides the most accurate view of the Earth's surface and shows changes in polar regions that are normally difficult to monitor. This aerial view of the Hubbard Glacier, near Yakutat in southeast Alaska, was taken during a very dramatic event, in May 1986, when the glacier advanced rapidly and sealed the entrance to Russell Fjord. The white glacier, with its compressed pressure ridges, dominates the upper portion of the photograph. It encroaches on the landmass known as Gilbert Point. Russell Fjord is on the right, and Disenchantment Bay is at the bottom. The vegetation appears red; the snow, bright white. The small ice dam closing the entrance to Russell Fjord has transformed the fjord into Russell Lake.

Four months after this picture was taken, the ice dam failed and discharged 1.3 cubic miles of lake water into the bay. The outburst was thought to have produced the greatest short-lived discharge of water in North America in the last ten thousand years.

▼ **Mendenhall Glacier, United States.** The foot of the Mendenhall Glacier, near Juneau, Alaska, as it enters the Lynn Canal.

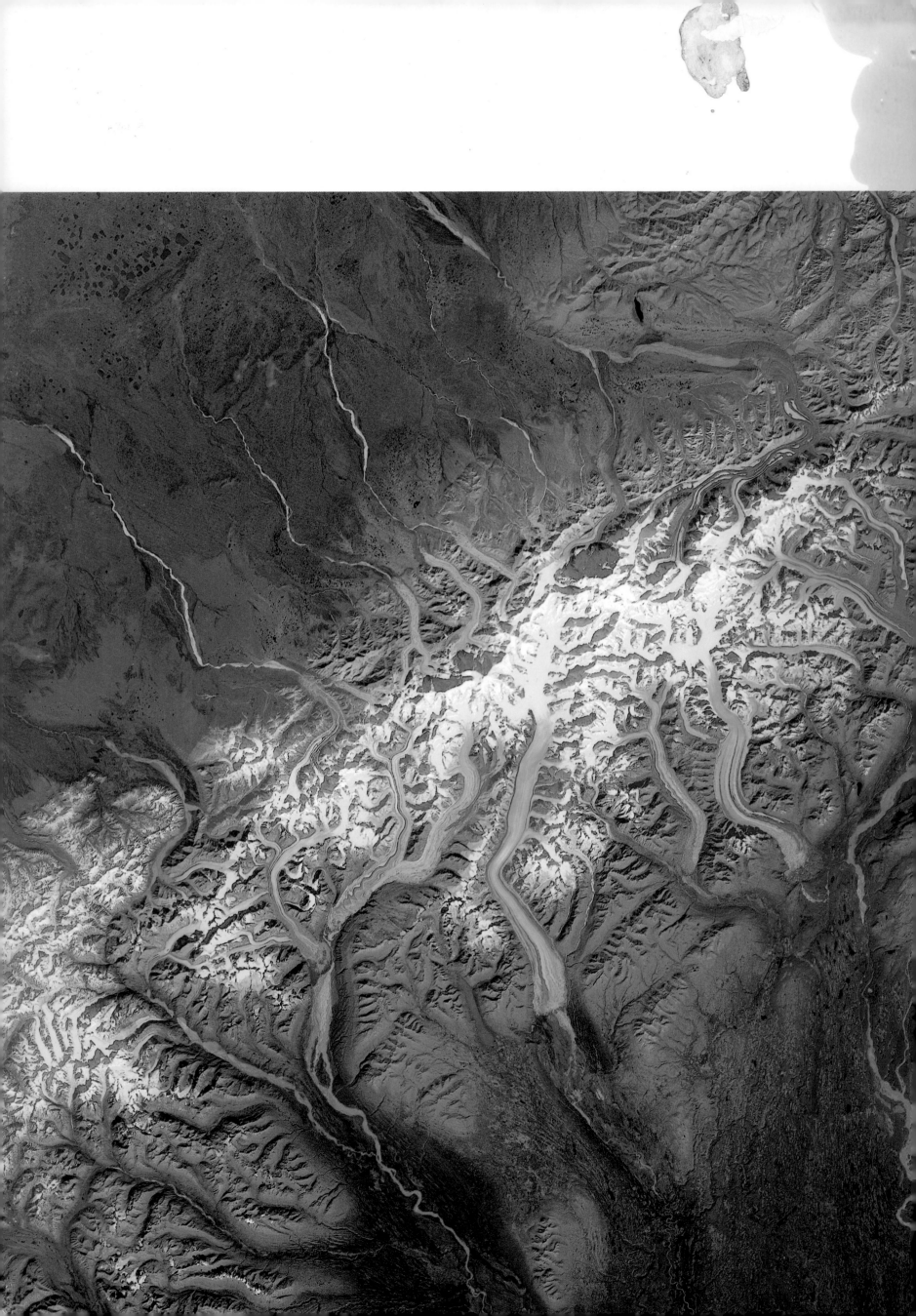

Denali National Park, United States. The Alaska Range is a magnificent chain of mountains towering over vast stretches of untouched wilderness. Although most of the mountains are between 7,000 and 9,000 feet in elevation, the range holds the highest mountain in North America. Reaching 20,320 feet, it is commonly known as Mount McKinley. To native Alaskans, it is Denali—"the high one."

Like other great mountain ranges, the Alaska Range is part of a region where geologic plates come in contact. Here they represent the largest crustal break in North America, running 1,300 miles across the full width of Alaska. The range also forms an important divide where rivers flow either to the south into the Gulf of Alaska or to the west into the Bering Sea.

In this false-color image, Denali National Park, with its many white-topped mountains, is in the center. Numerous blue-green glaciers flow to the northwest or the southeast. Mount McKinley is at the center of the mountain range, directly above Tokositma Glacier, which is to the right of the longer Kahiltna Glacier. The glaciers have helped sculpt the spectacular, sharp relief of Denali. Rivers fed by the glaciers are dark blue; vegetation is red.

TWENTY THOUSAND YEARS AGO, ICE COVERED
ONE-THIRD OF THE EARTH'S LAND SURFACE—MORE THAN THREE
TIMES THE AREA OF TODAY'S GLACIERS.

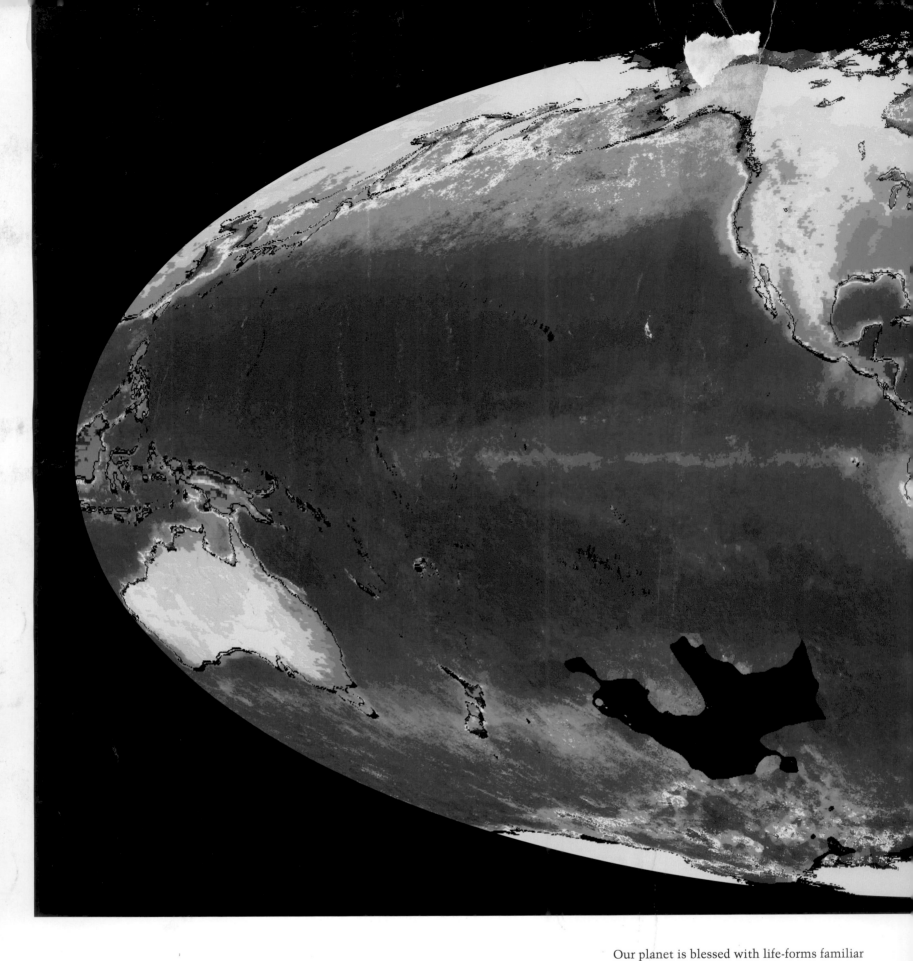

LIFE

Our planet is blessed with life-forms familiar and bizarre, in all sizes and shapes. Life has thundered through the past on the footsteps of giant dinosaurs and lies hidden as tiny bacteria living in thermal vents deep within the ocean. Plants provide the oxygen essential for all life on Earth and are the basis for almost all food chains. Animals create an intricate web of hunter and hunted, leading to wonderful adaptations of survival and ingenuity: from the acute vision of the soaring falcon to the complex social structure of the industrious ant. Some forms, such as the bristlecone pine, can live over four thousand years; others, such as bacteria, reproduce themselves within hours. Life has penetrated nearly all the regions of the planet, from lichens in frozen Antarctica to blue whales migrating throughout the oceans.

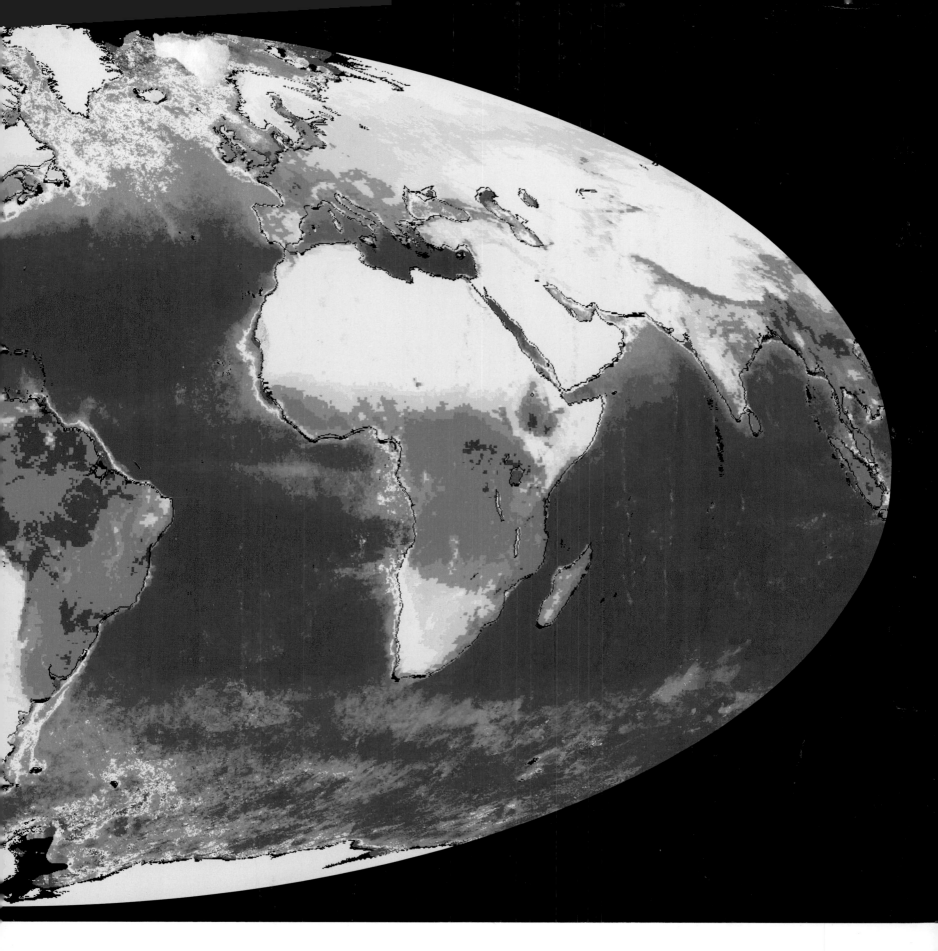

The plants and animals in this diverse tapestry have their own rhythms, with cycles of birth, maturity, reproduction, and death. Humans have observed these cycles for a long time and taken advantage of them to grow and harvest crops for food and medicine, and to hunt animals for nourishment and clothing.

Our fascination with and observations of life have had many expressions. In rural societies today, as in prehistory, women gather food to sustain the tribe between hunts. Shamans and medicine people collect wild herbs and barks to heal and soothe. Scientists observe life-forms in the field and the laboratory, seeking to decipher their natural history, physiology, and behavior.

We are only recently at the point where we can study life from space. It is not with the detail that enables us to count the number of corn stalks in a field or to observe the behavior of gorillas in the wild. Satellites can, however, track the movements of animals banded with radio receivers that emit a signal. Currently, the most powerful use of satellites is to measure the amount of vegetation covering the Earth. Sensors can measure the amount and type of plant cover on land and the total biomass of plant life in the water.

The satellite image shown above is the first truly global view of plant life on the planet. One of the most striking features is found in the oceans where vast areas are as unproductive as any desert (seen as violet and blue). The main productive plant life is in the coastal regions (seen as yellow-red-orange). Here river runoff and upwelling from within the ocean provide nutrients essential for marine plants, known as phytoplankton, to grow. On land, the most productive regions are green, while those areas with less vegetation are tan and yellow. Like the ocean, vast areas of land are deserts with very little productivity.

Eventually satellites will allow us to describe with great detail the types of vegetation on the ground. For now, these global and regional images are the first step in understanding the extent of vegetation and its annual cycles. They help to identify where deserts may be expanding, when the planet's annual greening begins, and how human impact through agriculture, forestry, and fishing is affecting the sustainability of these same resources.

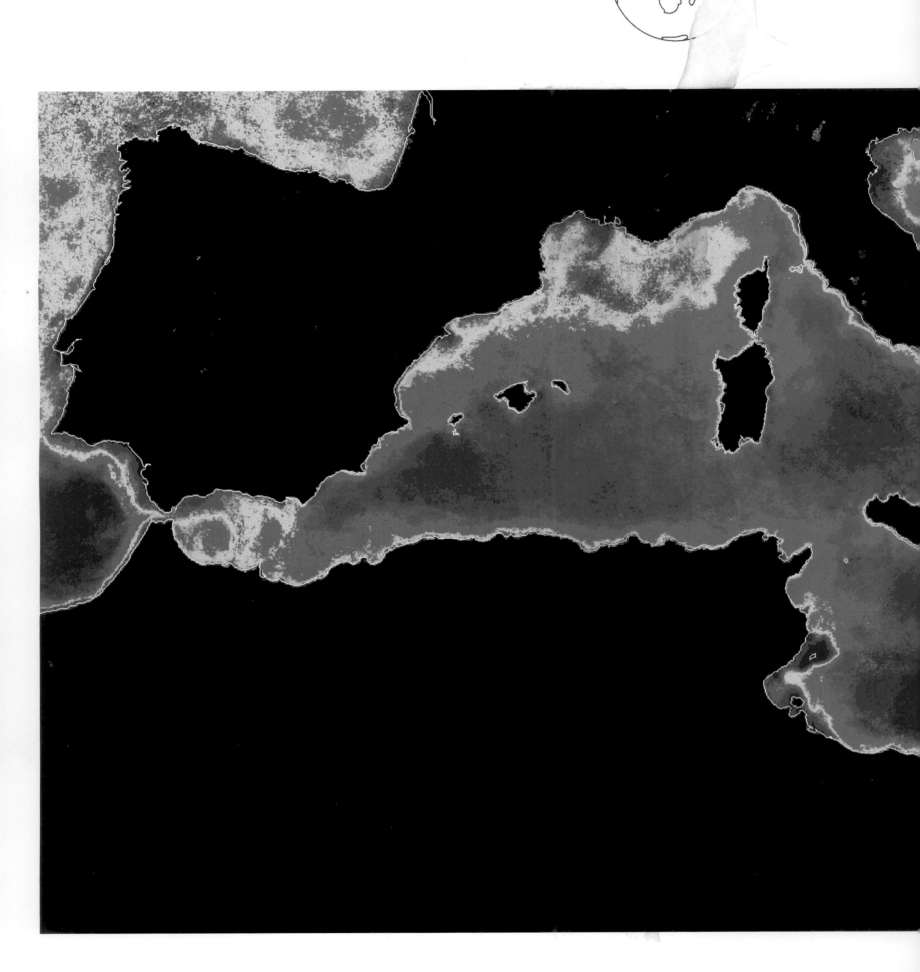

TWENTY PERCENT OF THE BEACHES ALONG THE MEDITERRANEAN
ARE TOO POLLUTED FOR SAFE SWIMMING.

Mediterranean Sea. A combination of geography, circulation patterns, and the effect of the narrow Strait of Gibraltar has limited the concentrations of marine plants, or phytoplankton, in the near shore regions of the Mediterranean.

The image here shows that the relatively clear, phytoplankton-poor waters (in blue) predominate as compared with the phytoplankton-rich waters of the Atlantic Ocean. The higher concentrations of phytoplankton

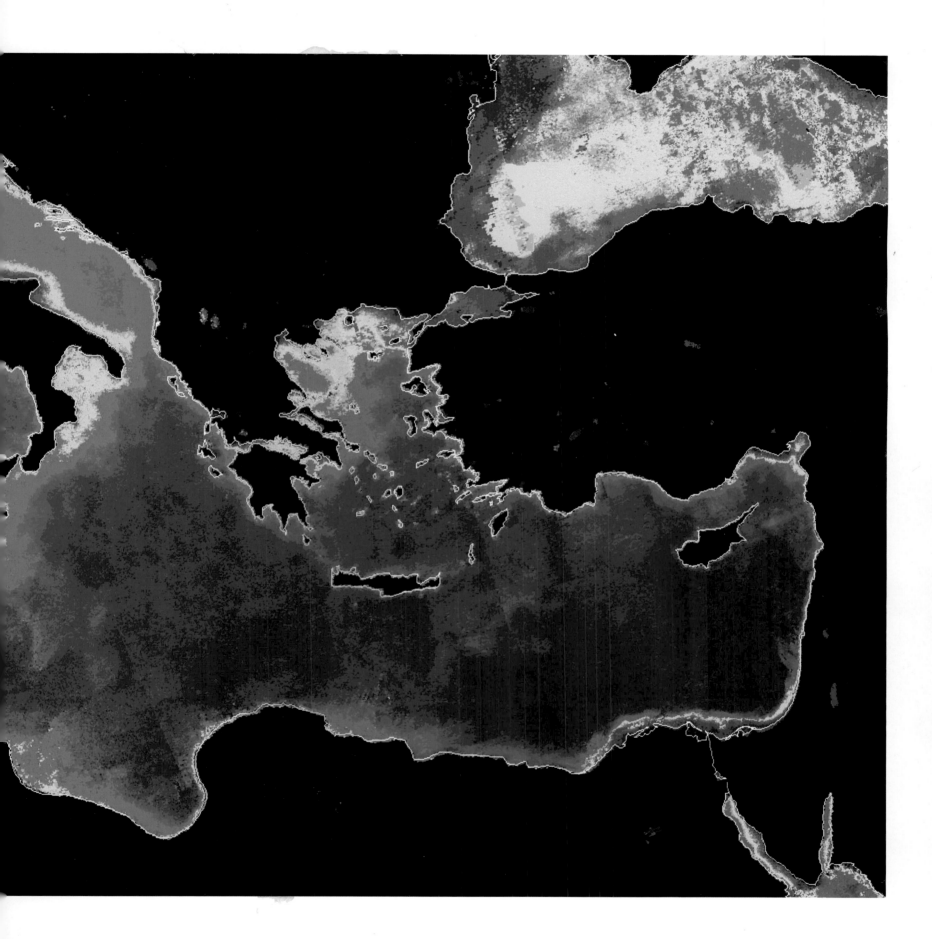

(in yellow, orange, and red) occur especially along the coasts of Spain and southern France and in the Black Sea. The circular pattern, or gyre, near the Strait of Gibraltar is caused by complex circulation patterns resulting from the exchange of water between the Mediterranean and the Atlantic Ocean. Surrounding countries are shown in black for reference.

As the cradle of Western civilization, the Mediterranean often provided an adequate marine bounty to a population much smaller than what it is today. Today this great sea has also been used as a sewer for the 350 million people who bound its shores—plus another 100 million annual tourists. A decade ago, 85 percent of the sewage that flowed into the Mediterranean was untreated. Ironically, this discharge helped to create some of the areas of high phytoplankton productivity, but it also often caused noxious carpets of algae that choked other marine life-forms and fouled beaches. Fortunately, some efforts are under way to improve the marine environment. Since 1978 seventeen Mediterranean nations have signed a series of protocols agreeing to stop dumping waste in the sea and to police land-based pollution. The April 1991 oil spill of 42 million gallons at Genoa, Italy, the largest such Mediterranean spill to date, indicates that this enclosed sea is still vulnerable to human activity.

Tropical Reef, Bahama Islands. Eleuthera Island, one of the Bahama Islands, rises above the water on the eastern edge of a submerged coral reef which is part of the Great Bahama Bank. Corals are small marine animals with hard calcium skeletons which live in association with marine plants and can grow only in shallow, sunlit waters. Reefs are the accumulation of coral skeletons, debris, and living corals. Each succeeding coral generation grows atop the skeletal remains of the preceding one. Eventually corals build up from the shallow seafloor to sea level. When sea levels drop, reefs can evolve into islands by accumulating sands, on which ocean-borne plants and animals establish themselves.

In this false-color image, the lush tropical vegetation of the 80-mile-long island appears bright red. Shallow water is aqua and deeper water is darker blue. The underwater, fringing reefs to the west of the island are seen as irregular bands of light and dark blue. Wave patterns in the Atlantic Ocean are also visible on the western side of the island. Reefs play an important role in protecting the fragile shorelines of islands by deflecting and dissipating the force of incoming waves.

Coral reefs can often be important indicators of past geologic and climatic conditions. Ancient reef remains have been found at depths beyond which corals can grow in the ocean, indicating the subsidence, or settling, of the seafloor through geologic time. The patterns of reefs and the depth of their growth can also reflect a rise or fall in sea level.

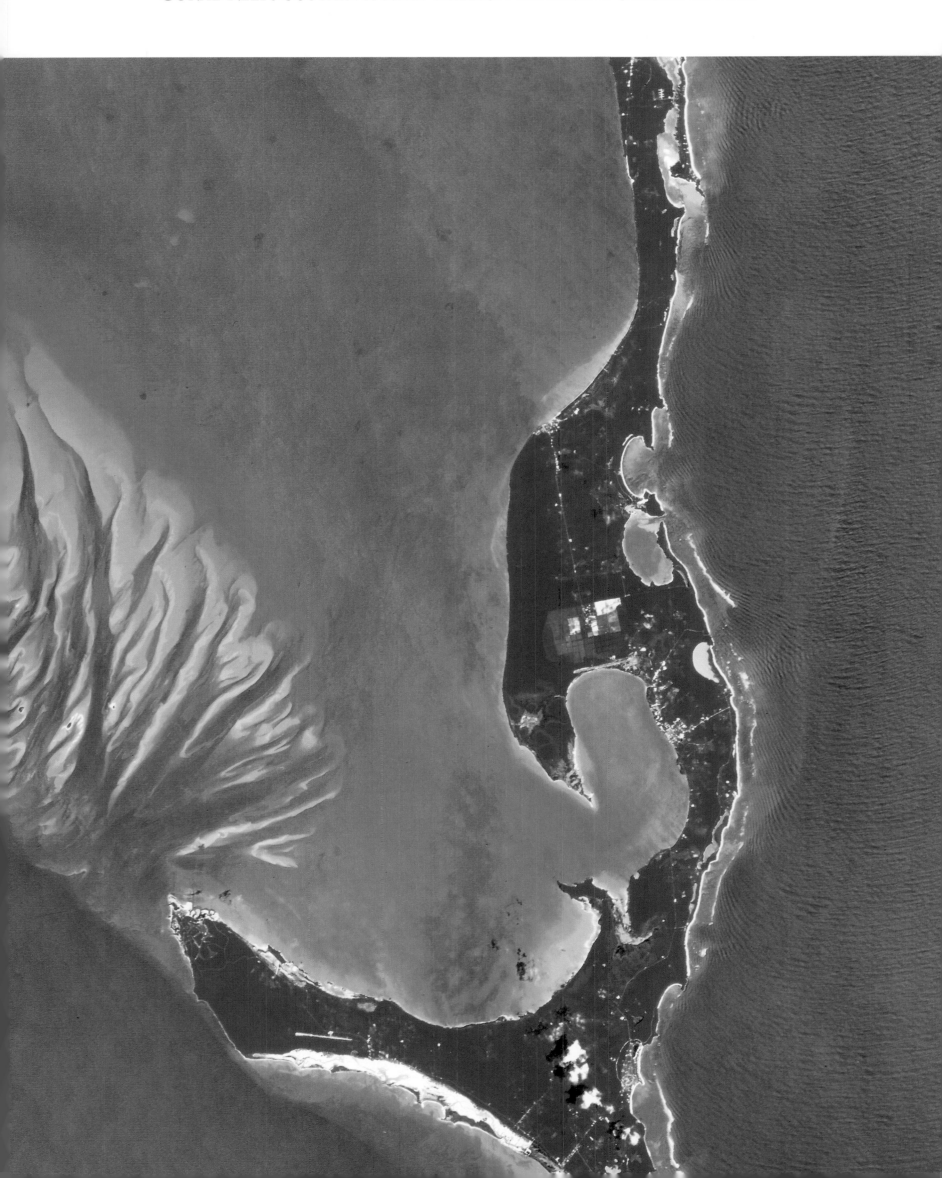

Ocean Seasons, Baja California, Mexico. Although most of us can watch the seasons change by observing leaves bud, grow, turn color, and finally fall, few can appreciate similar cycles in the sea. A special NASA sensor is able to measure chlorophyll—the pigment that colors plants green—and thus measure the cycles of marine plants. Because these plants, termed phytoplankton, are at the base of the food chain, satellite measurements are an indicator of ocean productivity.

The 800-mile-long Baja Peninsula of Mexico was created by forces that are still separating it from the mainland and opening up the long, narrow Gulf of California. The dynamics of the gulf's geography affect phytoplankton cycles.

▶ This image shows phytoplankton abundance as the satellite passed over the region for one day. Orange and red indicate high levels of plant life; green and yellow, intermediate levels; and purple and blue, low levels. Notice the high levels along the coasts and in the northern region of the gulf. Eddies and jets of water extend for hundreds of miles in long filaments of phytoplankton-rich water on the Pacific Ocean side of Baja. These high concentrations are caused by wind-driven upwelling that pulls up nutrients from deeper water. The southern area of the gulf contains low-nutrient surface water, while the northern regions above the Midriff Islands are rich in plant life due to strong tidal currents that mix the water and bring up nutrients.

▼ These two images, which average three months of data, reveal the seasonal variations in the distribution and abundance of phytoplankton. The most striking features are the low level of phytoplankton in the summer (left) and the high concentration in the fall (right). The increase is due to upwelling caused by strong northwest winds in the fall, in both the Pacific and the gulf regions. The satellite data upon which the observations here are based exceed all at-sea measurements of phytoplankton made in this area to date.

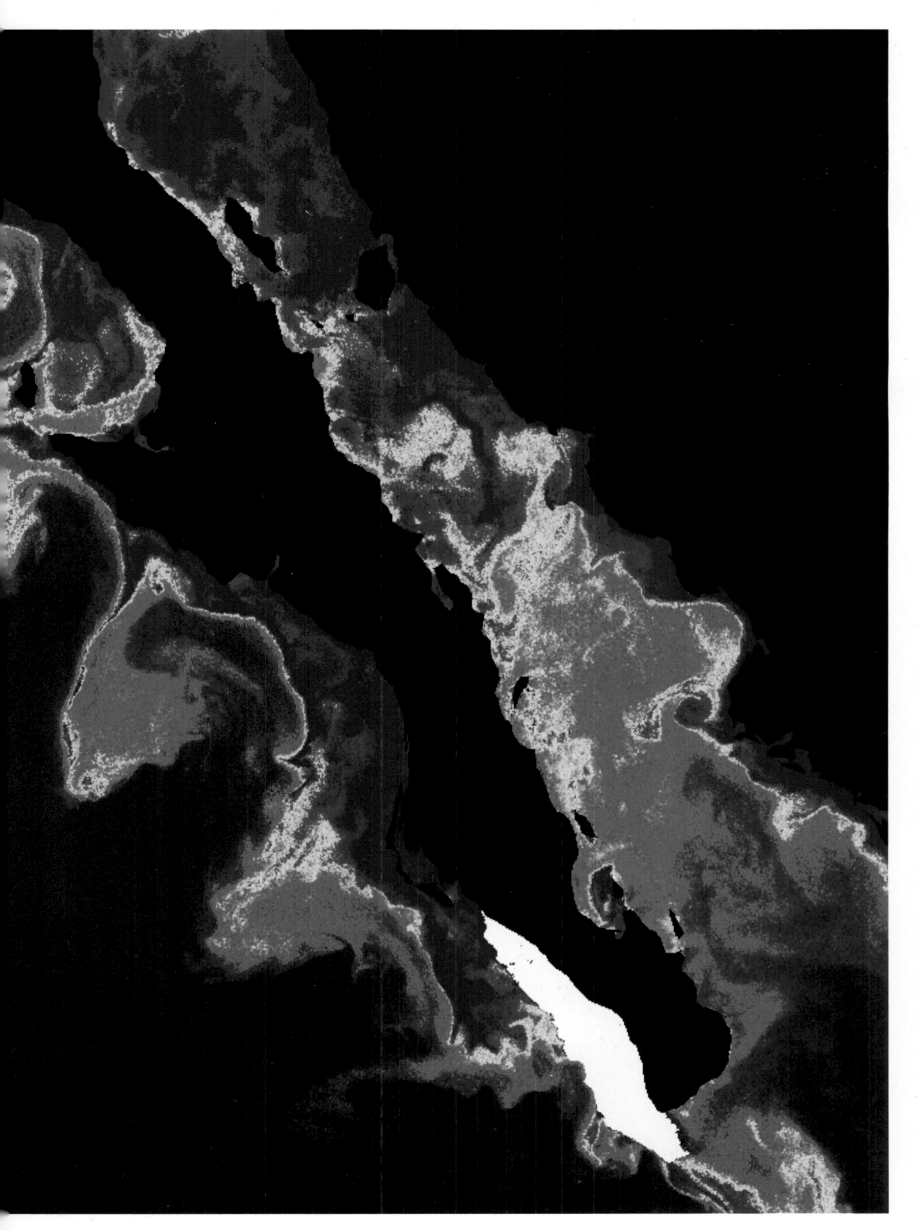

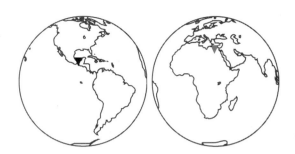

◄ **Forest Details, Central America.** One of the promising aspects of observing terrestrial vegetation by satellite is the ability to see not only the overview of a region but also the details. Newly developed techniques use airborne multifrequency radars to study tropical rain forest ecology. Shown here is a composite image of a 1,600-square-mile area of Central American forest. Parts of three countries are included: Mexico, on the top and bottom right; Guatemala, on the top left; and Belize, on the bottom left. A large portion of the image is undisturbed rain forest in Belize and Guatemala, which appears green. Forest that has been clear-cut for agriculture appears at the top center as dark blue, rectangular plots. Marshland formed by water flooding from the Booth River in Belize is at the right.

These sensor techniques are most sensitive to objects of about the same size as the radar wavelength. Thus, by using different wavelengths, the sensors can identify specific details of vegetation of different sizes. These distinctions can be enhanced by employing computer colors and sophisticated mathematical models so that eventually tree trunks, twigs, stems, and leaves in the upper forest canopy, as well as grasses, can all be distinguished. In this image grasses appear blue. By combining this data with information on the water content of vegetation gathered from the ground, the total biomass of the vegetation can be analyzed. All these observations further our regional and global understanding of the relationship between the living and nonliving components of our planet.

◄◄ **Nile River, Egypt** (previous pages). This great river in Africa is intimately associated with the civilization of ancient Egypt, which had its birth over five thousand years ago. The river's annual cycle of flooding ensured the fertility of the Nile Valley within the deserts that make up most of Egypt. Shown here is the Nile River where it forms a U-shaped bend north of the Aswan High Dam in southeast Egypt. The river is about 1/2 mile wide, with vegetation, shown in red, extending approximately 4 miles out from its banks. The desert is tan.

Yellowstone Fires, United States. When over 793,000 acres of Yellowstone National Park in Wyoming, Idaho, and Montana burned in the summer of 1988, many people were concerned that the first and most cherished national park in the United States lay in charred ruins. In the aftermath of the fires, there was serious debate about forest management practices: should a fire be controlled or allowed to burn? Fires, however, are an important process in the natural history of most forests. They allow different ecosystems to evolve in the forest life cycle. The Yellowstone fires, though spectacular, were part of an inevitable cycle. Within the soft ash lay seeds released from pinecones opened by the searing heat, waiting to sprout with the next heavy rains. Satellite imagery helped identify the progress of the Yellowstone fires and the extent of their damage.

▼ On July 22, the fires had already started, with a major fire burning to the northeast of the lake (right side of image).

► The large image shows the fires on September 8, when they were burning intensely in the park (outlined in red). White smoke plumes can be seen throughout the park. Burned forest areas are dark magenta; shrubs and grassland are light magenta; untouched pines are green. Yellowstone Lake is in the center of the image. The small image shows the park on October 2, when the fires had been extinguished by heavy rains, snow, and cooler temperatures. The extensive loss of trees and vegetation is seen in the red regions.

Global Seasonal Greening. The rhythms of the seasons sweep over the planet with cycles of greening of the Earth's vegetation. As winter subsides and days lengthen, the increase in temperature and light enables seeds to germinate and the soil to blossom with life.

Satellites monitor greening cycles on a global scale by using sensors that can measure the density of vegetation. These two false-color images comparing the summer and winter of 1987 are based on the seasonal duration of green vegetation. Regions with the most vegetation are green; those with less vegetation are shades of brown and tan; those with very little vegetation are gray. White indicates areas where the data have been omitted.

The winter image (January/February), at the top, shows little green vegetation throughout most of the Northern Hemisphere. The United States has very low levels of green vegetation, except for the southern states. The Southern Hemisphere, which is experiencing summer, has more green vegetation. The summer image (July/August), below, indicates a dramatic increase in green vegetation in the Northern Hemisphere. Regions of the world with long growing seasons, such as the equatorial rain forests of Africa and South America, have the greatest amounts of annual green vegetation. Satellite images showing seasonal vegetation are being used not only to monitor global vegetation but also to observe climatic conditions around the world.

Rain smell
*   I am full of hunger*
*   deep and longing to touch*
wet tall grass, green and strong beneath.
This woman loved a man
and she breathed to him
*   her damp earth song.*
*   …*
I remember it in the wide blue sky
when the rain smell comes with the wind.

Leslie Marmon Silko, poet

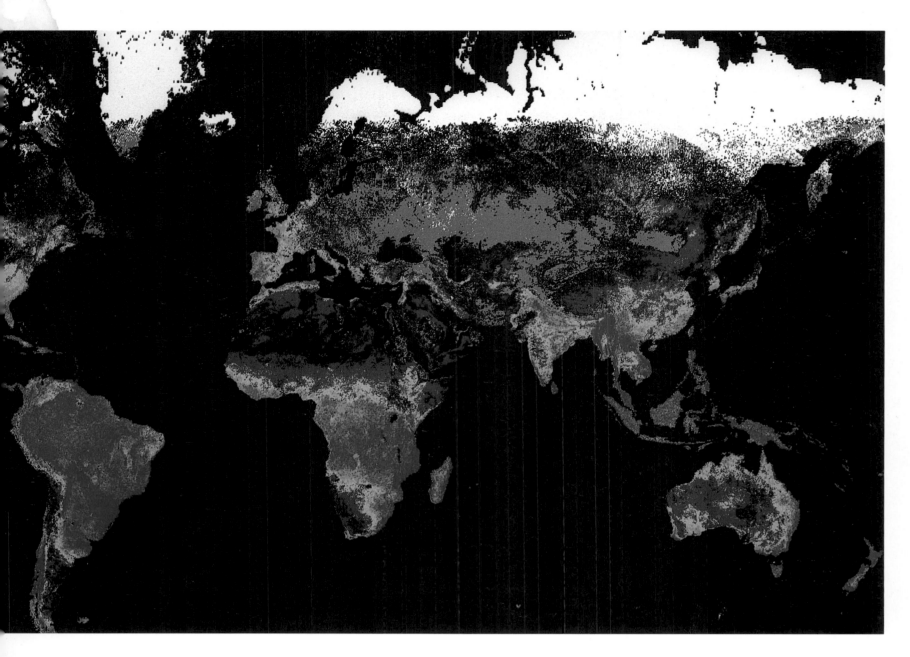

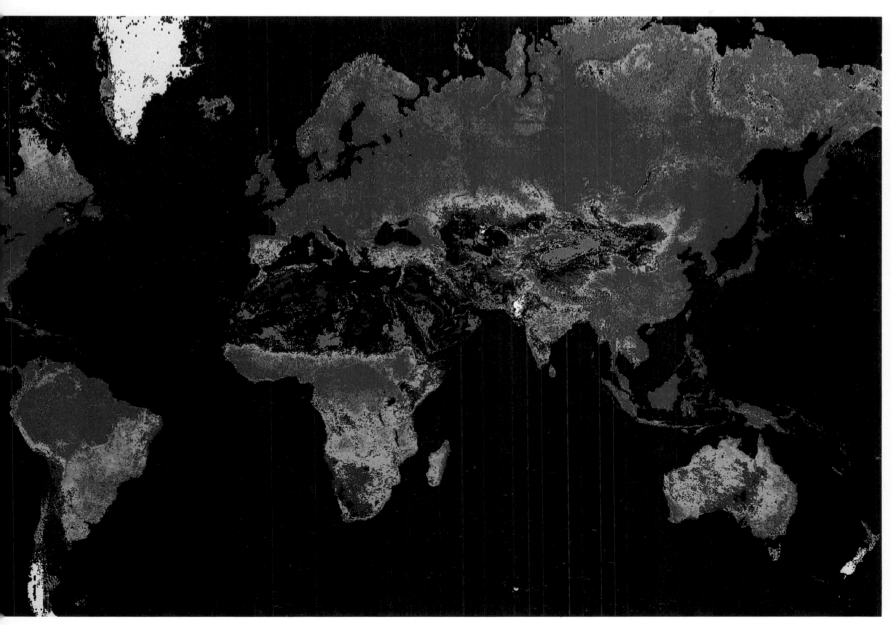

Nightlife, USA. The natural features of our planet in daylight are the main focus of this book. In contrast, this image shows the presence of human activities as reflected by computer composite satellite sensing that detects illumination at night. This electric tapestry of street and building lights leaking into space includes the main urban areas of the United States. Extensive metropolises glow brightly on both coasts, along the Gulf of Mexico, and around the Great Lakes.

HUMAN IMPACTS

We have hands that create tools and a mind that pushes the limits of their use. We leave our imprint everywhere we go, from cave paintings to footprints on the moon. Nature has been very forgiving. We have survived natural catastrophes and our own excesses. There has always been somewhere else to go. But now we are engaged in an environmental experiment on a global scale. And the Earth speaks to us with our greatest challenge: understand human impact; live in balance.

HUMAN
IMPACTS

The human species is at the evolutionary pinnacle of life on Earth. In the span of 1 to 2 million years, we have evolved from an intelligent primate standing upright on the African savannah to an organism that has been able to adapt to and colonize almost every region of the planet. In our search for security in the face of the uncertainties of the natural world, we have almost become the mythic gods we once worshipped. We harnessed fire to keep us warm and developed tools to expand our material capabilities. We pioneered agriculture and animal husbandry to provide us with a steady source of food. We created language, writing, art, and science to explore our world and to leave a record of the workings of our minds and the achievements of our cultures. For a young species, we have amassed an impressive list of accomplishments. Humans can plumb the depths of the oceans, fly though the air, visit the Moon, send probes to the end of the solar system, and watch the ebb and flow of daily events around the world by pushing a button and gazing at a glowing tube.

The evolution of our brain, and its thin cortex with billions of cells transmitting and storing messages, has given us wondrous skills. Yet our power to create is matched by our one great flaw: the power to destroy. Recorded throughout history are the civilizations whose cultural legacies have enriched our species. The ability of civilizations to thrive and expand their domains is sadly mirrored by their involvement in continual warfare and other self-destructive behaviors.

The human impact on our planet has been both positive and negative. Our widespread mark ranges from irrigation in the desert and freeways connecting whole continents to massive oil spills in the oceans and cities decimated by missiles raining from the air. Over thousands of years, we have evolved beyond being only one species among many in the natural world to having the ability to affect it on a global scale, with potentially disastrous results for ourselves and for other life-forms. So despite our technological prowess, the great philosophical questions are still with us: Who are we? Why are we here? Where are we going?

The satellite images in the previous chapter allow us to perceive some of the natural rhythms that constitute the pulse of the planet. The images in this chapter are like a report on the human impact on the Earth as viewed from space. They do not allow us to see the positive contributions of the many cultures inhabiting the planet. Yet what they do reveal is our ability to manipulate the natural world to achieve our own ends. In the process we have taken advantage of resources and opportunities. But we have also threatened the well-being of the environment that has served us so well. The most impressive aspect of the images is how they show the scale of our impact as seen from space and the magnitude of the patterns we are imposing on the Earth's surface. The images of urban centers can be seen as great accomplishments of our civilization, or they can also be seen as overextended systems that are not in balance, with their unhealthy levels of air pollution, traffic, and poverty. Ultimately, our interpretation of these images depends on our values and how we would ideally choose to live.

What is clear is that satellites enable us to track our impacts through time, and some of the portraits are disconcerting warnings. Fires viewed from space often indicate not only the destruction of forests but also the extinction of species. The ozone hole over Antarctica is enlarging, and the protective ozone layer of the atmosphere over the rest of the planet is thinning. The tiny glowing dot of heat energy from the April 1986 accident at the Chernobyl nuclear plant in the Soviet Union was seen from space. Satellites also record the forests destroyed by acid rain. These and other pressing environmental concerns are all functions of human impact.

The biggest immediate global challenge we now face is trying to assess whether—or how—the climate is changing due to our impact. We know that gases resulting in the greenhouse effect, such as carbon dioxide, warm the Earth and that their concentrations are increasing from the effects of industrial activities and our use of the automobile. These impacts will probably result in additional global warming. We can predict, using computer models, the general outcome of this scenario if it continues unaltered. Studies indicate that the global mean temperature will probably increase 5°F by the end of the twenty-first century. This could cause a global mean rise in sea level of up to one foot by 2030.

The satellites in place now and those planned for the future, such as NASA's Earth Observing System, will be watching the progress of our impacts. If sea levels rise, we will certainly see the coastal geography change for many regions. Island countries such as the Maldives in the Indian Ocean, which are close to sea level, may even disappear, as will low-lying delta regions. These satellite images are a record of our activities—a snapshot of where we are headed. They offer us a new perspective on the age-old questions of who we are and why we are here. They also offer a warning about where we are going. The warning resonates with truth: an unwelcome fate will be inflicted on those who do not consciously create their destiny.

Ozone Hole over Antarctica. Satellite and airborne sensors have recorded the growing hole in the ozone layer. The ozone hole is a dramatic example of the impact of human presence on the Earth. The threat to the ozone layer and the environment comes from man-made chemicals known as chlorofluorocarbons (CFCs).

Atmospheric ozone protects life from the harmful solar ultraviolet (UV) radiation. For humans, ozone depletion could mean increased incidence and severity of skin cancers, cataracts, and suppression of the immune system. Increasing UV light threatens the marine and aquatic microscopic plants that are the foundation of the food chain. CFC chemicals used in air-conditioning, spray cans, and blown foams are the main destroyers of ozone. In addition, CFCs are potent gases that add to the warming of the atmosphere. Each additional CFC molecule contributes to this greenhouse effect a thousand times more than a carbon dioxide molecule does.

This sequence of polar projections (with South America and Antarctica in black outline) shows, from below left to right, the ozone hole in 1979, 1987, 1988, and 1991 in October of each year, the time of maximum ozone loss. Very low levels are in purple, intermediate levels in blue-green, and higher levels in yellow-red. Antarctic ozone depletion varies from year to year, but a general trend showing decreasing levels is apparent. The lowest recorded levels of ozone occurred in 1991. Scientists have concluded that ozone depletion occurs year-round and worldwide, with a rate of loss in the 1980s that was triple the rate of the 1970s.

The ancient fear that fire from the sky would rain down and destroy the world has been supplanted today with the threat from CFCs, which is much more real. Fortunately, satellite observations have helped convince world leaders that the production and use of CFC chemicals need to be controlled and phased out. In 1990, ninety-three nations signed the Montreal Protocol, which will eliminate all CFC use by the year 2000. Although this is a good start for CFC control, many cities are enacting even more stringent limits that would take effect sooner.

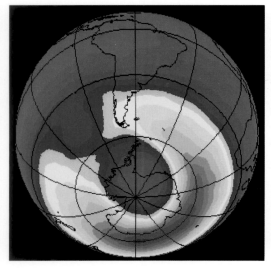

1979

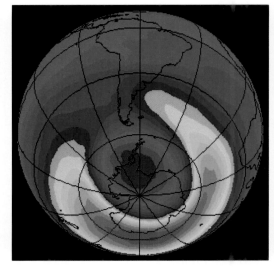

1987

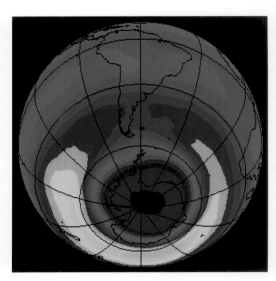

1988

Each Chlorofluorocarbon Molecule Destroys 100,000 Ozone Molecules.

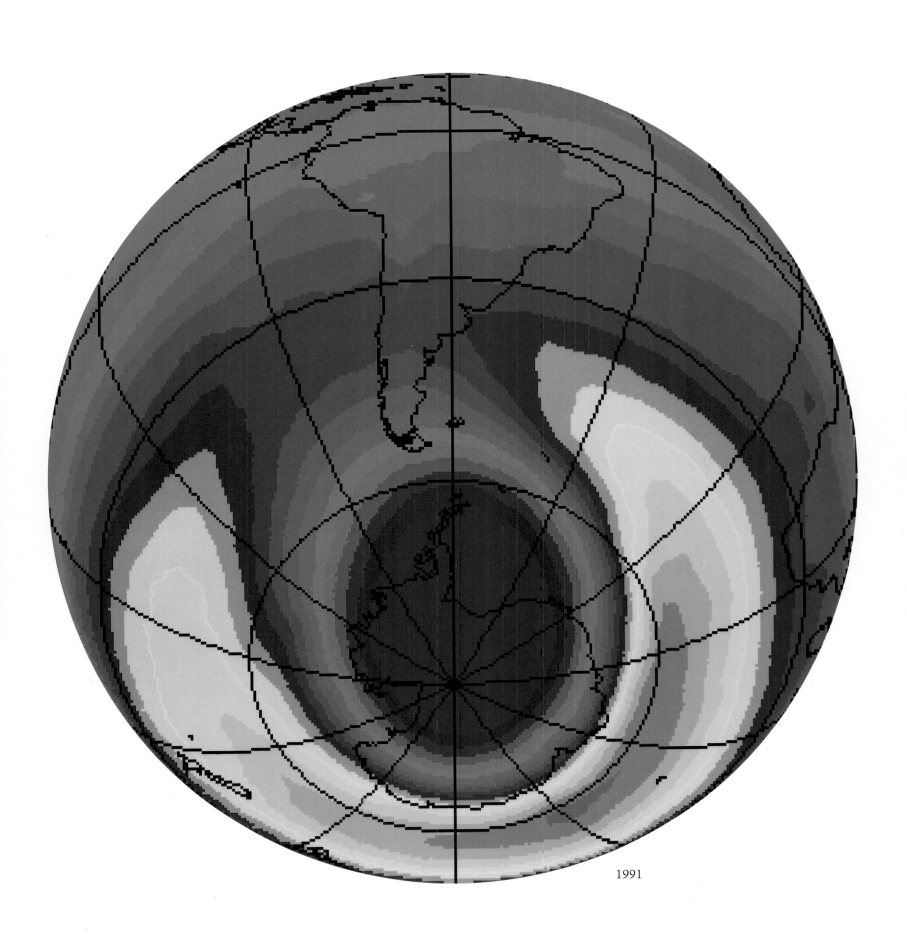

1991

New York City, United States. The large cities of the world are highly noticeable from space, as they are on the ground, because of their concentrations of man-made materials, and the often very linear appearance of streets and city grids. New York City has been growing for over three centuries, starting in 1626, when the small island of Manhattan was reputedly purchased for $24 by the Dutch from the Native Americans. At that time the region was all forested land.

Today, New York City is a densely populated metropolis and one of the cultural and economic magnets of the Western world. The island of Manhattan is visible in the center of this image, surrounded by the Hudson and East rivers. The only significant remaining vegetation on Manhattan, shown in red, lies in the long rectangle of Central Park, in the center of the island. The boroughs of Brooklyn and Queens are to the right of Manhattan, and the Bronx is above it. Jersey City is to the left. Staten Island, one the few areas of the city where there is still some farming, is below the center of the photograph and shows a greater amount of vegetation, also red. Kennedy Airport, in Queens, is the prominent geometric feature above Jamaica Bay, to the right of the center of the image.

Urban Clusters. Cities have always been the jewels of civilizations. Since early history, they have expressed the vital interplay of commerce and culture. These satellite images show four major cities and their unique attributes.

▶ **Los Angeles, United States.** Founded by the Spanish in the early eighteenth century, Los Angeles is one of the Pacific Rim cities bounding the Pacific Ocean. The many neighborhoods of the sprawling Southern California megapolis, covering 465 square miles, are connected by a vast system of freeways. Extensive use of the automobile in a city of 3-1/2 million has created a serious problem of ever-growing air pollution. Because the region is semiarid, Los Angeles depends on fresh water brought from northern California and Arizona. Blue-green indicates urban areas; dull red, vegetation in and around clearing fields; bright

Even if I were certain that the world would end tomorrow, I would plant a tree this very day.

Martin Luther King, Jr., civil rights leader

Deforestation, Brazil. Concern about global deforestation has raised awareness of how important trees are for the health of our planet. They remove from the atmosphere carbon dioxide—a potent gas that contributes to greenhouse warming. When a forest is cleared, fewer trees are left to absorb carbon dioxide for photosynthesis. Furthermore, burning the cut trees adds carbon dioxide to the atmosphere. Many countries besides those in the tropics have histories of intense logging or clearing. The United States was once heavily forested from the Atlantic Ocean to the Mississippi River. Lebanon long ago had abundant cedars. Today rain forests are being cleared at the rate of 50 acres per minute, and the loss of habitat is driving countless species into extinction.

Satellites have monitored much of the deforestation of the rain forest. Year-to-year comparisons of disturbed rain forest such as these images of the state of Rondônia in Brazil in 1975 (below) and 1986 (opposite) record the dramatic expansion of forest clearing. Clear-cutting has followed a systematic pattern: main roads reach into the rain forest, then fan out to create the feather pattern shown in 1986. Healthy forest is in red; deforested regions are in light green and blue. The discovery of gold in the Amazon basin has added to the destruction of the rain forest as new areas are cleared and mercury, a gold refinery by-product, has been allowed to pollute the region.

Agriculture in the Desert, United States.
The Salton Sea, in the Imperial Valley of southern California, was created in the early twentieth century when the Colorado River flooded its banks and irrigation channels, spilling into two deep washes. Like many semiarid regions of the world, this region has bloomed with the addition of life-giving water. Israel, Saudi Arabia, and the American Southwest have all benefited from irrigation to develop extensive agriculture.

Vegetation is shown in red, which creates the checkerboard pattern of farming plots. The surrounding desert is gray and tan. The widespread farming is the result of irrigation made possible by the All American Canal, which delivers water from the Colorado River across the desert floor. This intense agriculture has caused problems for Mexico, whose water supply from the Colorado River has diminished and is often polluted by salt buildup, pesticides, and fertilizers.

129

Mining Groundwater. The subsurface water stored within soil pores and rock formations is an important, often renewable resource that supports human activities. In many regions, however, groundwater is being depleted at rates faster than it can be replaced. Primarily used for agricultural irrigation and human consumption, groundwater represents an important supplement to the water supply of lakes, rivers, and reservoirs. This important resource not only is facing depletion, but is endangered by pollution. Agrichemicals, hazardous wastes, and harmful salts and minerals are all entering the groundwater, threatening its purity and its potential use.

These two sets of satellite images show changes in center pivot irrigation, which creates circular agricultural plots, in the midwestern United States and central Saudi Arabia from the early 1970s to the mid-1980s. In both cases there is a dramatic increase in the number of irrigation systems being used. Satellite images such as these play an important role in providing an inventory of irrigated crop acreage, which is essential for assessing the response of aquifers, or underground water, to changes in water use.

▶ **Western Kansas, United States.** This pair of images show farming and irrigation in 1972 (top) and 1988 (bottom). Crops, mainly corn, are red dots or rectangles. Fields not in cultivation are pale white. Irrigation in this area depends on the huge, underground Ogallala Aquifer—the largest source of groundwater in the United States. Extending from South Dakota to the Texas Panhandle, it irrigates over 36,000 square miles of the Great Plains, or one-fifth of all the cropland in the US. Depletion of the Ogallala Aquifer, some areas of which may only pump water for another decade, is a serious threat to crop production and the economy.

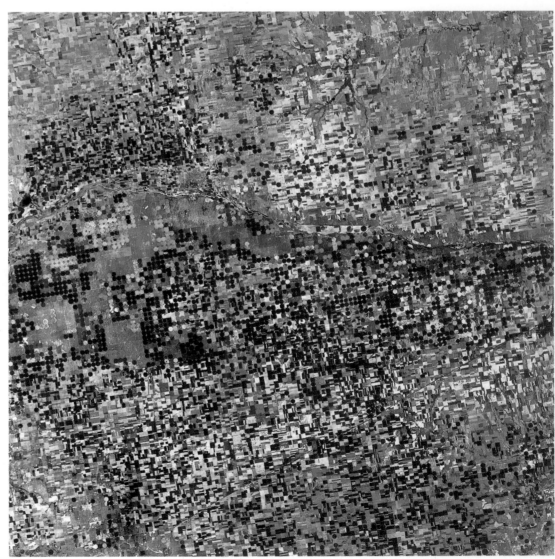

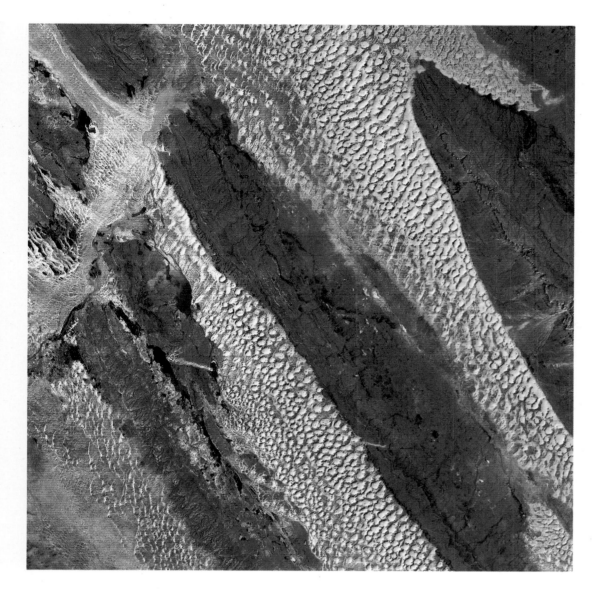

◄ **Saudi Arabia.** Striking development
of irrigation has occurred from 1972 (top),
when there were no center pivots, to 1986
(bottom), when there were hundreds. Pivots
are red dots; dunes are yellow; desert pavement
and wadis, or arroyos, are tan and purple.
This view includes the city of Buraydah
(top center). Oil revenues of the country have
been directed toward modernizing agriculture
and creating greater self-sufficiency in the
production of food. As a result, desert aquifers
have been mined for irrigation, predominantly of wheat. These reserves, like oil,
are nonrenewable resources and at current
rates of use may be depleted by the middle
of the twenty-first century.

Irrigated Cropland, Senegal. The population
of the world is projected to increase by almost
3-1/2 billion people by 2025, and the population of Africa is expected to pass 1 billion
by 2010. The plight of drought and human
starvation in Africa has been a global concern
for over a decade. Increased population,
persistent drought, and wars have prevented
any long-term solution to these problems for
many African countries. In order to meet the
food demands of this growing population,

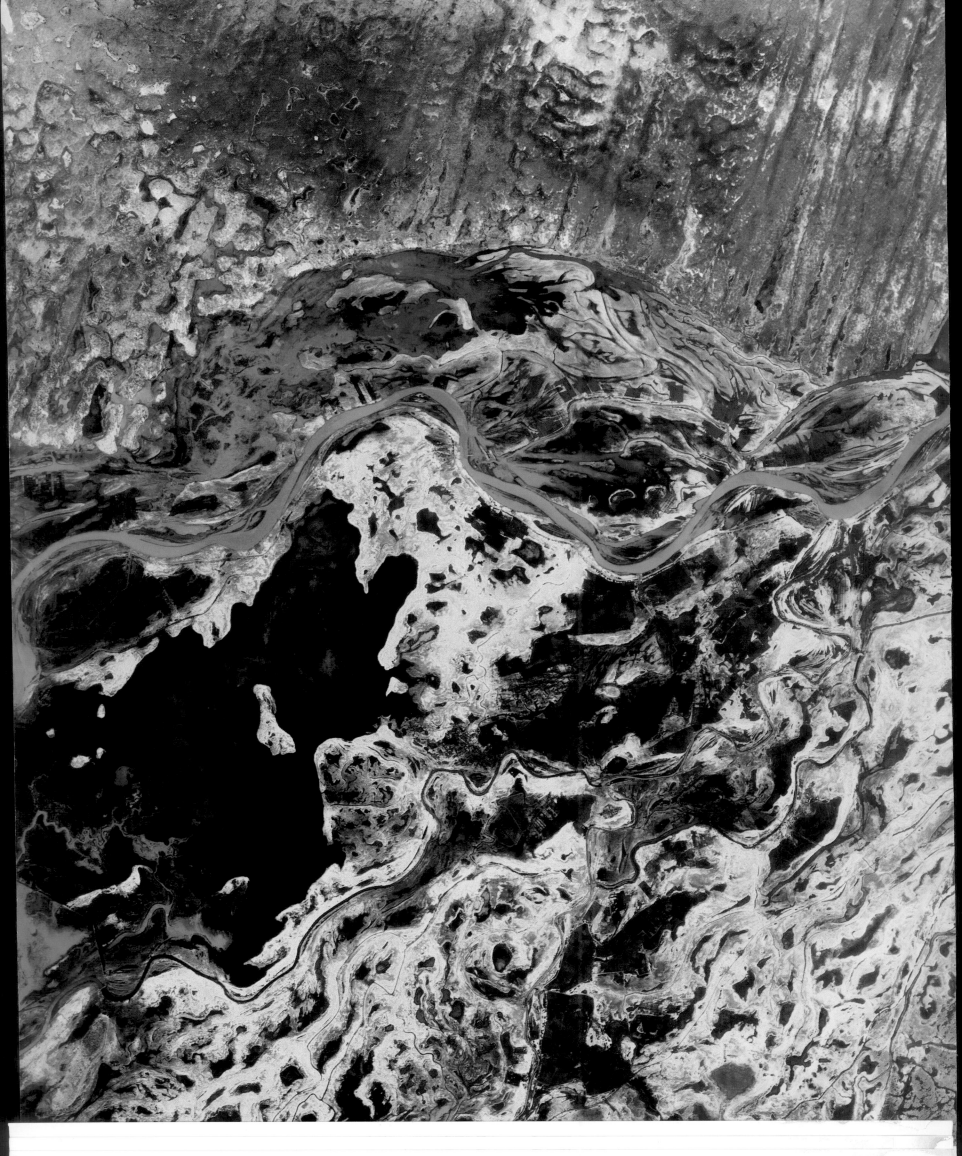

Before land was and sea—
    before air and sky
Arched over all, all Nature was
    all Chaos,
The rounded body of all things
    in one,

We urge that all people now determine that a wide untrammeled freedom shall remain to testify that this generation has love for the next.

Nancy Newhall, photohistorian

▶ **Irrawaddy River Delta, Myanmar.** Rivers flow to the sea, bringing their load from the land. In this false-color infrared image of the Irrawaddy River Delta in Myanmar (formerly Burma), healthy vegetation is red, and areas with considerably less vegetation are pink. Numerous plumes of sediment extend into the Andaman Sea, in the center, and into the Gulf of Martaban, at the bottom right. The Bay of Bengal is at the upper left.

◀◀ **Folded Mountains, Pakistan** (previous pages). As the enormous tectonic plates of the Earth move through geologic time, they crash into each other, creating mountains. Here, the view south over Pakistan reveals the fluid past of our seemingly solid Earth. The sinuous mountain ranges of Baluchistan, the dominant features in this image, were formed 40 to 60 million years ago. The Indus River and its valley are on the left, and the Arabian Sea is at the top, beyond the horizon.

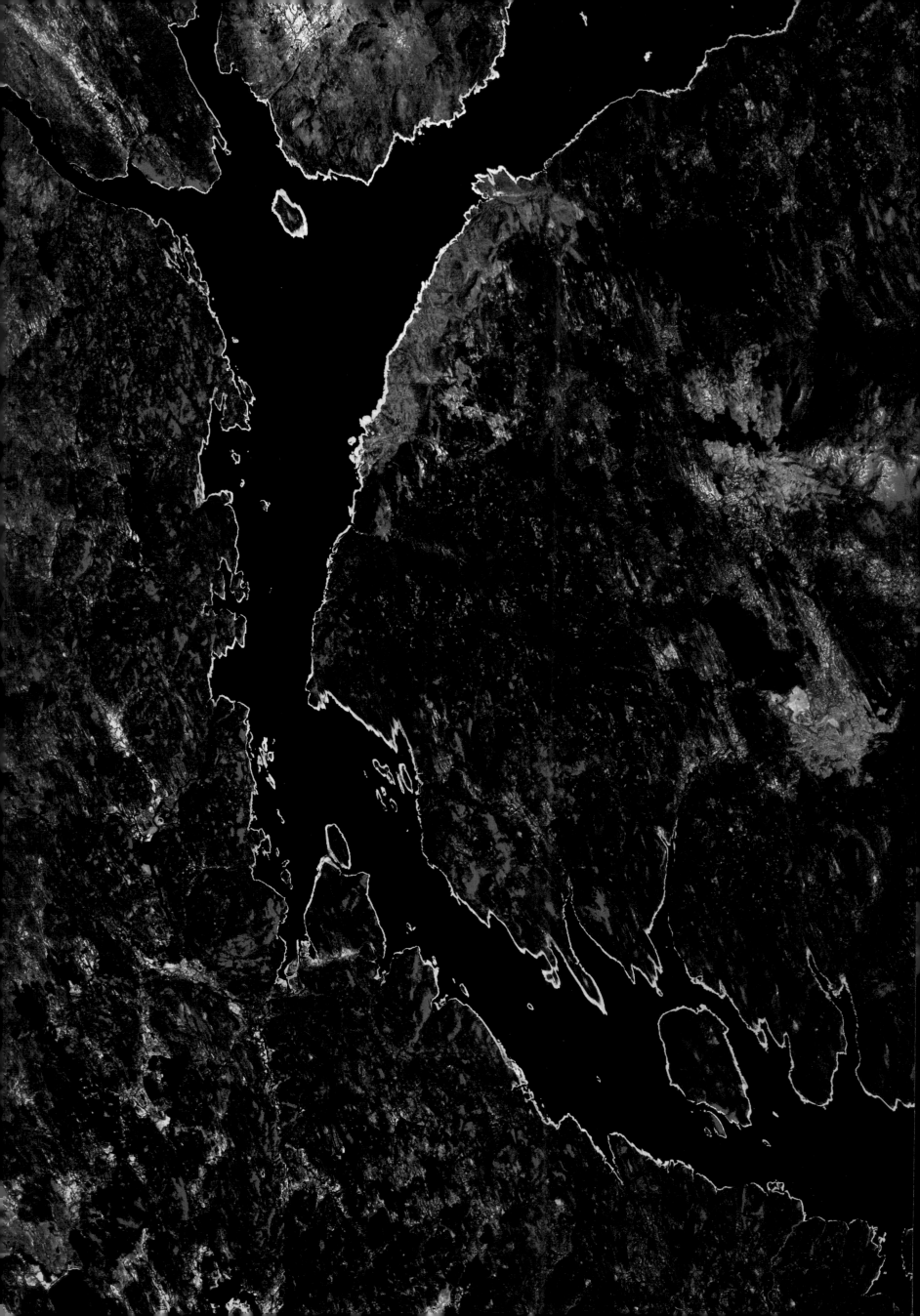

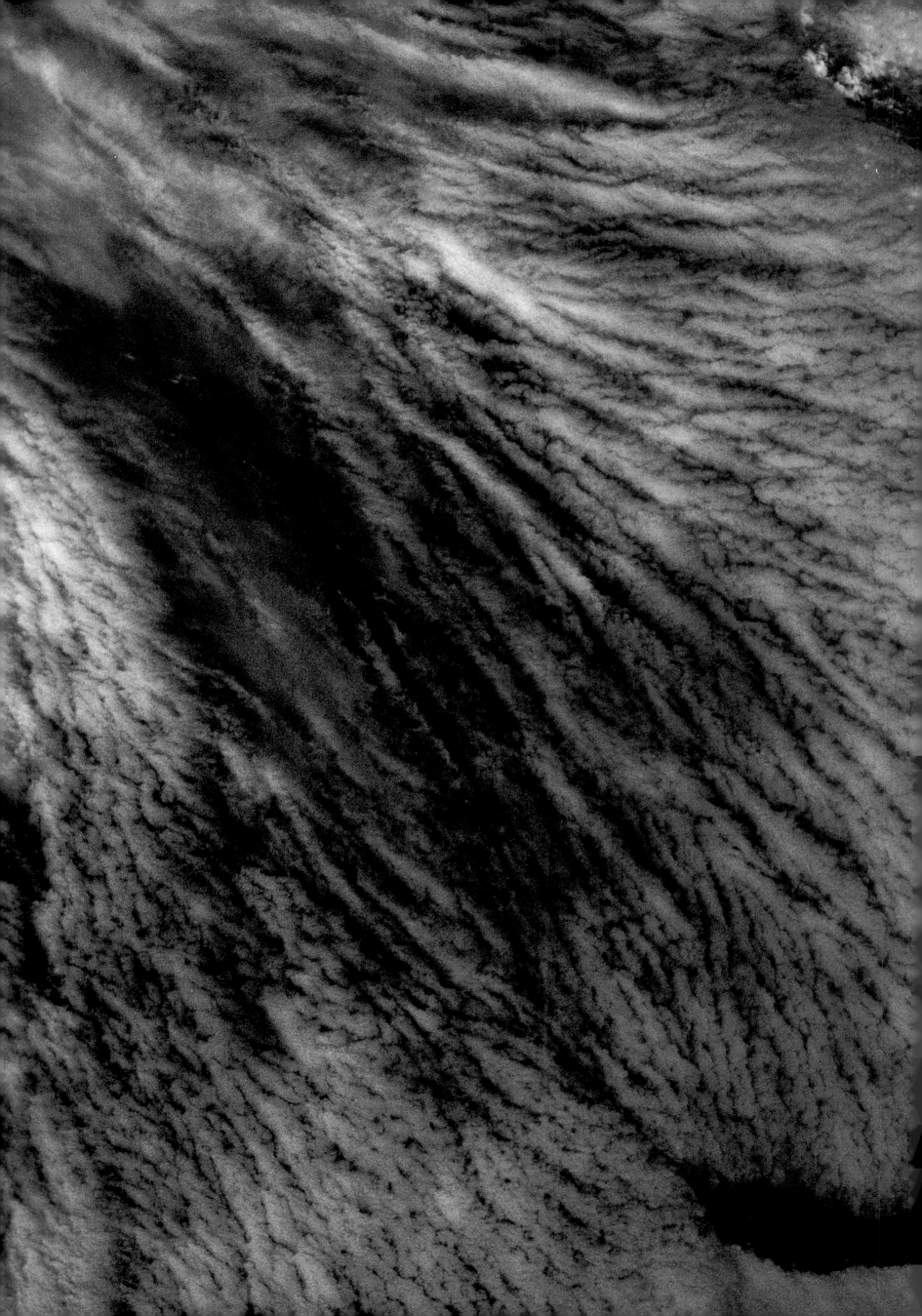

The softest of stuff in the world
Penetrates quickly the hardest;
Insubstantial, it enters
Where no room is.

Lao Tsu, philosopher

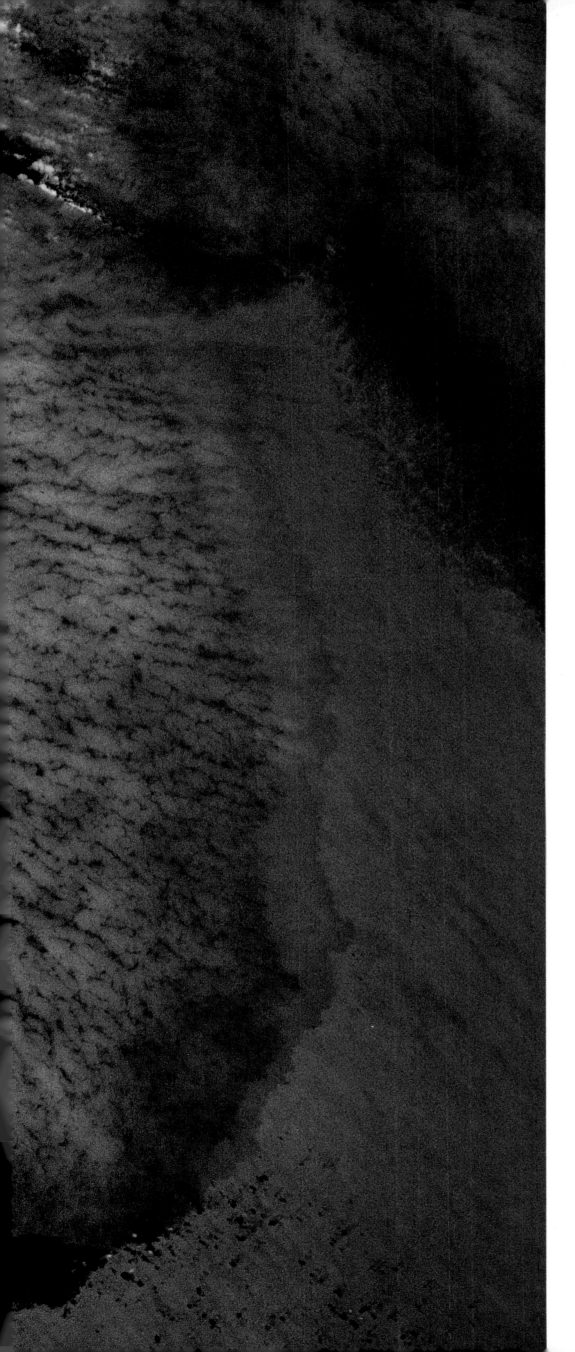

◄ **Cloud Front, Indian Ocean.** The ocean
and atmosphere interact in a dance of energy
and moisture. Here a tongue-like cloud front
rapidly moves forward to envelop a region
of the Indian Ocean.

◄◄ **Manicouagan Reservoir, Canada** (previous pages). Meteors leave scars from their
impact on Earth. This lake in northern
Quebec, a crater 40 miles in diameter, memo-
rializes the impact of a meteor that struck
the Earth 212 million years ago.

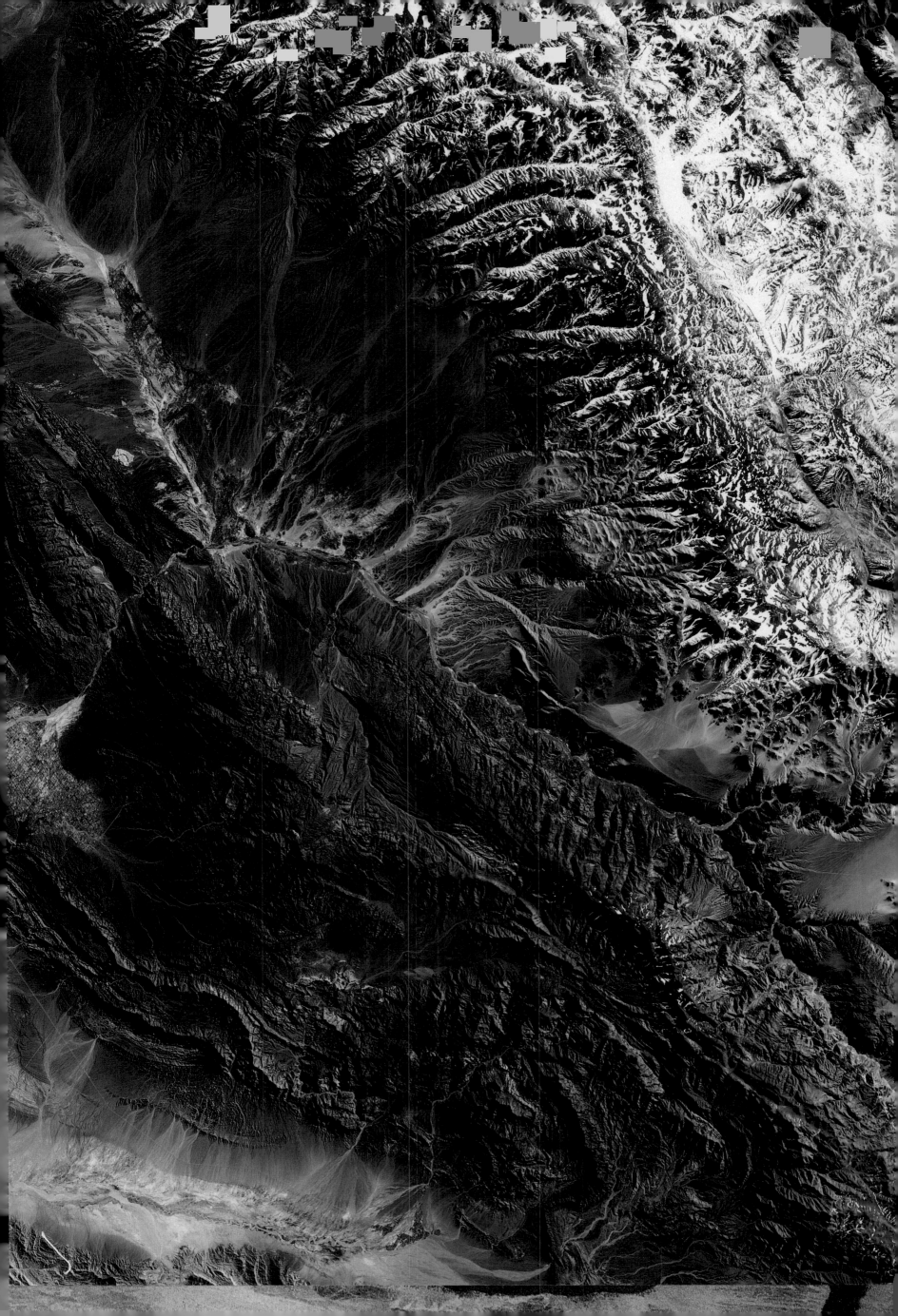

O Hidden Life vibrant in every atom,
O Hidden Light! shining in every creature;
O Hidden Love! embracing all in Oneness;
May each who feels himself as one with Thee,
Know he is also one with every other.

Annie Besant, spiritualist

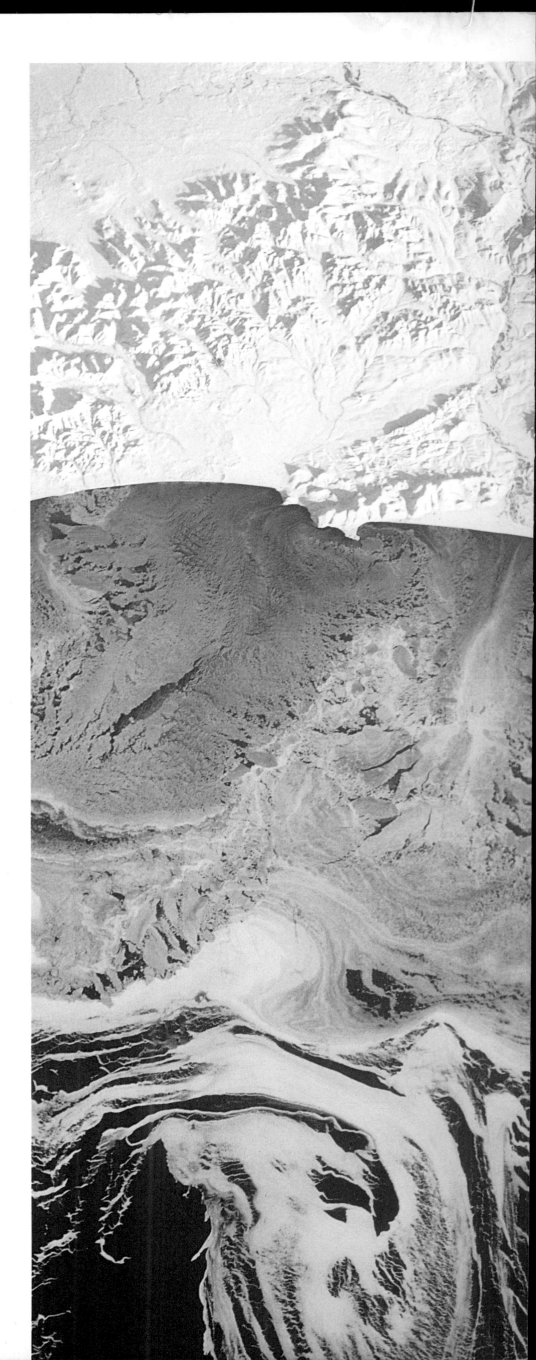

▶ **Siberian Winter, Kamchatka Peninsula.**
The polar regions have seasons of protracted
light and darkness and are the great heat sinks
that influence the Earth's climate. Cape
Olyutorskiy in the northeastern portion of the
Kamchatka Peninsula in the former Soviet
Union protrudes into the Bering Sea on the
Arctic Circle. A frozen ice sheet extends
from the point. Swirling ice and water mix
in the bottom half of the image. The surrounding Olyutorskiy Mountains are covered
with snow and ice.

◀◀ **Peace River, Canada** (previous pages). Rivers
are vital conduits bringing fresh water that
enables life to flourish. The Peace River flows
west through northern Alberta, Canada, surrounded by the checkerboard pattern of farms.

160

Earth Terminator and Limb. As the sun sets, the Earth sinks into shadow and darkness. The boundary of light and dark, at sunset and at sunrise, is called the termi- nator. The setting sun along the terminator accentuates the billowy clouds extending to the Earth's horizon, or limb.

We need to rest and allow the earth to rest. We need to
reflect and to rediscover the mystery that lives in us, that is
the ground of every unique expression of life, the source
of the fascination that calls all things to communion.

United Nations Environmental Sabbath Program

CREDITS

Image Credits
Endpaper: NASA Space Shuttle.
Page 2: NASA Space Shuttle.
4–5: METEOSAT-2, © SSC, Published with permission of the Swedish Space Corporation. **6**: NASA Space Shuttle. **8**: NASA Space Shuttle. **12–13**: © Payson R. Stevens. **16–17**: Courtesy James Marsh, NASA Goddard Space Flight Center. **18**: NASA Landsat. **19**: US Geological Survey. **20**: NASA Landsat, courtesy US Geological Survey/ EROS Data Center. **21**: © CNES, Provided by SPOT Image Corporation, Reston, Virginia. **22**: NASA Landsat. **23**: © Payson R. Stevens. **24–25**: NASA Space Shuttle. **26–27**: NASA, SIR-A Radar, courtesy John Ford, Jet Propulsion Laboratory, and Nicholas Short. **28**: © CNES, Provided by SPOT Image Corporation, Reston, Virginia. **29**: © Payson R. Stevens. **31**: NASA Landsat. **32**: NASA Space Shuttle. **33**: © Payson R. Stevens. **34–35**: © CNES, Provided by SPOT Image Corporation, Reston, Virginia. **36**: NASA Landsat. **38–39**: Courtesy Moustafa T. Chahine, Jet Propulsion Laboratory, and Joel Susskind, NASA/Goddard Space Flight Center. **40–41**: NASA Space Shuttle. **42**: Peter Woiceshyn, Jet Propulsion Laboratory; Morton Wuertle, University of California Los Angeles; Steven Peteherych, Atmospheric Environment Service of Canada. **43**: NOAA GOES-4. **44–45**: NOAA AVHRR, courtesy Gray Tappan, US Geological Survey/EROS Data Center. **46**: NOAA AVHRR. **47**: NASA Space Shuttle. **49**: NASA Space Shuttle. **50–51**: NASA Space Shuttle. **52**: NASA Space Shuttle. **53**: NASA Space Shuttle. **54**: NASA Apollo Mission. **55**: NOAA GOES-4. **56**: US Geological Survey/EROS Data Center. **57**: NOAA Satellite Research Laboratory, courtesy Larry Stowe and Robert Carey. **58–59**: Chet Koblinsky and Gene Carl Feldman, NASA Goddard Space Flight Center. **60**: NOAA AVHRR, courtesy Otis Brown, Robert Evans, and Mark Carle, University of Miami Rosentiel School of Marine and Atmospheric Science. **62**: NASA Space Shuttle, courtesy Larry Armi, Scripps Institution of Oceanography.

63: NASA Space Shuttle. **64**: NASA Space Shuttle. **65**: NASA Space Shuttle. **66**: © CNES, Provided by SPOT Image Corporation, Reston, Virginia. **67**: © CNES, Provided by SPOT Image Corporation, Reston, Virginia. **68**: © Payson R. Stevens. **69**: Courtesy Lee Fu and Benjamin Holt, NASA/Jet Propulsion Laboratory. **70–71**: NASA Space Shuttle. **72–73**: © CNES, Provided by SPOT Image Corporation, Reston, Virginia; and US Geological Survey/EROS Data Center. **75**: © CNES, Provided by SPOT Image Corporation, Reston, Virginia. **76–77**: NASA Landsat, courtesy Goddard Space Flight Center. **78–79**: Dorothy Hall, Donald Cavalieri, and Gene Carl Feldman, NASA/Goddard Space Flight Center. **80–81**: Jay H. Zwally/ NASA Goddard Space Flight Center. **82**: © Claire Parkinson/NASA Goddard Space Flight Center. **83**: © CNES, Provided by SPOT Image Corporation, Reston, Virginia. **84**: © Payson R. Stevens. **85**: Landsat, courtesy B. Lucchitta, US Geological Survey. **86–87**: NASA Space Shuttle. **88**: NASA, Jet Propulsion Laboratory, and University of Alaska, Fairbanks. **89**: © Bruce F. Molnia, US Geological Survey. **90–91**: © Radarsat International Inc. **92**: Alaska High-Altitude Aerial Photography Program, courtesy Paul D. Brooks, US Geological Survey. **93**: © Bruce F. Molnia, US Geological Survey. **94**: NASA Landsat, courtesy US Geological Survey/EROS Data Center. **96–97**: Gene Carl Feldman and Compton J. Tucker, NASA/ Goddard Space Flight Center. **98–99**: Gene Carl Feldman, NASA/ Goddard Space Flight Center. **100–101**: © CNES, Provided by SPOT Image Corporation, Reston, Virginia. **102–103**: NOAA, courtesy Dennis Clark. **104–105**: Image courtesy of Earth Satellite Corporation. **106–107**: Gregg Vane and Howard Zebker, NASA/Jet Propulsion Laboratory. **108**: Landsat, courtesy Donald Ohlen, US Geological Survey/EROS Data Center. **109**: Landsat, courtesy Donald Ohlen, US Geological Survey/EROS Data

Center. **111**: Courtesy Kevin P. Gallo, NOAA/NESDIS, EROS Data Center, and Jesslyn F. Brown, TGS Technology, Inc., EROS Data Center. **112–113**: Kevin P. Gallo and Jesslyn F. Brown, produced at US Geological Survey/EROS Data Center from data provided by the National Snow and Ice Data Center. **114–115**: © Payson R. Stevens. **118–119**: NASA/Goddard Space Flight Center, courtesy Mark Schoeberl and Gene Carl Feldman. **120**: NASA Landsat. **121**: © Payson R. Stevens. **122**: Los Angeles, © CNES, Provided by SPOT Image Corporation, Reston, Virginia; Mexico City, NASA Landsat. **123**: Paris, NASA Landsat; Cairo, NASA Landsat. **124**: NASA and NOAA Landsat, courtesy Barrett N. Rock and James Vogelmann, University of New Hampshire; David Zlotek, Cirrus Technology; and Hanan Kadro, University of Freiburg/FRG. **125**: NASA and NOAA Landsat, courtesy Barrett N. Rock and James Vogelmann, University of New Hampshire. **126**: NASA Landsat, courtesy Gray Tappan, US Geological Survey/EROS Data Center. **127**: NASA Landsat, courtesy Gray Tappan, US Geological Survey/EROS Data Center. **128–129**: NASA Landsat. **130**: NASA Landsat, courtesy Gray Tappan US Geological Survey/EROS Data Center. **131**: NASA Landsat, courtesy Gray Tappan, US Geological Survey/EROS Data Center. **132–133**: © CNES, Provided by SPOT Image Corporation, Reston, Virginia. **134**: NASA Landsat, courtesy Gray Tappan, US Geological Survey/EROS Data Center. **135**: NASA Landsat, courtesy Gray Tappan, US Geological Survey/EROS Data Center. **136**: NASA Landsat, courtesy US Geological Survey/EROS Data Center. **137**: © Payson R. Stevens. **138**: US Geological Survey/Eros Data Center. **139**: US Geological Survey/ Eros Data Center. **140–141**: © Payson R. Stevens. **144–145**: NASA Space Shuttle. **146–147**: NASA Space Shuttle. **148–149**: NASA Space Shuttle. **150–151**: © Radarsat International Inc. **152–153**: NASA Space Shuttle. **154–155**: NASA Space

Shuttle. **157**: NASA Space Shuttle. **158–159**: © Radarsat International Inc. **160–161**: NASA Space Shuttle. **162–163**: NASA Space Shuttle. **164**: Courtesy Woods Hole Oceanographic Institute. **165–168**: NASA. **169**: NASA Space Shuttle. **169**: NASA Space Shuttle. **171**: NASA Space Shuttle. **176**: NASA/Jet Propulsion Laboratory.

For information on how to obtain single images in this book contact:
World Perspectives, PO Box 709, Bolinas, California, 94924, 415-868-0670 Tel, 415-868-1944 Fax

Quote Attributions
Page 24: The Dalai Lama and Galen Rowell, *My Tibet*. **33**: William Blake, *The Marriage of Heaven and Hell*. **40**: Krishnamurti, *Think on These Things*. **61**: Rachel L. Carson, *The Sea Around Us*. **74**: Loren Eiseley, *The Immense Journey*. **91**: Samuel Taylor Coleridge, "Hymn before Sun-rise, in the Vale of Chamouni." **110**: "Love Poem" by Leslie Marmon Silko. From *Sisters of the Earth*, edited by Lorraine Anderson. © 1991 by Lorraine Anderson. **144**: Ovid, *The Metamorphoses, Book I*. **148**: © 1991 by Beaumont Newhall. Reprinted with permission of the Estate of Nancy Newhall, Courtesy of Beaumont Newhall. **153**: Lao Tsu, *The Way of Life*. **160**: Annie Besant, "O Hidden Life." **169**: Adlai E. Stevenson, speech, July 9, 1965.

Captions for images in introductory and concluding pages:
2: Clouds over South America.
4–5: Planet Earth. The yellow areas highlight northern Africa and the Middle East. The Mediterranean and Europe lie north of the African continent.
6: Atlantic Ocean sunglint.
8: Saudi Arabia coast with clouds and sunglint.
169: Indian Ocean sunglint.
171: Peruvian coast and Andes Mountains looking south.
173: Aurora over the Arctic.

ACKNOWLEDGMENTS

Embracing Earth: New Views of Our Changing Planet was a labor of love that could not have happened without the support of many people. We appreciate the encouragement we received from the people at Chronicle Books. Our senior editor, Jay Schaefer, pushed us beyond our limits. He helped to stimulate the conceptual framework of the book and to draw out the best in our design. Judith Dunham, our text editor, brought to the book a knowledge of geography and natural science, as well as an attention to detail, which added to the refinement of the text. Karen Silver made sure everything moved forward in a timely fashion and kept the book on schedule.

Special thanks to Brad Bunnin, our lawyer, for his unflagging support, creative ideas, and enthusiasm. Additional legal thanks go to Roberta Cairney and Walt Hansell for their counsel and to Anne Hiaring for her last-minute advice and help.

The designers at InterNetwork, Inc., worked under intense time pressures. Leonard Sirota was a constant resource for design ideas and buoyant enthusiasm. Patrick Howell gave elegance to the design. Eric Altson demonstrated powerful organizational skills and contributed to refining the design concepts. Monica Cruz organized all the editing, word processing, and research.

We also acknowledge Colleen Hicks for her astute advice, her unwavering cheerfulness, and the broad range of her support, including quote research and office administration.

The major science agencies in the United States that develop and work with satellite technologies—NASA, NOAA, the United States Geological Survey's Earth Resources Observation Systems Data Center (EDC)—provided important imagery for the book. These agencies are ultimately supported by the people of the United States, who have an opportunity to see the results of such vast research in an accessible form, as the wonderful images in this book. Images were also kindly provided by the SPOT Image Corporation of France, Radarsat International Inc. of Canada, Swedish Space Corporation, and Earth Satellite Corporation in the United States.

Many organizations and individuals were responsive to and supportive of our efforts to assemble this book in a relatively short time. First, we thank Stan Wilson at NASA Headquarters, who has written the essay "Remote Sensing: Striving for a Global View," which adds an important overview to the technical aspects of remote sensing. Other individuals at NASA who were especially helpful or provided technical review include Shelby Tilford, Dixon Butler, Ming-Ying Wei, David Adamec, Ghassem Asrar, Bob Brakenridge, Joe Engeln, Jack Kaye, Mike Kurylo, Tony Janetos, Joe McNeal, Greg Mitchell, Bob Murphy, Bill Patzert, Bob Thomas, Lou Walter, and Diane Wickland.

The United States Geological Survey's EDC also provided essential image support, for which we thank Al Watkins, Chief of the National Mapping Division. We also thank Dave Carneggie, for working with EDC contributors on image research; Gray Tappan, for enthusiastically suggesting a variety of imagery; and Rose Tyrell, for responding efficiently to our image requests. Other EDC personnel who were helpful in recommending or providing imagery include Norman Bliss, Mathew Cross, Kevin Gallo (NOAA), Tom Loveland, Rich McKinney, Don Ohlen, Russ Pohl, Wayne Rohde, Frank Sadowski, Mark Shasby, and K. C. Wehde. In addition, we acknowledge the valuable contributions of Richie Williams, Doug Posson, Denise Wiltshire, and Bruce Molnia, USGS personnel from the National Center in Reston, Virginia, who offered suggestions and encouragement, as well as images.

At NASA's Goddard Space Flight Center thanks go to Gene Carl Feldman, for the ocean color images as

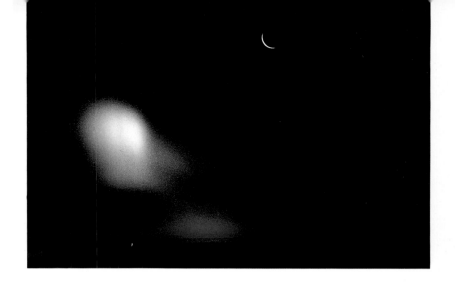

well as the beautiful images that introduce the sections on water, ice, and life; Compton J. Tucker, for images of vegetation; and Arlin Krueger, Courtney Scott, and Scott Doiron, for images of the Mount Pinatubo eruption. Lisa Rexrode was extremely helpful in organizing and providing Landsat imagery. NASA's Johnson Space Center also gave us support, and we thank Kamlesh Llula and Dave Pitts for their suggestions on environmental Space Shuttle imagery.

Individuals at NOAA who provided image support include Mike Hall, Eileen Shea, and Frank Lepore, and Laura K. Metcalf and Laurence W. Arnold (NOAA/NESDIS). Larry Stowe and Robert Carey of NOAA's Satellite Research Laboratory assisted us with imagery of the Mount Pinatubo eruption.

Other scientists who were extremely helpful in sharing imagery from their research include Moustafa Chahine, Kevin Hussey, Peter Woiceshyn, Ben Holt, John Ford, Howard Zebker, and Gregg Vane at the Jet Propulsion Laboratory; Barrett Rock at the University of New Hampshire; Yann Kerr at Laboratoire d'Études et de Recherches en Télédétection Spatiale; Otis Brown and Robert Evans at the University of Miami; and Nicholas Short at Bloomdale College.

We thank the following individuals in the private sector who suggested and provided beautiful images: Clark Nelson at SPOT Image Corporation, Susan Ross at Radarsat International Inc., Max Miller at Earth Satellite Corporation.

We also appreciate the help of Richard Underwood, who supplied photography suggestions and identified many of the Space Shuttle images, and Paul Grabhorn, Amy Budge, and Ben Shedd, who researched Space Shuttle imagery. Leonard Frank generously shared quotations from his book in progress, and Sayre Van Young and Kelly Zinkowski helped with quotation research.

Each of the authors individually also extend special appreciations.

Kevin Kelley is deeply grateful to Payson Stevens, who had the frontline responsibility for writing and designing the book. Payson drafted the text with great discipline and focus, and artfully, gracefully, and forcefully carried the book to its conclusion. Payson is a man of extraordinary energy and talent, and it has been a privilege to collaborate with him and with his team at InterNetwork. I am also pleased to acknowledge Barry Fishman, Bill Arthur, Robert Johnston, Joseph Miller, and Alia Johnson for their advice and guidance. I also thank my daughter, Vanessa, and my son, Aaron, for their enthusiasm and perceptive comments. Special thanks to my wife, Susan, for her advice, encouragement, and love.

Payson Stevens expresses his sincere gratitude to Kevin Kelley, whose book *The Home Planet* was an inspiration for this book and for our collective efforts to expand awareness and appreciation of the Earth. I also thank Roger Revelle, my mentor, who died while this book was being written. Roger devoted much of his professional career to science in the service of people and taught me that the most important thing is to learn how to ask the right questions. The images in this book are visual questions about process and patterns. He would have enjoyed them being made available to the public. Thanks, too, to my friends Richard Carter, Carmela Corallo, Barry Fishman, Cornelia von Mengershausen, Jon Phetteplace, Richard Rosow, and Larry Siegel, who provided spiritual and practical advice, and to my family, Naomi Coval-Apel, Eric Stevens, Larry Stevens, and Bob Apel, for their encouragement. Renée Hobi deserves the deepest appreciation and love for her understanding of what it takes to create an endeavor such as this book.

INDEX

ONE EARTH, ONE WORLD

Home Planet. A view of our planet from 1.3 million
miles away, as taken by the Galileo spacecraft on its course to
Jupiter in December 1990.

Designed and Produced by InterNetwork, Inc.

Book Team:
Art Director: Payson R. Stevens
Senior Designers: Patrick Howell, Leonard Sirota
Associate Designer & Electronic Manager: Eric Altson
Research & Word Processing: Monica Cruz
Copyeditor: Judith Dunham

*To replace the trees needed to manufacture the paper
for this book, the authors and publisher will arrange to plant trees
in endangered rainforests.*